THE
VELVETEEN
FATHER

ALSO BY JESSE GREEN

O Beautiful

"A BRAVE, BIG-HEARTED CHRONICLE."
—*Los Angeles Times*

"[*The Velveteen Father*] pierces the familiar cants and cutesies of books about parenthood . . . Green's observations are sound and dry, observed with sly wit. . . . There are observations here sure to resonate with the childed, the childless, and the childfree; and Green's contemplative view of parenthood is all the stronger for his resistance to see this ultimate responsibility through the gauzy lens employed by many of his contemporaries."

— *The Washington Post Book World*

"Green is a fine storyteller. . . . The baby boy, Erez, presents him with challenges that are nearly overwhelming. Through them all, however, he maintains a sharp wit. . . . His most powerful writing . . . is saved for heartfelt passages on what it means to be Jewish, in love and responsible for a young life."

— *Detroit Free Press*

"It is a work from the heart, and it alternately touched and wrenched and broke my own. Green, a gifted essayist . . . presents his memoir as an exploration of who he is, as a gay man and as the father he never expected to be. In so doing he offers an unblinking picture of the discrimination and stereotypical expectations that continue to torment gay men, and he arrives at a surprising but entirely fitting conclusion: that parenthood transcends all labels."

— *The Cincinnati Post*

"Remarkable . . . Powerful reading . . . Insightful, eloquent, and clever . . . A standout comment on the eternal and contemporary implications of family emerges from this enjoyable story that is far too good not to be true."

— *Kirkus Reviews*

"A glorious love story. By page 10 you'll be choosing baby names."

— *Out Magazine*

"Intensely personal, moving, and often humorous."

— *The Advocate*

Please turn the page for more reviews. . . .

THE VELVETEEN FATHER

An Unexpected Journey
to Parenthood

JESSE GREEN

BALLANTINE BOOKS / NEW YORK

*For my parents
and for Andy:
origin and destination*

"Real isn't how you are made," said the Skin Horse.
"It's a thing that happens to you.
When a child loves you for a long, long time,
not just to play with, but really loves you,
then you become Real."

"Does it hurt?" asked the Rabbit.

"Sometimes," said the Skin Horse.

Contents

I. The Designated Daughter   1

II. The Tear Beat   61

III. Éminence Mauve   119

IV. Dreft and Kwell   179

Acknowledgments   241

I

The Designated Daughter

ONE

"Mommy," he said.

In the summer after his third birthday, Erez started asking for his mother, or at any rate for something he referred to by that name. "I'm going outside to find Mommy," he informed us one day, quite jauntily, as if he were announcing a trip to his toy box. And then, as an afterthought: "Where is she?" Of course he could not reach the deadbolt yet, and anyway he was not quite sure what the word "mommy" meant. But he knew that his friend Aaron had one and that his friend Rosalie had two. And that he didn't have any, at least not in the house.

It was, Andy tells me, among Erez's first sounds — "ma" — just as it is for most children. "Ma" is the sound of first recourse, of merely opening the lips. It is the name that is there whether you speak it or not, "the invisible breath between every line," as the poet James Merrill put it. But for Erez, the bleating syllable lacked a referent. Andy was his father; he had no mother; no one came when he uttered the world's oldest word. Very soon after he started speaking it, the sound naturally fell into disuse, until it was hijacked several months later as the name for his favorite stuffed animal, a black-and-white cat even now called Ma'am — from the sound he had learned cats make, we assume.

He had no mother, but of course he did. Andy often told him the story, or part of the story, in the dark as Erez lay curling for sleep: *One day I walked from work and took the subway train to the bus and the bus to a plane, and the plane took me far away to another state, where a woman who was able to grow you inside her but could not take care of you was looking for a daddy to love you for*

*the rest of your life. And I was that daddy. And I took you back to
the plane to the bus and the bus to the subway—well, actually, this
time, we took a cab—and brought you here to Brooklyn to be my
son forever.* Which perhaps explains Erez's mania for transporta-
tion, his every-night dreaming of trains.

For a while he asks a few times a week: "Where's Mommy?"
Other times he says definitively: "Daddy is my mommy." This
seems a piece of wisdom, but it is the wisdom of the stopped
clock, correct twice a day. In the category of family relationships he is apt to say anything. "Mommy?" he says to a passing
stranger. "Mommy?" he says to a woman whose child has just
called her that. Or at television time, this: "Let's watch *Grandma
Yankees!*"—inexplicably having altered the title of the musical
Damn Yankees to suit some subterranean agenda. Wallace and
Gromit, characters in a favorite video, have similarly turned into
Wallace and Grandma. And I sometimes get turned into Uncle—
a term someone must have used in his presence, or even deliberately taught him to use. But I'm not his uncle, any more than
Gromit (a claymation dog) is his grandma. I'm his . . . well, no
wonder he's confused.

He finds a picture in the drawer of a flea-market dry sink—a
drawer so rarely opened by adults that it still contains news clippings and liquor bills from the man who owned it decades ago.
What a party Sink Man threw in May of 1963! Here is an order
for twenty-five bottles of wine plus an assortment of spirits and
thick green liqueurs. But suddenly it's 1967 and here is a letter expressing sorrow over Sink Man's recent "tragedy": "I hope that
time will enable you to overcome your present sadness. Fortunately, you are still very young so that much of your life is before
you." The condolence—is it possible?—still reeks of pipe to-
bacco. And here is a photograph.

But before we even see what it is, Erez has torn the tiny picture
in four. This is not surprising; he shreds, juliennes, or otherwise
dismembers almost anything he particularly likes. Playing cards
and the pasteboard sleeves of videotapes are helpless in his path;
pop-up books may be totally harvested of their pop-ups within
minutes if left undefended. Now he hands over the remains of a
woman, taken in a photo booth in what seems, from her hairdo

and Peter Pan collar when reassembled, to be the late 1950s. She is young, a bit bulbous, smiling through lipstick; she has not yet had a child—and would she ever get to, before her "tragedy"? For she is the wife (or so I imagine) for whom Sink Man threw such a bibulous party, whom Sink Man lost not four years later.

"Mommy?" Erez says, dropping the bits merrily in my hand.

TWO

We do in fact have a photograph of Erez's mother—his "birth mother," as we are careful to call her, though it is a peculiar and somewhat defensive retronym. In the four-by-six glossy she is seated in a hospital chair in a hospital room, wearing a hospital gown and holding her newborn but looking at the camera, not even a half-smile but a quarter-smile on her face. She is not pretty and not ugly and has a bad shingle haircut, but there is an intense, magnetic, Carly Simon quality to her features—that is, if Carly Simon had just given birth and were holding the infant whom she had irrevocably agreed to give up to a stranger.

In the months since Andy had decided to seek an adoption, he took to calling the anonymous woman who would bear his child Concepción. In part this reflected a desire to define her by her biological role in the endeavor, to restrict her significance to that moment, some months earlier, when she had—what? Forgotten her diaphragm? Refused to use the one she had? And in part this reflected his assumption that she would be Hispanic, because the agency he was dealing with had a largely Hispanic clientele. But Erez's birth mother (it turned out) was herself adopted and of unknown ethnic parentage. From the photograph you cannot tell; her face is pale with the exhaustion of labor and her features are too idiosyncratic to interpret. But if she was never sure of her background before, her newborn boy would have filled her in, for even at birth he had the high almond eyes and light-brown-sugar skin so typical of the Latin American mélange.

Well, she must already have known. She and the man who impregnated her—a man not merely white but Mormon—already had a child, an eighteen-month-old girl being raised by Concepción's adoptive mother. Indeed, the girl was the reason Concepción had elected to give her newborn away in exchange for five thousand dollars in what the agency calls "expenses related to the pregnancy." As Concepción saw it, she was faced with a kind of Sophie's choice. "I have to take care of *myself* now," she wrote in her adoption plan, explaining why she would sign the papers. "I want to get myself into college, so I can get my daughter back." In another photograph we see that girl, Erez's full sister: a pretty little toddler with the same mixed features. She grins while clasping her father's blue jeans, though you cannot make him out because he's facing away, into a mirror, and the camera's flash obscures the reflection. Besides, like too many fathers, he has largely been cropped out of the picture; he is little more than a pair of pants.

But we have learned through various channels that Don (as I call him, short for "donor") was twenty years old, installed aluminum siding for a living, was tall, blond, very attractive and, unlikely as it seems, chipper and cheerful. Concepción, darker and moodier, held powerful sway over her handsome young boyfriend. At her command, and despite misgivings, he appeared at the adoption agency's office and obediently signed away his parental rights. Should we even know about this private drama? It was retailed sub rosa, for in a "closed" adoption the flow of information is tightly controlled so as to prevent the adopting parents from ever knowing the birth parents and, especially, vice versa. As a result, everything that was more than dull prose came to us unofficially or unexpectedly or around some more or less improper bend. What came to us straight, in Concepción's own hand and on lightly censored medical forms, was the kind of featureless, filled-with-holes story you might expect to read in a death notice. She was thirty-two—twelve years younger than Andy at the time, twelve years older than Don. She lived in the Southwest, working as a cashier in a state I won't name. She smoked cigarettes but didn't drink and had recently been taking cough medicine for a cold. She liked to ride motorcycles and also liked to read.

Perhaps it was because she felt she was relinquishing everything else that Concepción decided to reserve the most salient piece of information to herself. It was a social worker from the adoption agency who told Andy that Concepción, having evaded drug screening through most of her pregnancy, finally tested positive for cocaine a few weeks before going into labor. Which may be why Andy, a single man who had just started waiting, was offered Baby Boy Blank (Concepción's last name has been obliterated in the medical records) five days after the child was born on March 4, 1994. Several other prospective parents—couples who had been waiting longer—had already declined. "He's very pretty," the social worker told Andy over the phone, trying to close the deal. "But there's a tremulousness which could be the result of his mother's drug use."

Tremulousness?

"He shakes," said the social worker. "As if he were nervous. It may go away. Do you still want him?"

THREE

Had he ever *not* wanted him? In Andy's file cabinet, among folders of clippings about foreign countries he hoped to visit—Chile, Turkey, India—I find a folder labeled ADOPTION, and in it news articles dating back to 1983. Even before that, it appears in retrospect, he had been shaping his life toward this unlikely moment, this most foreign of destinations. Or, for too long, misshaping.

Andy was born in the last week of 1949 to a Brooklyn Jewish family steeped in the traditions of small private enterprise and vast public education. His mother, unable to get a job as a buyer at Macy's at the beginning of the Depression, went on instead to teach high school English for thirty-six years. His father ran factories that made, among other apparel, cheap children's clothing. They worked hard and, in the manner of such stories, prospered sufficiently to give Andy and his older brother trumpet lessons, college educations, and, posthumously, two Brooklyn brownstones. They did not, however, give Andy the fundamental sensation of perfect safety that deludes some children into growing up happy. They couldn't; they hadn't had it themselves and wouldn't have known how to invent it from scratch. Instead they educated and clothed other children, came home exhausted, drank casually but continuously until they fell asleep.

When Andy tells me this last detail I have trouble believing him; my parents still have, in a closet, liquor from my bar mitzvah luncheon. I had always previously subscribed to the message of the great, scary joke: *Why don't Jews drink? Because it blunts the pain of living.*

And yet Andy's parents do not disprove the joke. Janet and Lewis were witty, principled people who loved their sons but numbed themselves so successfully that despite their love, and expertise, they couldn't help Andy with his math. Could they have helped what happened when he was seven, when his brother, Frank, sprayed lighter fluid at the smoldering barbecue while Andy leaned over the coals, watching? Janet and Lewis were inside, upstairs, preparing the hamburgers and greeting the guests, as the barbecue exploded in Andy's face. Many years and several painful debriding procedures later, the flames still fork, albeit faintly, across his neck and jawline, only now they are made of ropy scar tissue instead of substanceless heat and light. The best care was obtained, of course, but what had happened and what it meant were never discussed. Even so, the accident helped to shape at least one person: Frank eventually became a scientist, specializing in industrial health and safety.

In a way, though, we are all shaped by our accidents. Once burned, twice shy. Andy did not ever again venture far from his parents' purview. Rather, he confined himself quite narrowly within the contours they had drawn: He went into small private enterprise and vast public education. He runs the family business, which is no longer clothing but the two handsome buildings that clothing bought. And he has been an employee of the New York City Board of Education since he was twenty, as an English teacher until 1984 and as a guidance counselor thereafter. Where I grew up, in an affluent suburb of Philadelphia, guidance counselors were administrative nonentities who signed your schedule and occasionally said things like "Brown's got a good reputation, have you thought of Brown?" At Andy's school in the Brooklyn neighborhood of Crown Heights, he is more likely to find himself saying things like "What did the others do while your father beat you up?" The afternoon club he runs isn't Little Theater or Junior Achievement but the Pregnancy Prevention Program. For a fair number of the fifteen-year-old girls enrolled at his school, the club is already too late.

In his commitment to teaching and in his love of cheap clothing, Andy was living out his parents' priorities; he even lived in one of their houses. But he was, in at least one fundamental way, quite different from them: He would not, it appeared, be a parent himself. Having (as he puts it) dated women chronically and men intermittently, having stepped gingerly out of and back into the closet several times during early adulthood—his was a closet with a revolving door—Andy identified himself as a gay man for good by 1980. Thereafter, periods of relative monogamy alternated with periods of intense (albeit safe) promiscuity, leaving him by 1994 with a ghostly address book of dead acquaintances but also with a small solar system of former lovers in rather close orbit. He no longer questioned his sexuality; he was active in gay politics and AIDS charities and wore a modest earring and marched in liberation parades. What he had begun to question was what liberation had liberated him for.

FOUR

At the time Concepción was giving birth, Andy was living with a man he called, somewhat coolly, his "ex-lover-to-be." It had already been decided that Elliot would be moving out, though the date kept not getting set. Elliot and Andy had been a couple for six years by then. For most of that time they had clacked off each other like billiard balls, making the relationship feel, at least to Andy, intimate and yet somehow provisional. Looking back on it now, I think it was a case of two people who had not really figured out what their life's goals were separately—who could therefore not figure out what they might be together.

There had already been, for instance, the Debacle of the Karens, as I'll call them here—though in fact the name the two women shared was a different, if equally plain one. Andy had gone to high school with Karen One, a slim, witty, swaggering woman whose eyes were perpetually rimmed with kohl. They were classmates but not contemporaries; having been a December baby and having skipped a year somewhere along the way, Andy was quite a bit younger than most of the kids he spent time with. As a result, he had adopted a reflexive posture of awe toward them, especially insofar as they participated in the fast revolutions of the time. Karen had been avant-garde in high school and was, to some extent, avant-garde still; when Andy read that an East Village women's theater was presenting her lesbian version of *Cinderella*, he attended in hopes of renewing their acquaintance. Soon enough he was standing in the kitchen of the apartment Karen One shared with Karen Two and saying, over the noise of the party that was going on around them, "You know, I would be a good person to father a child for someone." And the Karens stared at him.

Andy said it casually; by 1989, he had said the same words, or words like them, to a number of women, mostly lesbians. What he meant was not entirely clear, even to himself. Certainly it included providing sperm, not through sexual contact but through "alternative insemination"—a phrase generally shortened to "A.I." in conversation, thus leading to an unfortunate confusion with artificial intelligence. Indeed, it would take some form of artificial intelligence to believe that such an arrangement would work out well. Or some artificial hope.

In any case, the Karens were staring because they had been thinking about Andy for just such a role. Later, during a phone call, they asked him officially: Would he like to help them conceive and raise a child? Andy, looking out his kitchen door to the shifting concrete of his empty backyard, said something like "Yeah, that sounds great" and left it at that. But if he wasn't one for pinning down details ahead of time (or even after), the Karens were. Months of discussions ensued concerning HIV testing, how to pay for the insemination procedures, responsibility for and rights to the child that might result. The Karens' lawyer drew up a contract outlining all this. It was never signed.

As Andy tells me this story—as I pick it out of him, like bits of glass—he closes his eyes frequently and rubs his forehead; undoing the work, or antiwork, of forgetting these events is almost as painful as the events were themselves. He now sees what should have been warning lights and wonders how he could have been so foolish as to drive right through them. The Karens, for instance, didn't trust what he told them about his sexual practices, though he had been exclusively safe without even one deviation since 1983 and had repeatedly tested HIV negative. They wanted more tests; they wanted him to store up sperm for six months and then be tested again. And then they wanted to start over again: more collecting, more testing. Andy easily managed to ignore their mistrust but could not so easily ignore another looming problem about the Karens: His friends, especially Elliot, didn't like them. Karen Two, a very quiet bookkeeper with a pudding-basin hairdo, attempted to make nice, but Karen One, with her cutting imperiousness, drove Elliot mad.

Nevertheless, starting in the fall of 1989, Andy went to a mid-town sperm bank every other week, paid his eighty dollars, and masturbated in a weird little room that was stocked with heterosexual pornography and reeked of air freshener. Six months later, after another HIV test, he began withdrawing these deposits monthly; for another fee, the bank handed over a tank of liquid nitrogen in which three little straws of semen were frozen. These he toted to the Karens' apartment in lower Manhattan—although he once attended a political benefit on the way, nervously leaving his expensive parcel with the coat check girl while he nibbled on cheese. What exactly the women did with the straws Andy never quite knew; in any case Karen One kept not getting pregnant. They consulted conception specialists, and Andy tried other sperm banks, all to no avail. As it turned out, Andy was subfertile because of a backed-up testicular artery; the freezing process killed what few good sperm he had.

Andy decided to have the problem corrected surgically but the Karens didn't feel like waiting. The process had been going on for two years already, and Karen One was now past forty. She seemed to blame Andy. One night, in anger, Karen Two revealed that the women had secretly arranged for another donor to replace him;

his services were no longer required. "I didn't do this to you," Andy cried. "I didn't go looking for a woman younger or richer or who got along with my friends!" But the affair was over. The Karens, noting that Andy had fronted much of the money for the sperm banking and the fertility consultations, promised to pay him the half they owed—between one thousand and two thousand dollars, Andy estimates. But they never did.

A year later the birth announcement arrived: a gesture perhaps lacking in thoughtfulness. Andy tried to be happy for them, but was not entirely surprised to learn that the Karens broke up soon thereafter. Time wounds all heels.

FIVE

If you believe a child will save your relationship, it will destroy your relationship. Whether it ever arrives or not.

I don't know if this is what happened to the Karens, but I know how it played out for Andy. He was a few months shy of forty when the discussions with the two women began, and though he had initiated the process almost casually, with an apparently off-the-cuff remark, this was merely a ruse for outwitting his own anxieties. In fact, as he found out all too well during the months of visits to the air-freshened room, during the hours of waiting for the results of repeated HIV tests, during the otherwise unnecessary testicular surgery to enhance his fertility, he wanted to have a child more than he wanted anything else. That it didn't happen under those circumstances may have been a blessing, but now he was forty-two.

Elliot must have sensed Andy's shifting priorities. Their relationship had started off well enough but, like a bad family vacation, lost its way in side streets and back roads almost at once. There was much bickering in the car along the way: *We should have taken the exit back there!* And *Where have you driven us now?* Neither of them had a keen sense of direction. Andy is spatially dyslexic (I may have invented this term); when he tells me to get in the left lane on the expressway I have to ask, "Do you mean the *left* left or the *right* left?" And Elliot, who had been struggling for years to turn his beautiful singing voice into a viable career, seemed to be stricken with paralysis when it came time to make important decisions.

The alternative insemination scheme did not help matters between them. For one thing, while Andy was sperm banking, he was instructed not to make deposits anywhere but in the bank. This can have a dampening effect on any lovemaking that does not involve a plastic cup. Beyond that, Elliot, with good cause, did not trust the Karens—and yet Andy desperately needed to. *Why can't you support me in this?* was Andy's theme; he was adhering, for the moment, to the romantic notion that couples must share everything, including their delusions. Elliot couldn't comply. "What do you need them for?" he was always saying. "You could find other women to do this with, or why don't you just adopt? We could adopt together."

This was not technically true. It was not then—and is now only rarely—legal anywhere in the United States for an unmarried couple, especially a gay couple (unmarried of necessity), to adopt a child together, no matter how long they've been partners, no matter how fit they might be as parents. Though the laws in some states would change over the next few years, in 1991 public and private adoption agencies still favored married couples, as they had throughout history; the modern prototype adoptive family was an infertile middle-aged cop and his stay-at-home wife in a semi-detached house in Queens. Failing that, the agencies favored single women, especially minority single women for hard-to-place minority children. So strong was the maternal prejudice that a single man, even one who said he was heterosexual, could expect to wait longer for a child than a similarly situated woman, or perhaps forever. In that environment, an openly homosexual single man might well have concluded that honesty was the worst policy. In Florida, for instance, a 1977 statute—inspired by Anita Bryant and repeatedly upheld over the years—specified that "no person eligible to adopt . . . may adopt if that person is homosexual." Even in those states where gay men and lesbians were not prohibited by law from adopting, they were often prohibited by custom.

Still, the doors were opening slightly; many gay men in New York knew someone who knew someone who knew one of the handful of guys who had succeeded in adopting a child. Often this would be an older child, or a "special needs" child (usually meaning hyperactive or borderline retarded) or a child with a cleft palate or fetal alcohol syndrome or HIV. In other cases the so-called adoption was actually just a foster placement: a baby awaiting a more "appropriate" adoptive family, or a runaway gay teen deliberately (if temporarily) placed in the home of a "stable" gay man or couple. But sometimes it meant something at once more ordinary and more extraordinary. In 1990, a medical administrator named Sal Iacullo became the first openly gay man to be granted a decree of adoption in the state of New York. He and his partner, a municipal grant officer named Wayne Steinman, whom Andy knew from political circles, had already been raising the healthy three-year-old girl as foster parents; now she became Sal's legal daughter, if not Wayne's. The inequity disturbed them, but there was time to fight that battle later. And the girl's name was Hope.

SIX

The opening of the adoption doors was not the result of a new national commitment to the needs of parentless babies. Nor was it the result of a change in attitude toward homosexuals, although that helped. It was not even the result of a greater demand by homosexuals themselves; lesbians generally preferred to bear their own children, and most gay men, if the idea of adoption even occurred to them, knew better than to apply. It was no bright force that made the difference, but a dark one: desperation.

It began with the publicly managed foster care system in large cities like New York. Whereas many private adoption agencies dealt almost exclusively with the healthy newborns of embarrassed young white women—and had waiting lists that could easily stretch to half a decade—foster care programs like the one run by New York's Child Welfare Administration had a much more difficult task. It fell to them to find homes for older, darker, or sicker children who had been legally wrested from their abusive, incompetent, or absent birth parents, or merely abandoned like so much garbage. The supply so far outstripped the demand for these wards of the state that there was no waiting list at all; very few parents, given the choice, would elect to take in a pair of eight-year-old twins with learning disabilities. Still, for decades, the CWA had managed to place these kids, efficiently if not always happily, in private or group homes, where, for a fee, they were fed, clothed, and raised to majority.

But the simultaneous debut of crack and AIDS in the early 1980s threw the already unbalanced supply-and-demand adoption economy entirely out of whack. At some New York City hospitals—Harlem, Metropolitan, and Bellevue among them—nearly five percent of all newborns tested positive for HIV: as many as a thousand a year. Mostly, these babies were black or Hispanic; only one in ten was white. They were the offspring of intravenous drug users or their sexual partners—women who were themselves infected. Some of these women were already sick, some addicted to drugs, some jobless, homeless, or all of the above. The fathers were usually out of the picture. In most cases the city had no choice but to step in and find a place for the babies to live, babies even worse off than the previous generation's hard-to-place wards.

By 1987, despite its efforts, the CWA (or perhaps by then it was the Administration for Children's Services; like a criminal, the office changed its name with each ensuing scandal) was floundering badly. The disease, the drugs, and an unprecedented increase in reports of child abuse had combined to overload the system. The five o'clock news shows were having a field day with the so-called boarder baby crisis: hundreds of kids abandoned in hospitals, being raised in jam-packed nurseries, tethered to their beds, crawling around in circles. Despite their disabilities, many were healthy enough to go home, at least temporarily, if only there were homes to go to. But there weren't enough cops in Queens to take up the slack, let alone middle-class black families with money to spare. And even if there were, they would not be looking for babies like these. Who would be so desperate for a child that they would invite the probability of death into their freshly painted nurseries?

During the two years ending in 1989, the number of children

needing foster care in New York City doubled, to thirty-nine thousand. That December, as it had for the previous ten years, the CWA sponsored what it called a foster care and adoption fair. On a bitter Sunday, many of the seventy agencies that administered foster care in the city set up booths in the student commons at Manhattan Community College. There they displayed photographs, fliers, and videos of the kids they had in stock. Four hundred children were ready for homes that day; only one match was made. And if the blatant pathos that produced this meager result was unsettling, it was by no means the most desperate advertisement produced for a good cause. Earlier that same year, the National Association of Black Social Workers had sponsored its own fair at the Fashion Institute of Technology on Manhattan's West Side. The Black Social Workers had perhaps the most daunting problem of all, given American attitudes toward race, and they had further painted themselves into a corner by establishing a policy adamantly opposing transracial placements. At their fashion show, dozens of available kids paraded down a runway in their Sunday best—some merely toddled—while rock music played and prospective parents took notes. The mistress of ceremonies kept up a slightly desperate patter ("Jaekwan likes to sing, eat, and read comic books") as if to disguise the horrible necessity of what was going on.

SEVEN

If placement policy at the Child Welfare Administration was, even then, blind to sexuality, CWA workers were not. Like their counterparts at private adoption agencies, they had for years, subtly or unsubtly, discouraged unmarried men like Andy from applying, especially if the man in question showed alarming indications of good taste. Oh, a few had made it through the process successfully, but only by closeting themselves: sequestering their lovers, stashing their earrings, temporarily deaccessioning the Mapplethorpe above the fireplace. By 1988, however, the city, ridiculed on the news and threatened with lawsuits, could no longer afford to turn away any minimally competent applicants, especially those willing to consider a child with HIV. Gay men were willing. Perhaps some placement officers felt this made for a rough kind of justice: Weren't gay men the cause of the problem in the first place? Others surely believed they had no choice but to hold their noses and take emergency measures. Gay men couldn't have normal children, but they might be entrusted, briefly, with dying ones.

And yet there must also have been some in the CWA who had been waiting many years for an opportunity like this to breach the taboo. In the struggle for equal rights of any kind it has often been assumed that the bureaucrats on one side of the ramparts and the complainants on the other are utterly discrete entities. They are not. As it happens, and not accidentally, the child-helping professions are teeming with homosexuals and their fellow travelers. Within the CWA, within the placement agencies, within the pediatric hospital wards, gay men and lesbians awaited the propitious moment.

On April 5, 1987, a half-black, half-Hispanic boy named Alex was born at Bronx Municipal Hospital. Despite an early bout with pneumonia—and a diagnosis of full-blown AIDS—he was soon healthy enough to go home. But his mother had left the hospital without him. A drug addict suffering from AIDS herself, she was incapable of providing the child with proper care. Alex was remanded into the custody of the CWA.

Alex was ten months old and still boarding at Bronx Municipal when a gay couple from Queens came for a visit. Frank and Dante had been together for ten years at that point; both from large Catholic families, they were uncles and godfathers many times over. In their picture-lined apartment, they had tried to cobble together a miniature family of their own: two parakeets, two Chihuahuas, the two of them in their double bed. But Dante had become depressed of late. His job in real estate had long since grown stale, as had earlier jobs in nursing and imports. While Frank was out teaching, he sometimes just sat in the kitchen for hours, drinking coffee and wondering what was missing. Then one day a call came from an old nursing friend with a new job at an adoption agency in Yonkers. She told Dante about the exciting work she was doing, implementing the city's expanded effort to find families for babies with HIV.

Over the next several months Frank and Dante underwent the investigative process set up to screen foster parents. A social worker from the agency visited them to look into their motives, their relationship, the apartment itself. A child abuse clearance was obtained after a computer search of criminal files. And Dante's old nursing friend reviewed the medical issues, explaining the precautions they would need to take, should they get a child, against transmission of HIV. She also warned them that many—in those days, most—babies with AIDS die before the age of two.

Frank and Dante were the first gay couple to apply for a foster child through this program, and among the first in the city. The head of the agency took the unusual step of interviewing the couple at home herself; if something went wrong with this placement, the backlash could destroy the program. But Frank and Dante were unassailable. They were responsible, stable, hearty, optimistic, sturdy, comfortable, clear-eyed. They had energy and time. And they wanted a child.

By the time I met Frank and Dante in the fall of 1989, Alex, who had lived with them for ten difficult months, was buried at Calvary Cemetery. Buried there, too, was Mickey, another baby they'd taken in. But Michael and Jonathan, two more boys eventually placed with them, were alive and moderately healthy. Frank and Dante had their family at last, precarious though it was. And even though their own families had largely deserted them—it was one thing to be gay, another to be gay and have children—the two men felt blessed. This sense of blessing, which I found as moving as it was incomprehensible, was what drew me to write about them the following year. The article appeared in *7 Days*, a now-defunct New York City weekly, under the headline "Lullaby and Goodnight," though my working title had been "Dream Babies"—by which I meant that these children were long desired and soon vanished. I thought Frank and Dante were saints. "Taking care of kids nobody else wants is more a sign of a community's decency than of any newfound rights," I wrote,

more mildly than I felt. Gay men being allowed to clean up society's messes, and then being left with nothing: What kind of ad-
vance was that beyond being pigeonholed as hairdressers, florists,
and decorators?

EIGHT

Mercifully, the TV movie of "Lullaby and Goodnight" was never
made. One producer's bright idea was to "turn Dante into a girl."
Another wanted to give the babies, instead of AIDS, a scary-but-
in-the-last-act-curable disease. Another thought (now here's the
switch) that Frank and Dante, not the babies, should die; the babies could end up with some heterosexual relative—a happy ending! In any case, I was excised from the project when my saints
cut a private deal and sold it from under me. If this was selfish of
them, perhaps they were entitled to own their loss outright.

Back in Brooklyn the issue of selfishness was troubling Andy,
too. The expense of spirit wasted on the Karens had naturally left
him feeling bankrupt, and yet, since he had trouble thinking ill of
anyone, especially two women seeking a child, he could not con
clusively face their betrayal. Was selfishness somehow inherent in
the biology of reproduction? Did you *need* to be greedy to create
a child? It wasn't until the following winter, when he contracted
a life-threatening form of pneumonia and was hospitalized for
several weeks, that he understood the Karens' narcissism as char-
acterological, not generic. "It isn't *AIDS* pneumonia," he explained to Karen One, alluding to pneumocystis carinii, which
was then everywhere in the news, filling the lungs of HIV-positive
gay men until they essentially drowned. "I'm very sick but I'm
going to be fine." Karen responded glibly that, oh, she wasn't concerned at all: She'd already had herself tested again and knew she
wasn't in danger.

This was a woman who understood her priorities, or at any rate
understood what they weren't. Andy was not so efficient in his desires. He had tended in his life to follow his impulses without
studying them too deeply; a true child of the sixties, he hitched a

ride with whatever people and whatever passions drifted into his vision. Some of the people were difficult and some of the passions unpromising, and the path of least resistance turned out to be a poorly maintained road. But if Andy was diffuse, he was also determined: For the most part he managed, through the application of a nearly tireless enthusiasm, to turn risky, impulsive investments into net gains, albeit slight ones. The difficult friends came through sometimes, in their difficult ways. The passions did not make the world much better but did not make it worse. As a result he didn't really know how to process a total wipeout like the perfidy of the Karens, and so he sulked.

His experience with alternative insemination was far from atypical. It seemed, upon closer examination, that this procedure led in most cases to one of two outcomes: failure and acrimony or success and acrimony. Contractual obligations were as unlikely to produce happy results in the manufacture of babies as they were in custody cases later, and the geometry of the lesbian couple at two points of the triangle with the lone sperm donor at the third enforced certain inequities. The inequities were at base biological, of course. The one thing a man lacked in order to give birth to a child was so vast and mysterious that religions were built around it; a woman lacked only a teaspoonful of something men wasted by the gallon. This gave the whole production an unsavory black widow–meets–D. H. Lawrence odor: Come and then die. The putatively virile man so central to the process was actually in the women's employ: a hired hand, as it were.

Is it disloyal of me to surmise that Andy contributed to the disaster, if only through a lack of self-knowledge? Looking at him now, I don't think he could have been happy with the arrangement, even if it had somehow worked out. What he wanted out of fathering a child was more than would be likely to result from vacation visits and paying for college. Unfortunately, he knew less about what he wanted than about what he *didn't* want. He didn't want (for instance) to get involved with any more contractual masturbation schemes. He didn't, of course, want a dishonest marriage: It was hard to say who was saddest in such ménages, the sneaking husband, the unfulfilled wife, or the anxious children.

And yet Andy had somehow come to believe that he didn't want to adopt a baby, either. It's hard now to credit his reasoning: that babies should be breast-fed and that an adopted newborn, dependent on a bottle, was cruelly deprived of an important, perhaps a crucial, experience. "Something about immunity," he now mutters in defense of that position. "Immunity was in the air."

NINE

All due respect to the breast; it's a wonderful organ and undoubtedly a more esthetically pleasing vending system for nourishment than latex nipples and presterilized liners in plastic bottles with teddy bear designs. But a distaste for the bottle could only have been covering some other, more substantial distaste. Was the antiadoption prejudice of previous generations reasserting itself? Andy's mother, who had breast-fed her two sons, seemed to have felt that adoption, with its bottle feedings, was deeply unnatural: not direct and biological like the flow of milk from mother to newborn, but disjoint, synthetic—an abstract formula. The liquid involved was even *called* formula, which seemed to suggest all sorts of potentially mathematical exertions. Andy had never been good at math, but he'd loved mythology, and mythology (see Oedipus) did not speak well of adoption.

Even *my* mother and father, mild and liberal though they are, permitted themselves this casual bigotry. Little spoken of except as slander, adoption was vaguely understood in my house as a procedure occasioned by a physical defect in the parents—infertility, a lack of robustness—and prefiguring emotional defects in the children. The fact that emotional defects were rampant among the biological offspring of their friends and acquaintances did not seem to threaten the connection they made between stranger and strangeness, for ancient clan issues were involved here. Perhaps especially among the descendants of Moses (himself adopted, by Pharaoh's daughter) the distinction between insider and outsider, and thus the legibility of bloodlines, became a talisman of safety in an unsafe world. Which is why none but the most fanatical

Lubavitcher sects proselytize; to the contrary: In the game of "Is It Good for the Jews?" (Einstein, yes; Roy Cohn, no) it was often noted with an asterisk of relief that psychopaths like David "Son of Sam" Berkowitz turned out to have been landsmen only by accident—that is, by adoption.

In such an environment, the only thing more unnatural than a couple choosing adoption would be a man choosing adoption on his own. As a source of passion—the kind of passion mothers are admired for possessing and vilified for lacking—fatherhood, even biological fatherhood, was suspicious. Women needed to have children to be seen as normal and fulfilled, but too much child-lust in a man made him a freak: a possible pedophile, or at least homosexual. What are we to make of those fathers who, desperately wanting to nurse their own babies, convince quack doctors to inject them with hormones? We think them ridiculous, perhaps disgusting, especially since the halfhearted lactation thus stimulated could not nourish a guinea pig. The pleasure, if any, derived by the man—ah, pleasure, that American criminal—seals the sin, though the pleasures of female breast-feeding are tolerated as an unavoidable side effect of biology. A man who wants to adopt a child is often seen in a similar role: stealing from a woman the one thing society allows (indeed forces) her to keep for herself. Was it finally unnatural—that is, unhealthy—for a man to raise a child without a woman? Was it *selfish*?

On the other hand, if the television of my youth was to be believed, many men—widowers, that is—raised children alone, although they had a habit of hiring nannies whom they later married. Other TV dads fell in love with widows and adopted their brood, raising the kids (the phrase went) *as their own*. The unspoken anxiety to which these youthful deaths and family reconfigurations alluded was divorce, which by 1965 was beginning its Sherman's march through the American familyland. In its opaque and syrupy story lines, television was answering the question of what to do with the kids displaced by the fires along the way. Blend them, merge them, fold them into the corporation—a subtext that spoke to the underlying scariness of an unclaimed child. Adoption seemed to challenge the ownership fixations (and the anxieties beneath those fixations) of a postwar American consumer society whose icon of successful adulthood was a paid-off mortgage. Who really owned an adopted child? It was never asked who really owned the other kind.

However strongly these ideas influenced Andy's thinking on the matter, there were plenty of other obstacles. One of them was Elliot, who in the spring of 1992 was once again suggesting they adopt a child together—more accurately, that Andy adopt as a single man, as Sal Iacullo had done, and let Elliot become a de facto coparent. Andy knew the relationship with Elliot was on its last legs; he could not consider moving forward under that circumstance. "I don't want to do this with anybody ever again," he decided, once his pneumonia had cleared. "In fact, I don't want to think about it at all." And so he didn't. Instead, with some of the money he had earmarked for a child, he bought a small summer house in eastern Long Island, from two men who were both dying of AIDS.

TEN

Well, that's what gay men did instead of having children: They had houses. If a couple could afford it, they bought and renovated a charming three-bedroom cottage in the country, turning nurseries into guest rooms and installing a pergola on the site of the rusty swing set. Down came the cowboy wallpaper (or maybe not) and up went the flea-market chandelier. If a friend showed up for housewarming with a set of chased-silver bobeches, you may be sure our couple knew what they were: wax-catching collars to protect candlesticks from candles. A couple without offspring must, after all, make themselves useful, or busy at least. Oh, their taxes still helped to finance the local schools, and their Halloween decorations were the wittiest in town, but few children knocked at the door for their homemade candy apples, and their pre-empty nest stayed empty.

Or they gardened: comprehensive assemblages of every legitimate iris, tomatoes shameless on their stakes, and months of sauces from them. Or they collected: Roseville ceramics from the drought month of July 1947, when the celadon glaze acquired a valuable golden aura. Or they made children of their pets, or pets of each other. "Kiss! Kiss! Papa wants a kiss," I remember over-hearing a friend croon, while I froze in embarrassment in the doorway where I stood—but was it his human partner or his spaniel being addressed? It was his spaniel.

Or they traveled or they cooked or they pruned and pumped until their big hairless breasts resembled the breasts of women. Or they stayed at the office even after the heat was shut off, doing the job of two family men and saving their ungrateful employers the expense of adequate staffing. Or they went on the road for thirty-seven weeks with a bus-and-truck tour of *Paint Your Wagon*, rack-ing up Friends and Family credits on their gigantic MCI bills. Time was what they could offer the world instead of offspring, and with it, they made the world interesting or efficient and oc-casionally even beautiful.

But it is in the nature of substitution manias that the substitu-tions never suffice; since the fundamental conflict remains unre-solved—how do I make an adult identity in a world that constricts the concept so narrowly?—the distractions just grow more impor-tunate. The garden can always be quainter, the body leaner, the lover even lovelier in a madras shirt from Barneys. Any job can be done even better: can be, and must. Which is why, at least for this particular stratum of bon ton gay men, process is all. Without children they can afford to be perfectionists. Or do I mean: Per-fectionists, they cannot afford to have children.

Neither Andy's house nor garden (nor pet, for that matter) would win him prizes in a gay Olympics. He *was*, in fact, living in the "garden" apartment of one of his parents' two Brooklyn brownstones, though the concrete expanse to which the term al-luded had long since begun to heave, displacing the daisies and inviting lawsuits. The building itself had for years been a rooming house and still featured one floor of shell-shocked veterans paying nominal rent because Andy refused to dislodge them until death did, and maybe not even then. His own floor he had halfheartedly renovated when he turned thirty—perhaps too young to escape the whiff of the dormitory. It was long and low-ceilinged and very dim in its deep interior. Formica, that substance dread of gay men, was not unknown there, and wood-grained, too. Except for the Keith Haring SILENCE=DEATH poster you would not have thought a gay man lived there, let alone two; perhaps you might have imagined a graduate student on a small stipend who liked to cook but did not mind that his pots and pans featured rust instead of Teflon and that his bathroom resembled a tiled oubliette.

Andy liked it like that. Andy liked that it wasn't fussy, that it was instead the opposite of fussy, furnished from yard sales and aunts' attics with haphazard aplomb and nary a bobeche. Andy liked his *life* like that. He liked that his dog was not a trembling, overbred toy but a shepherd-husky-cocker mutt who'd been abused by a previous owner and therefore loved Andy the more devoutly. So what if Chauncey shed profusely, stank occasionally, barked incessantly until he went deaf? He fit right in. Andy's life was a congenial mess—congenial, at any rate, if you didn't look too closely, which seemed to be the aim. Things too neatly arranged invited too much examination, and too much examination provided too much information. And so, in the manner of rebels everywhere, he cultivated the lapse, the mischance, and the leather jacket as if these were morally good per se. Perfectionists are commonly understood to be maniacs of one kind or another, confusing orderliness with goodness, but you can have a mania for *dis*order, too. You can have an indiscriminate drive to magnetize everything, and you can apply to the fulfillment of that drive the same zealous energy others apply to editing the irises and dusting the Roseville. That was Andy: the imperfectionist. And he liked it like that.

ELEVEN

But even imperfectionism can be daunting, hard work. The things and people you drag into orbit tend to need a lot of maintenance; otherwise they wouldn't be so draggable. Andy didn't mind it when he was paid for the service; ever since he'd upgraded himself from English teacher to guidance counselor, he seemed to spend as much of his day handling the social crises of his four hundred charges as he spent jury-rigging their byzantine schedules. Nor did he mind it when the service was utterly simple to perform: The aunties he collected (his mother's friends, really) were delighted with a chatty call now and then; a gentle scratching behind the jaw was all it took to solve Chauncey's life problems. But difficult, depressed humans could not be scratched into satiety, and sometimes Andy resented their importunings. He was not paid, he told himself, to rescue them—which is not to say he wasn't trained.

And trained by the best. Andy's mother had been, by all accounts, an excellent, if imposing, teacher. Pictures of her among her students—toughs at an all-boys "vocational and technical" high school—suggest a stern and idealistic woman, feared but loved, just like in the movies. Is Andy gilding or defacing the lily when he says she was not in fact a Mrs. Chips but a terrifying battle-ax? She knew what she wanted from her pupils, enunciated it rather too plainly, and was wholly unaccepting of any sort of defiance. She practiced a sort of incorporal punishment: no raps with rulers, but a freezing glance or withering remark for those who failed to measure up. It hardly seems an accident that she served for a time (in the quaint administrative parlance of New York public schools) as "cutting dean"—and was she ever. Unfortunately, her sharpness was not reserved for truants. Shoppers may feel grateful that she never got the job she sought at Macy's back in 1930: Retail was not perhaps the most suitable career for a woman whose attitudinal repertoire ran from *prove it* to *I don't think so*. The taming of rowdy boys, on the other hand, provided a socially useful outlet for her cleverness and hauteur. The kiss of her whip helped tenderize thick skulls for *Ethan Frome*; crumb by crumb, she managed to feed her future mechanics the Shakespeare she loved.

This was not a mask Janet could take on and off at will: She was the cutting dean with Andy, too. When he brought home mediocre grades, she said, "Why don't you bring home grades like your brother?" And when he did bring home grades like Frank, she said, "Why don't you bring home grades like this all the time?" The problem with high standards is not that they're high but that they're standard. They support one truth at the expense of others. No trumpeting of Frank's excellent qualities could make Andy more like him, but it could make him less like himself. His own excellent qualities, untrumpeted, would naturally go into a kind of internal exile. Janet's fierce certainties left the whole family, but especially Andy, in a state of suspended reality. If she said a thing, it would be true, by the sheer implacability of her will. But if a thing she said had the temerity to persist in *not* being true, if it *wasn't* right, there was no choice for it but to disappear. The accident that left Andy scarred at seven was recategorized, according to one of Janet's typical diktats, as an example of parental neglect pure and simple; that there was a more direct agency in the matter was never to be discussed and was therefore not so. This unilaterally legislated reality, meant to spare Frank an unmanageable guilt, had the effect of denying Andy a manageable truth.

Well, it's an old Jewish story—actually, it's several old Jewish stories, all jumbled together illegibly. There is the contest of the night-and-day offspring, ancient as the Bible. There is the apparently affable but strangely mute father, an unindicted co-conspirator. There is the second-generation immigrant's drive for excellence, narrowly defined, in her children. And there is, above all, the high drama of the magnificent, overbearing mother and the cowed, inadequate son. This is the part of the story Andy feels most viscerally, despite adversions to his mother's wit, her compassion (when dealing with people outside the family), her fierce intelligence. The way she seemed to *need* him to be inadequate in all his dealings with the outer world. The way she brought down the guillotine on plans that might take him away from her. And if this was nothing more than a Yiddish penny dreadful, it was none the less powerful. In her storminess, in her egoism, in her aphoristic pith, she must have sometimes seemed like a brownstone-belt Queen Lear. Never more so than when Andy eventually told her he was thinking of having a child. "God forbid," she spat. "Wait until I die."

Andy tried to discuss the subject: "Wouldn't you like a grandchild nearby?" (He lived only three blocks from his mother; Frank and his family lived in Detroit.) "I *have* two grandchildren," came the reply. After a while he gave up. He understood, in part, the source of her fury. It wasn't so much her prejudice against adoption, or even against men usurping motherly prerogatives. It wasn't her reasonable concern that a single person — especially one as callow as she believed Andy to be — might be squashed by the burden. It was simpler, starker, and unaddressable: She was afraid. Who would take care of her if the boy she had groomed since birth for the job suddenly, in the fifth act, upped and quit?

TWELVE

By then Janet had been widowed for many years, but hidden behind her widowhood was a complication. She had first been jilted. Andy's father, whether suffering a belated midlife crisis or just tired, after twenty-four years, of his wife's insatiety, decamped from the marriage in 1969, taking up with the woman who had been (surprise! — for the children had not known) his first wife long ago. Janet was destroyed, and yet not so destroyed that she couldn't mobilize a hasty counterinsurgency. Or was it a court-martial? Andy, who had plans to spend the months between his junior and senior years of college in an off-campus apartment at the University of Wisconsin, was summoned to Brooklyn without explanation to appear as evidence in Janet's case. Which was, in brief: *The children! The children! Where is your sense of duty to the children!* Well, actually, the children were twenty-three and nineteen, and Frank was safely ensconced in graduate school at Harvard. But Andy (Janet pleaded) still required the kind of guidance only a father, a properly married father, could provide — and look, here the boy was, with long hair, no plans, and a coterie of pretentious, pot-smoking friends. Her argument prevailed and, as punishment for his crime, Lewis agreed to return to his accuser. Once again he left his first wife and returned to the sad, the difficult house in Brooklyn. But if the return was for good, it was not for long; he died eight years later, of the rare blood disease purpura, at sixty-six. Frank wondered if his father had been done in by the toxic solvents he'd once used for refinishing woodwork around the house. Andy wondered if the solvent was merely regret.

Janet rallied for a while. She donned a beret and went to the theater—not to glitzy Broadway spectaculars but to Beckett and Chekhov at unupholstered dives. When Ingmar Bergman brought his Swedish *Hamlet* to the Brooklyn Academy of Music she whispered along in English, verbatim: "When sorrows come, they come not single spies, but in battalions." She had Andy escort her to campy satires and was curious to visit the louche clubs afterward, but Andy drew the line at that. She annotated her encyclopedias with articles clipped from magazines and for a time managed her properties sharply.

But the outer sharpness began to collapse without the structure of her work and unhappy marriage beneath it. She became more and more dependent on Andy, not only for company but to assuage her lurking terror. She staged repeat performances of the disappearing-husband drama, only now Andy was double-cast: He played himself and his father, too. His plan to get a doctorate in 1989 was interrupted by one such summer-stock revival; summoned back to New York from New Mexico, he found Janet on the brink of collapse. Truth be told, his doctoral ambition must not have been very powerful if it could so easily be diverted by his mother's familiar antics. And yet his ambition, however tenuous, was at least his. He let it go.

He had let so much go. To be a gay man of his generation almost *required* you to let so much go. You let go of your purchase on a clear path in life, unless you chose instead to let go of your integrity. You let go of your entitlement to respect in the world. Now you began to let go of friends not even forty. And yet Andy had let go of even more, more than what the times and the accident of his orientation required. He'd let go of the priceless human assumption of perfectibility: that some part of what existed, or could exist, was unblemished and beautiful. No. The only thing real for Andy was what was broken, what required him.

As Janet aged and sickened, Andy gradually realized that this mania for rescue—as played out repeatedly in his love life, his social life, his very occupation—had its source and destination in the same magnetic, disagreeable woman. He may have spent half an adulthood erecting various bulwarks against the feminine in his personality (why else the leather jackets?) but in the end the feminine came crashing in from the other side. Helping Janet in and out of a hospital bed, her thin gown flapping, he remembered a phrase an old boyfriend had used to describe how gay sons get trained, for better or worse and till death do them part, to tend to their powerful mothers. "Designated daughter," the friend had said. And that's what Andy was: the designated daughter.

THIRTEEN

Once upon a time there was a difficult queen in a land of pleasant men. Now, this queen had certain powers; she was much admired for her metamorphoses. She could turn coal into gold and, more amazingly yet, gold into coal. People from other lands came to see her perform her magic, which in fact was very difficult work; they applauded, paid her tribute, and stayed out of the way of her wand. But among her own people, no matter how many transformations she managed—food from nothing, blood from a stone—no one clapped.

Who were these pleasant, undemonstrative men? Though she could not say how it might have happened, they seemed to own her, or at any rate her powers. For she had a husband and, oh, at least a thousand sons. Naturally, the first was a gleaming jewel (she did not know, when he came along, just how many more there would be). The second—well, we'll get to him. The rest were indistinguishably ductile, at least in response to lashes of her tongue. And her tongue had a mind of its own.

There was nothing soft in this queen's life, not even herself. She had so many children (and she knew what to do); but after the firstborn they occasioned only the most abstract kind of satisfaction. Sometimes she wondered if she had been cursed. Pricked with a poison thorn, perhaps, or abducted from her native people, or pointed in the wrong direction by the maleficent goon of a higher power.

Maybe if she had been born a bit earlier—or much, much later. Maybe if she hadn't panicked at thirty-five and married after so many years of satisfactory self-rule. Maybe she could have been a bohemian. A poet? A lesbian? An actress in a garret?

Or maybe if she'd had a daughter.

For it befell one day that the gleaming jewel (quite naturally) removed himself to another setting. A little while later, the husband defected to a nearby country; when eventually he was remanded into her custody, he promptly died of a strange disease with a murmuring name that seemed a kind of farewell affectation. Purpura, purpura, purpura . . . You might think that the queen would at last be happy in herself, but at sixty-eight she knew something she had not known before: A queen is owned by her subjects, without whom she has no one to rule. Without ruling, she has no one to be.

She needed a daughter, and fast; the only question was how to get one. Well, the old queen still had a bit of magic left: Perhaps she could perform one last metamorphosis. But on whom? She looked around the remains of her land, now consisting mostly of paying tenants. And then she remembered: the second son. Why, he didn't seem very busy at all; perhaps he could be put to good use. What else was he doing that was so important? True, he didn't seem ideally suited to the role; with his butch finery, his leathery carapace, he was almost as masculine as the queen herself. But she asked her mirror, which knew deep things: "Who's the feyest of them all?" The mirror reflected a tall pale flame, the emblem of the second son.

And so one day the queen commanded him to come, which he promptly did. "You will care for me now," she said, "and no one else."

"What will I get in return?" he asked.

"In return, you will be allowed to care for me," she replied, closing her eyes tightly, emptying her vial of fairy dust, and reciting her spell over and over: Purpura, purpura, purpura . . .

Perhaps she shouldn't have closed her eyes so tightly, for some of the fairy dust dispersed in the wind—resulting in much confusion elsewhere—and the spell only worked partway. The second son did not grow breasts, nor did his penis fall off, but a hollow opened up inside him that did the queen no good. Or did it?

The second son attended his mother until she died. He fed her, amused her, called every morning. And if he sometimes looked right through her, toward something else on the horizon, was that such a terrible price to pay? She had not meant to, but she'd given him something deeper than breasts: She'd given him back his heart. In her last year, when she began to lose him, she must have understood the moral: Don't teach your children to care for you unless you want them to care for someone else.

FOURTEEN

For a while Andy said nothing more about becoming a parent. But he did continue to think about it. "Think" may not be the right word, however: On the one hand there was a single, almost atomic beam of feeling, which could not be picked apart or diverted; on the other hand there was a thicket of hyperthought, so dense and rambling as to admit no light. His attempts to prune the thicket kept getting stuck in the same three places. By what method would he have a child? Alternative insemination had been a disaster, and adoption—even if it was possible—still made him queasy. With whose help? He did not feel he could handle the responsibilities of child-rearing without support, and yet what support was available (from Elliot) he would not take and what help he would take (from his mother) was unavailable.

Last, there was what seemed at the time the most critical question: Why? The teenaged girls in his after-school Pregnancy Prevention Program (he sometimes thought it should be called the Second Pregnancy Prevention Program) talked casually about having children almost as something to do instead of homework, or as a fit punishment for sex (since they didn't like birth control and didn't "believe in" abortion), or as a way of creating something of their own—something unsullied, at least for a little while, by the unhappy conditions of their lives. These motivations were obviously repellent or delusional, and the babies produced in consequence appeared to be—what was the mildest way to put it?—underserved. But Andy couldn't come up with anything much more convincing, and in the absence of a good reason he suspected himself of bad faith.

It's not surprising that he could not identify a credible, honorable motive for having children. Few people can. Ask the parents in a traditional family why they bothered to reproduce and you will most likely get the tautological imperative ("We always wanted to") or a confused collection of rusty saws ("We felt we should give something back to the next generation"). Ask a gay man why he might want to have a child and you're likely to get an uncomprehending stare. For it cannot be overstated how hamhandedly American culture pushes parenthood on heterosexuals and how stingily it withholds the idea from gay men, like an unscrupulous mountebank. Are you unable to afford a meal, let alone a child? Good, have a baby. Are you fourteen years old and illiterate? Good, have a baby. Are you miserable in your marriage? Good, have a baby. Are you mature and well off and responsible but gay? Good, collect Roseville.

There are few officially sanctioned prejudices left in America but this is one. Behind it lurks the idea that gay men are at heart—one must say the terrible thing frankly—pedophiles. Like the blood libel of the Jews, gay men's supposed sexual appetite for children has been advanced for years as proof of an almost Satanic turpitude. And while the incoming tide of sexual liberalization has done much to expand civil rights for homosexuals—not to mention their appearance on sitcoms—by 1990 it had not yet managed to overwhelm that nasty, unsinkable canard. Indeed, the history of the idea is remarkably consistent. As far back as the 1930s, tabloids used the mostly trumped-up "sex murders" of young boys as an opportunity to inflame public hysteria under the guise of sober lecturing on the dangers of homosexuality. Anita Bryant did much the same in her seventies crusade, and today Colorado for Family Values, in its guide to antigay initiatives, flatly states that "73 percent of homosexuals incorporate children into their sexual practices." Gay rights groups, helpless in the face of such ludicrous smears, have responded with some unfounded statistics of their own; it is commonly held and fervently repeated that ninety percent of pedophiles are heterosexual men. And while no reliable study I've seen confirms this famous figure, the literature does seem to support the idea that the vast majority of pedophiles are adult males having sex with underage girls.

Why then has the animus toward homosexuals focused itself more and more narrowly over the years, despite all evidence, on their relations with children? So-called queer theorists have made convincing arguments connecting the pedophilia slur to sexual envy: Gay men must be punished for their freedoms *within the context of their freedoms*—see also AIDS. Sociologists connect the slur to a generalized cultural lust for youth that is severely repressed and then hatefully projected. And anthropologists cite an atavistic fear of behaviors that do not replenish the clan: homosexuality, par excellence. All these theories are probably true; all are interesting, at least. But whatever the underlying cause, the result is that gay men are trapped in a catch-22: They can't disprove the lie unless they become parents, but they can hardly become parents because of the lie. If the desire to have children nevertheless arises, the most sensible thing for gay men to do is to crush it.

FIFTEEN

Which is essentially what the gay movement as a whole did throughout its early years. The subject of children was virtually taboo, so deeply internalized had the pedophile slur become. It did not help matters that newspapers began covering a pathetic organization called NAMBLA—the North American Man/Boy Love Association—as if it were some sort of pervert internationale, instead of a tiny clique of ill-socialized and mostly unpracticing paraphiliacs. Gay men cringed at the acronym and yet, themselves so often the subject of sexual stigmatization, could not bring themselves to speak much against it. The result was a kind of age paralysis: Don't deal with young people; instead, stay young yourself. When, in 1983, a college professor named A. Damien Martin and a psychiatrist named Emery S. Hetrick first sought financing for a program to help gay kids—kids who were being abused in shelters, schools, and foster homes—they could hardly bring up the notion at cocktail parties before the potential donors on whom the project would depend had fled to the crudités. A well-known gay leader attempted to dissuade Martin from the plan by saying, "If you go near the schools, we'll *all* be thrown in jail!" Even those who came through with money took pains to cover their tracks. One man, perhaps fetishizing his desire for discretion, insisted on delivering a fifty-thousand-dollar contribution in cash he'd stuffed in his cowboy boots.

By 1990, the Hetrick-Martin Institute (as it was eventually known) was well established as the country's leading service-and-advocacy organization for gay youth. An often overlooked but obvious and telling point is that most of its clients were the children of heterosexuals. Organizations for homosexuals who wanted to have children of their own were only just beginning to appear, and most were overwhelmingly female in membership. While no longer exactly taboo, the subject of family was simply not high on gay men's political agenda, especially at a time when AIDS was sucking up most of the energy and money (not to mention the bodies) available to an increasingly exhausted community. (Hetrick and Martin, longtime companions, had both succumbed by 1992.) Activists who had been dealing with death for over a decade did not have much patience to spare for those few men who sought any opportunity to talk—moonily, sunnily—about birth.

If Andy had not voluntarily taken a vow of silence on the subject, he might have been driven to it by the dreamy, purple tones of the seekers. These were men who said they wanted children but whose attitude toward family (as toward so much else, for that matter) was painfully confectionary, glazed with clichés. Whenever I heard them, I had the sense that the glaze was designed to seal over a rather unsavory history. *How beautiful is the perfect innocence of a child!* their rapturous expressions proclaimed, but their own childhoods, upon closer inspection, often proved to have been insufficiently innocent. This was typical enough for gay men, but most other gay men displayed their painful childhoods unwhitewashed—or even, preferably, exaggerated, accoutred, and turned into a personal style. The seekers, on the other hand, denied the past and at the same time sought to reinvent it; they were priests of a religion that had defrocked them and in which they believed all the more.

Of course, I knew women like this as well, but there was something doubly disturbing about men who preached the cult. Harmless if helpless, they ascribed too much power to the thing from which they felt shut out—and in this they bore an unfortunate and unfair resemblance to pedophiles. Oh, they would never hurt a child, unless by cooing it to death. But like every NAMBLA member I've interviewed, they seemed inanely evangelical; something dense and drippy in their utterance, something longing in their gaze, suggested a deluded romance. For the pedophiles this romance was all too literal (if one-sided); their descriptions of even the most glancing encounter with a youthful love object tended to be filled with images of flowers responding to celestial dew and blossoms about to burst into bloom. The child-seekers were romantic in a much less interesting way: They were naive.

From his years in the classroom and in the guidance office, Andy had enough experience of real children to know they were not innocent, not powerful, not the source of the strong feelings people contrived to have about them. For better or worse, they were always pawns in what was inevitably an adult's (or at any rate a parent's) game. It was only by talking to actual parents—friends of friends, or strangers with Snuglis—that Andy began to work his way toward a resolution. Oh, these parents had as many damp notions about the sanctity of childhood as anyone else, and were just as capable of waxing rhapsodic over shrieking Junior, at least as long as Junior was engaged in the sandbox thirty feet away. But they also knew about colic and tantrums and how important it was to get back to work. The child-seekers never seemed to *want* to get back to work, if they had any work in the first place. Like Andy, they were looking for something more compelling than what their lives currently provided. But there is a fine line between needing a child to fulfill your identity and needing a child to give you an identity in the first place.

SIXTEEN

Only by understanding where that line, that tightrope, lay was it possible to predict whether you would walk it successfully. On the one hand, you needed to want a child enough to pay the agency or get someone pregnant and in any case put up with two to three decades of nearly constant anxiety. On the other hand, if you wanted a child *too* much—if a child was *all* you wanted in life— you might have nothing more than the wanting to offer him if and when he arrived.

Andy wasn't quite sure where he stood. Friends told him that he got depressed whenever he spent time with other people's children, that he seemed to feel envious and inferior. This at first surprised him, because he hadn't thought of himself as a person who particularly *liked* kids, merely as a person who *wanted* them. But the friends were right: Andy did get sullen when he went to Philadelphia, say, and saw his old pals the Furstenburg sisters, each with her own pair of appealing children. It was not the children per se he envied but the accomplishment of their mothers: Professional women in satisfying long-term relationships, they had identified their core goals and in a timely manner met them. This was, of course, the key act of adulthood, and Andy had not completed it; that is, he had identified the goal but failed to reach it. Hence his sense of inferiority—notwithstanding whatever excuses he could make about how hard it was for a gay man. "For all my countercultural pretensions," he tells me now, "I had always been a Jewish prince who wanted to do what he wanted to do and didn't want to be stopped." And yet he had let himself be stopped.

Who had stopped him? Who hadn't? The dream we find so becoming in women, so touching in husbands, we label a deformity in openly gay men. His mother, desirous of grandchildren otherwise, wanted none from her son who refused to get married. ("God forbid! Wait until I die!") His gay friends were less hostile if not more helpful. "I spoke with lots of guys who would say, 'That's a wonderful thing to want to do but, God, who would want to do it?' " Andy remembers. "I thought they must find their lives a little more interesting than I found mine, they must be really engaged with the things they do. But I didn't need another tchotchke or another trip or trick someplace. Nothing like that was going to make the second half of my life significantly different and better than the first. The first half, well . . . there wasn't anything there I couldn't let go of.

"I didn't want those things anymore. I wanted meaning in my

life in the absence of being an artist or writer or revolutionary, which I now figured out I wasn't going to be—which I don't think I ever really *wanted* to be. And yet I was becoming selfish enough to see that I didn't want, forever and always, to be taking care of people who had very little to offer me back. Truculent students, dying AIDS patients, lovers too needy or too remote. Least of all my mother! Gay men are magnets for people in need and I wasn't going to spend the rest of my life just doing that out of enforced saintliness. I wanted *unconditional* love, which seemed a kind of immortality. I mean, if I was going to be taking care of people anyway, I might as well get something for it."

Unconditional love. Immortality. Were they good reasons for wanting a child? They sounded a lot like the reasons given by girls at school. But Andy no longer cared about reasons. What he finally realized was that having children was *in all cases* ill-founded. Motives were never unimpeachable, and so he did not need to have an unimpeachable motive. Had he not been a gay man, no one would ever have asked him to explain. Since he *was* a gay man, he had been forced to do much more thinking than most people do—certainly more than his own parents had—if to no better conclusion. Like everyone else with their mixtures of terrible thinking and fantasy and hope, and something perhaps theological, if you will (or biological, if you won't), he had what reasons he had. He was human; it was enough to say he wanted— not so much to fill a hole as to tend to something untended in himself. He was rich but fallow. He wanted a child because he wanted a chance, at last, to love well: not to receive unconditional love, but give it.

SEVENTEEN

With this realization, the concerns that had shut Andy down for almost a year dissolved surprisingly quickly, like a May storm that rages for hours but blows away in minutes. What had once seemed the most difficult question—Why?—now seemed the most simple, or perhaps just moot. The questions of how, and with whose help, were the ones that actually mattered, and they soon fell into place as well. He would adopt; babies grew up fine on formula. And Janet or no Janet, Elliot or no Elliot, he would raise the child alone.

Going it alone came simply. Why not? He was now forty-three and had managed most of his life alone: cooked for himself, cleaned for himself, bought a car and a little house without anyone's help or approval. He cared for himself (and his retinue); surely he could care for a child. Single women did it all the time — why, there was Murphy Brown even now, sassing the vice president on TV. Why couldn't he do something she could? Something a resourceless teenager could? His resources were substantial. Not that he had saved much money over the years, but he had a pension fund he could borrow against. And how much could the thing cost, anyway? Well, there was child care, of course, but he could rent out the house on Long Island to help pay for a housekeeper. Plus, having served so long in the school system, he was due for a sabbatical; although that would mean a thirty-percent reduction in salary for a year, it would also allow him to be home with the child. And if he timed it right . . . but he was getting ahead of himself. At this point all he had was the resolve. He did not know the first thing about adoption itself.

Well, he knew the first thing. Adoption was (or could be) clean. It did not require him to jerk off into test tubes or triangulate with willful lesbians. It did not, he hoped, require him to lie or compromise his identity. And it had a certain ecological appeal. Adoption allowed you to take care of a child who already needed it, rather than wrangle with biology and hardware just to make another life on earth. It was like going to the pound for a dog: a rescue maneuver. Indeed, adopting Chauncey when the mutt was already three years old, Andy had thought it could be a dry run for parenting. So, to their horror, did his friends, who said, "What are you doing? You can't take care of a dog!" — as if Andy would forget to feed him or to make arrangements when he went on vacation. Perhaps it's not surprising that people thought Andy was a lightfoot bon vivant; that's what he wanted them to think. But he was actually foot-heavy. He lived in a building owned by his mother. His "ex-lover-to-be" still slept in his bed, albeit curled in the opposite direction. As an imperfectionist, Andy allowed loose ends to flap where they might, but the knots he made, for better or worse, stayed tied. In any case, Chauncey, now thirteen, had managed all right. The leg broken by the previous owner had turned arthritic, but that seemed proof of Andy's goodness in rescuing him. He gladly helped Chauncey onto the sofa, onto the bed: one less lonely creature in the world.

If adoption seemed like the right thing to do ecologically, that was secondary. It was the right thing for Andy. Andy liked clean slates, if he could get them; he was not at his best with history. History always seemed to implicate someone. Andy did better with people when the inscrutable wrongs of their past were kept shrouded, were at any rate unattributable to him. Starting new, you could not be made to feel guilty about the broken leg of an earlier life; you could only be made to feel good for the rescue. An anonymous sexual escapade was therefore, in a way, the safest kind: not because it had no future but because it had no past. *You come to me with whatever pain I did not cause; do not say what it is and I will kiss it.* This was the love without history, just as adoption was the birth without history, or with a history permanently obscured. An adoptive child's story begins over, at least as far as his new parent is concerned, on the day he's turned over with his box of diapers and complimentary car seat. No past, only future — or so Andy thought.

EIGHTEEN

If Andy knew the first thing about adoption, he did not know the second, which was how, in fact, you got a child.

He spent most of 1993 finding out: attending meetings and conferences and workshops while consulting with people who had been through the process before. Usually he was the only unmarried man in the room, sometimes the only man at all, and it was unclear whether the methods being discussed would even work for him. Private adoption, for instance, was a process that typically involved placing advertisements for yourself in newspapers around the country and perhaps obtaining an 800 number so that a nice Catholic girl who had made a mistake might call you toll-free and offer you her child. You essentially marketed yourself as a desirable alternative to abortion. Unfortunately, such girls were more likely to be drawn to an ad featuring "loving childless wealthy couple married ten years eagerly seeks to provide a happy home for your beautiful baby girl" than to one featuring "single gay man, mid-forties, seeks to piss off disapproving mother."

The alternative to a private adoption was an agency adoption, which seemed just as likely to run into trouble. Whether operated by states, foundations, or just as family businesses, most agencies had the same preferences in prospective parents as the women who were their clients—and had better antennae for picking up subtleties and obfuscations in the application. Andy could state, truthfully, that he was a single man and not a front for a homosexual couple, but an agency, especially a church-based agency, would make its own assumptions. And if the agency dealt in "highly desirable" children—healthy white newborns—they had plenty of highly desirable parents to choose among before they got down to the Andys of the world. It seemed that his only hope for an agency adoption, therefore, would be to find one whose clients were somewhat less Caucasian.

By 1993 many single women and discreet lesbians had successfully adopted baby girls from China—only girls, because the country's misogyny and "one-child" policy encouraged poor families to hold out for a son. Yet even here single men were suspect, just as they were in most of the countries to which increasingly desperate couples, exhausted from their regimens of drugs, surgeries, and micromanaged intercourse, applied for children. The social workers and lawyers who facilitated such international adoptions might themselves see no problem with the kind of placement Andy sought, but it was harder to get a single man through Bolivia (say) than a llama through the eye of a needle. So it would have to be—how comforting the name!—a domestic adoption. But domestic where? There were no agencies on Christopher Street.

Andy's research seemed to be turning up more questions than answers. Did he prefer a boy or a girl, or did he not care? Would he accept a child with a medical problem? What about an older child, or a sibling pair? How much was he willing to lie and how much was he willing to spend? (Domestic adoption agencies, he was learning, could charge as much as twenty thousand dollars— or, if you would take a black child, as little as twenty-five hundred.) But no question was as powerful as the one at the heart of the psychology of adoption: Did he want the procedure to be "open"—in which case the birth family and the adoptive family had some degree of interaction, might know each other's names and whereabouts, might even exchange letters and photos and visits? Or did he want it "closed"—in which case they were forever strangers?

Open adoptions were, at least for married couples, easier to obtain. But they were also, in general, more subject to disturbance. Birth mothers had been known to seek more contact than originally agreed upon, or more money. They became importunate, threatening. Adoptive parents had been known to renege on their promise to share news of, or time with, the baby. They became hostile, defensive. Of course, closed adoptions could be painful, too. There was the birth mother's pain—but that pain was at least anonymous, sealed away not just from the adoptive parent but, more important, from the baby. And there was the pain of the adopted child himself, who, later in life, might be tormented (people surmised) by questions about the birth family he could never know.

Pain, pain everywhere, or so it seemed from the five o'clock news and the very special Movie of the Week. And yet that was a distortion. Adoption wasn't the problem; life was the problem. Life was full of regrets and unanswerable questions regardless of who your family was. The thing to do, Andy realized, was to counteract unavoidable pain by planning, as much as possible, for unassailable joy.

NINETEEN

And so, on January 10, 1994, a man describing himself accurately if narrowly as a single, Jewish, forty-four-year-old guidance counselor, with brown eyes and salt-and-pepper hair, six feet tall and weighing (though this seems wishful) one hundred and sixty-five pounds, the possessor of life insurance, a small mortgage, a master's degree in education, and a 1987 Dodge Lancer worth about twenty-seven hundred dollars—a man, moreover, who was energetic, sociable, and socially conscious, with a well-developed sense of responsibility toward other people, who took things seriously but liked to laugh and who spent much time outdoors with his dog—made application to become a father.

The agency to which he applied was known to have given children to single gay men, or even, with one blind eye, to gay couples. Apparently, like the armed forces, they had a "Don't ask, don't tell" policy. Certainly there was no question on their forms, nor did they ever inquire in person, about sexual orientation, although there was a line labeled "other persons living in household," which might have turned up dirt. Andy winced and in his best hand wrote: "none." This was not completely a lie, since Elliot was planning (as always) to move out. Still, he was there. He shared Andy's bed, even if nothing but sleep and sleeplessness ever happened in it. To say he was Andy's lover or partner by this point would have been false, and not incidentally might have jinxed the adoption. So Elliot was elided. Elsewhere, as if in compensation, he did make an appearance, under the heading "Child Care Arrangements," as someone who would help out when Andy was "absent from the home." "How is this person related to you?" the form wondered mildly. "Tenant," Andy wrote.

Well, Elliot did pay rent. And, in a deeper sense, he was one who held on—and on. This trait, so surprising and disturbing to heterosexuals who want nothing to do with their exes, is a commonplace of gay (and especially lesbian) relationships. Sometimes it seemed there was no choice. The gay world, whatever statistics you favored, was small and insular and besieged; it required, as much as possible, that no one be wasted, that burned bridges be rebuilt. Consequently, people bending away from each other, like Andy and Elliot, had learned to tolerate—or even promote—a great deal of ambiguity; the ambiguity could in some cases serve to postpone necessary change, and thus be stultifying, but it could also reflect a commitment to manage and endure conflict instead of violently disconnecting. It was, in any case, a useful trait in facing the process of adoption, which asks of you that you remain in a state of perpetual readiness for an event that may happen at any moment, or never; the agency told Andy that nine months was standard, just as if it were a real pregnancy.

Nine months seemed comparatively quick, and the reason was simple if brutal: The agency, located in a southwestern state, dealt primarily with birth mothers who described themselves as Latino, Hispanic, Chicano, or mixed-race. If you wanted a white child (whatever that meant), you might wait five years, and the agency politely suggested you take your search elsewhere. If you didn't care about the baby's skin color, though, the agency didn't care about yours—or about the gender of persons who might touch it, either. To Andy, this seemed more than fair. An unreconstructed (not to say knee-jerk) liberal, a member of a junior version of the Congress of Racial Equality at thirteen, he was not only undeterred by society's (and even his friends') lingering prejudice, but was, in a way, spurred on by it. He was himself a member of a suspect minority, or possibly even two.

Which may or may not be the reason why, filling out the forms, Andy specifically requested a child of Hispanic or mixed origin. Can he be forgiven if his imperfectionism, his rescue mania, extended no further? For the child, in many people's eyes, would already be burdened with the fact of adoption, and, worse, adoption by a single, gay parent. That was enough for one small life; beyond it, there should be as little cause for scrutiny as possible. Andy asked for a newborn boy, tall if such a thing could be predicted, for Andy was tall and he hoped his son would not look up to him too far. And he specified a child without handicaps or health problems, with a birth mother who was drug and alcohol free—surely the same qualities Concepción would have chosen, were she in a position to choose.

Children are always overdetermined. The simplest biological birth arises from an impenetrable complex of motivations: personal and social, animal and moral—however you wish to parse them. But a simple biological birth does not require its authors to fill out forms, to examine their impulses and choose words to describe the indescribable. Adoption does. The agency asks you to fill in blanks, some of them rather ominously large: "What are your feelings regarding adoption?" ("Adoption unites what is good for individuals with what is good for society, and makes a bond between strangers," Andy wrote.) "What are your reasons for adopting a child?" ("When I was a child, my parents cared for me. As an adult, I care for myself. I want to complete the circle now.") "What are your expectations for a child you adopt?" ("My dreams for my child include him being an accomplished student, musician and athlete, emotionally warm and honest, creative, curious, humorous and kind, with a professional career and a satisfying personal life. My expectations are that he will meet his potential, whatever it may be, with support and encouragement from me.")

And then finally: "Describe yourself." But—except for the "musician and athlete" part—he just had.

TWENTY

Instead of a sonogram, an adoptive parent undergoes a home study: a picture not of the place the baby comes from, but of where he will be going. "Home study" sounds somewhat ominous, as if a white-gloved blue blood will be examining the fireplace mantel for dust and the spines on the bookshelves for smut. But the procedure is in fact performed by a social worker, licensed by the state, who is probably as sloppy a housekeeper as her subjects. She is not, in general, interested in the dishes; she is hired by the adoption agency, which may be thousands of miles away, merely (merely!) to see that the house is in satisfactory condition to accommodate a new life, and to see that its occupant is, too.

Except for having a cleaning lady in, Andy barely prepared for the social worker's visit one Saturday afternoon in January. Certainly he didn't tuck in the loose corners of his gay life, let alone try to recloset himself; he left the SILENCE=DEATH poster up, left his modest earring in, and introduced Elliot in passing. Of course, Andy already knew that the social worker wouldn't care; when he'd met her, for a preliminary interview in her office, she had shown him photographs of kids she'd helped to place with gay men. Like most people who do the hands-on work of trying to find good homes for children (she was a single adoptive mother herself) she did not trouble herself with the abstract policies of politicians and boards. She was practical. If in her report she had to fudge the details a little, she didn't mind; she knew that such placements, however unorthodox, were good for kids—not just because all the studies showed this, but because she had seen for herself. A gay person with the emotional, intellectual, and financial resources to navigate his way, despite all obstacles, to a successful adoption was probably better suited than most to navigate his way to a successful parenthood.

What she was really concerned with during her hour-long visit was where the crib would go, who would take care of the baby when Andy worked, and how the child would be disciplined when the time came. (Andy had revealed his unfamiliarity with this last subject, and perhaps his distaste for it as well, in his application: "Certainly there will be no physical punishment," he wrote. "I will probably use 'time outs' in conjunction with other methods that I don't know about yet.") She liked that art and music were everywhere in evidence. She apparently even liked Andy's shall-we-say-eclectic taste: "The house is very warm and comfortably furnished," she wrote in her report to the agency— and then, somewhat improbably, added: "The house is immaculately maintained."

By the time a baby arrives in an adoptive parent's house, that parent has been repeatedly described, redacted, and entered into the public record. Authorship of this record is unclear: Many hands seem to have fashioned the strange prose, which veers in tone, like the Bible's, from the magisterial to the dotty, even within one sentence. Like the Bible, too, it is filled with riddles of perspective ("Andrew was observed . . . to have a very pleasant personality") and koanlike conundrums ("Andy describes his relationship with his parents while growing up as hard to characterize"). It is equally emphatic about facts and dreams, which makes them seem equally true: "Andrew has never been married. He states that there is no potential relationship on the horizon. He feels that perhaps one day he will find the right person and will marry if this person comes along." Is the record moving only in retrospect, and only to interested parties? (Is the Bible?) Or is there something in its perseverative attempt to domesticate the most mysterious subjects—attachment, faith—that is, in its very inadequacy, moving?

But the law is not a literary critic. On February 16, 1994, Andy was informed in plainest prose that the adoption agency had "accepted" his home study and considered him ready for placement—ready, that is, upon payment of the next five-thousand-dollar installment of its fee. Once his interstate child-abuse clearance was complete (and assuming it determined that Andy had never been convicted of a sex crime), they were "expecting placement within three to six months."

Time seemed to be contracting: Nine months had become as few as three. Andy at once applied for and was granted a one-year sabbatical from work, to begin that September. Having done so, he fretted that the child would not arrive in time and that the sabbatical would, in effect, be wasted. But if he was nervous, he was also frankly aglow. After years of fruitless attempts, he was finally, as the agency itself had put it, expecting.

TWENTY-ONE

Among all the thousand-and-one listings in the book of baby names, Andy could not find one that wasn't dull or outlandish. If it wasn't Steven it was Stirling—not that the names he'd been considering on his own lacked for outlandishness. His favorite was Wolf, which in his ear sounded lean and kinetic and virile. It was also a "brown" name, befitting what he assumed would be a brown child; according to this logic he also toyed with Mediterranean monikers like Carlo and Zev. What he wanted to avoid was a nerdy name, a name that didn't sit squarely in the mouth, a name, in short, that could be perceived as weak.

Which is, alas, how he had perceived his own name, at least when he was a boy. The long version was, in his part of Brooklyn, still odd and formal; the short version marred by a quick final "y" that hung down, he felt, like a stubby, useless tail. It isn't hard to see through these complaints to the homosexual panic beneath—and to the reason he as a gay parent would want a name for his son that was unassailable. *The child is father to the man.* For most heterosexual men, the birth of a child, a son especially, seems to confirm their masculinity, however idiotic the connection may be. Was it possible that, for a gay man, adopting a son would have the opposite effect? A single father would first be a mother, and thus, in a way, *less* of a man. And yet what had been the point of gay liberation if not to storm such gender Bastilles? Wolf, it seemed clear, was an overcompensation, and asking too much of the boy besides.

But how was it possible *not* to ask too much in a name? The only ones that regularly escaped the life sentence of wishful thinking were those too unfamiliar to have connotations, except insofar as their unfamiliarity might *become* their connotation. At work, Andy almost never encountered a Mike or a Sue; there were African names like Omotunde and Nunoo, faux-African names like Shamika and Aquanda, Creole names like Fabiola and Nesly, Indian names like Taiwattie and Jasoda—all of which, however strange, seemed to his ear light and new and unburdened with gender expectation. That they may have been expressive of other kinds of striving was a subtlety not lost on a man whose brother had been named for Franklin Delano Roosevelt, but you could not avoid striving on every axis at once. Humans strove. The point was to avoid handing down to your child the heaviest of your burdens, and it occurred to Andy that a way out of the gender dilemma, *his* heaviest burden, was to find a name unusual enough to be unclassifiable. Like Linden, perhaps—which was what some of the Guyanan boys at school were called, after the hearty tree.

Linden was perhaps too close to the name of a certain reviled president from Texas, but while visiting Israel in 1993, Andy had encountered, twice in two days, a name that seemed similarly fresh and arboreal. The first Erez had washed Andy's hair in a Tel Aviv salon. The second was the son of an army general whose obituary appeared in the *Jerusalem Post*; in an accompanying photograph the dead man's boy looked kind and stalwart despite his mourning. Later Andy learned that the name the two very different men shared—the shampooist and the hero's son—was a simple Hebrew noun meaning "cedar." Well, not entirely simple; though it was a modern invention as a man's name (there is no character in the Bible named Erez) it came with its own set of connotations, at least for Jews who had ever sung the Ninety-second Psalm on Sabbath:

> The righteous . . . shall grow tall like a cedar in Lebanon.
> Planted in the house of the Lord, they shall blossom in the courts
> of our God.
> They shall still shoot forth in old age; they shall be full of sap and
> green.

Erez ba-livanon: a cedar in Lebanon. Though elsewhere deployed as an image of God's destructive power (Psalm 29: "The voice of the Lord breaketh . . . the cedars of Lebanon; He maketh them also to skip like a calf"), these tall and fragrant and long-lived trees had served for centuries as symbols of strength, of the indomitability of the righteous—a concept more vibrant in hope than in fact.

For the first time in years, it seemed, Andy's hopes *were* vibrant, untrampled by leadfoot reality. He thought of the cedar trees at his little house on Long Island: the house he had bought when he thought he would not have a child. They were shorter, no doubt, than the ones in Lebanon, but they certainly adapted well after transplant and grew steadily in any good soil. That they were a symbol of strength was all the better; with a single gay Jewish father, the boy would need it.

TWENTY-TWO

The needle didn't hurt—too much. A little pointy pressure, a buzzing sensation, a radiating heat as the ink went in. Not that Andy could watch; he may have been drawn to the disreputability of it (it was a *wolfy* thing to do) but he wasn't, after all, a wolf. He was a sheep in wolf's clothing. Thank God the parlor, located in an ugly New Jersey strip mall (tattooing was as yet illegal anywhere closer), was bright and airy, filled with light chatter. And that the "artist" had an MFA from NYU.

Mostly, Andy was relieved that the procedure hurt less than going to the dentist—bridgework being what Jews did instead of getting tattoos. Beyond that he didn't try to explore the implications. Yes, it was against Jewish law, but what wasn't? Wearing earrings, throwing away clipped toenails, doing anything (with the strange exception of male circumcision) that altered and thus desecrated the body were all proscribed. In a middle-aged man, what's there to sully, anyway? And if a tattooed Jew could not be buried in a Jewish cemetery, this (Andy liked to joke) was not in itself reason enough for having the pin stuck in your arm. Nor was his mother's sure disapproval. Or was it? His attitude toward things forbidden in Jewish and matriarchal law was much the same, somewhere between indifference and thumbing his nose. "My whole life I tried to be a bad boy," he now admits, "but I could never get it together to be as bad as I wanted. I had the same job for more than twenty years, working second and third jobs for what reason I don't know, being good to everybody—dogs, children, old ladies. If I was ever going to do something louche, it had better be something that would stay with me forever, and I had better do it now, while I still could, because I wouldn't get to do it again."

If there was a little bit of pain involved, so much the better; it would connect Andy symbolically to the immensely greater pain of labor he could never experience directly. Or maybe, in its tininess, the tattoo prick was more like the putative prick of conception: Somewhere, if not in his own body, a microscopic egg was being pierced by an even smaller sperm. Perhaps this was happening even now, as he winced with each touch of the needle. After all, the letter approving him for adoption had arrived just a few days earlier. Three to six months, they had said, but it surely could be nine; was Concepción feeling what he did now, seeing what he saw in the purple behind his eyelids?

Probably not. It was impossible to generalize about such matters, but Andy imagined that Concepción and Don were not seeking to become parents as assiduously as he was. Probably they were not seeking to become parents at all. The pang at the moment of fusion inside her would be irrelevant, the side effect of whatever joy or solace was being sought in the act of intercourse. Reproduction was her body's idea, not her own; only unnatural measures—condoms, pills, vows of chastity—would have prevented her conceiving a child. For Andy, though, conceiving a child *was* the unnatural measure, no matter how much it might make him look natural to the rest of the world. "A gay man needs children like a fish needs a bicycle," one friend had said. "You are trying to live out a dream that is false." Well, if it weren't false, it wouldn't be a dream. And what should you do with your dreams if not live them out?

Still, to the extent he was abandoning the appearance of unnaturalness by conceiving of Erez, Andy did not want to forget that he would never be the same as other parents. Like the HIV-positive people now showing up on Benetton billboards, he would mark himself before others did it for him; his tattoo would be a way of asserting, if only to himself, the otherwise unobvious fact that he was outside the mainstream. Strangely, he saw it as a kind of memo, best written down in an unmistakable place: *Pick up milk; remember who you are.*

There was, of course, one group of tattooed Jews allowed to be buried in Jewish cemeteries; for them, the concentration camp survivors, the idea that you might need to be reminded of the way society had branded you would seem, at best, naive. Many spent years awaiting the laser techniques that would finally erase the numbers printed on their forearms. Only a person who was afraid he might not be different *enough* would choose to make the point on his biceps. In this, Andy was living out an ambivalence built in to gay liberation (and, for that matter, American Judaism): Are we different? Should we be? If I play golf, drive a Mercedes, hire a maid, am I still a Jew? If I father a child, push a stroller, and, one day, pay orthodontist bills, am I still gay?

Am I still me?

For Andy was also living out the last phase of his own trial by fire. As he sat there in the tattoo parlor, he was not unaware that only a few inches separated the work-in-progress from the long-complete work of the barbecue flame. If he had once been marked for life without his consent, now he would mark himself instead. Before the change (his child, that is) came, he would finish the old business of the sad little boy who flung his arms over his eyes to save them. There was so little time. Six months? Nine months? The flame was upon him once again, but this time it was Andy who told it what to draw: a frolicking blue cherub unfurling a banner on which is written the name of the rescuer. The rescuer and the rescued both: *Andrew,* it said.

TWENTY-THREE

Waiting. We think of waiting as a passive time—a time to keep as still as possible so that the thing we're waiting for will be able to find us. But that stillness is actually quite an exertion, like balancing a glass of water on your head while performing all your normal chores. *Yes, hello, pleased to meet you, I have a glass of water on my head.* It is nothing, and yet it is the central fact. And not just for you. Everyone sees that you are waiting. They see the bubble in your eye, seeking level. When a woman is pregnant, her stomach makes it literal: She is balancing a glass of water within her.

Andy prepared himself for the long wait. It was now the end of February; was it too much to hope that a child would find him before the fall? Just to have something to aim for, he picked a "due date" of July 1, knowing that the agency's guess ranged out as far as Christmas. Even the near date seemed impossibly far—and what should he do in the meantime? Buy equipment: a crib, a stroller, and, what did you call it, a Bathinette? But he was suddenly as superstitious as one of his aunties, who believed it invited the evil eye to furnish a nursery before the baby was imminent. So he bought nothing, and even declined, at least for the moment, the baby shower offered by the proprietor of a local gay bar. Instead, he just looked at his apartment and imagined how it would feel with another life inside it. Would it suddenly be full? Too full?

Of course there already *was* another life inside the apartment, or two if you counted Chauncey. After a few sniffs, the dog would do fine with the new arrival, or so Andy assumed; he was comfortable with children and deeply committed to serial napping. Surely he would just park himself on the couch as usual and absorb the change into the precious unchangingness of his days. The other life, Elliot's, was another story—but what *was* the story? Supportive of Andy's decision, glad for his success so far, he took a great interest in the upcoming adoption while understanding that it would not be his child. If he could ever find a new apartment, he would not even be living with Andy by the time the boy arrived. He would be—what? A quasi-stepparent? A friend? An "uncle"?

As they had never been keen on definitions before, they let this one slide. Elliot would be whatever he was. In any case, with that glass of water on Andy's head, it was no time for sudden, decisive movements. Even in ordinary circumstances, external change seemed to Andy somehow threatening, untoward. Certainly, change of any sort was something friends generally discouraged, even when the change was meant to make one's deepest wishes come true. *Don't give up your job for art! Don't give up your art for a child!* The fear seemed to be that if you moved on in one way you might move on in other ways, too, leaving your friends alone in your wake. And if this was partly selfish, it was partly protective, too: People who have seen you through pain or penury don't want to see you that way again. *Why must you change? You're imperfect, but I like you that way.*

Immediately, in his first week of waiting, Andy realized he would have to steel himself to such responses, which came mostly (it was sad to note) from gay men. They looked pained, bee-stung, almost betrayed, but Andy could not help them. Straight women were more practical: "Get out a pen," they instructed him. "Here's what you'll need." Mothers or otherwise, they took for granted that someone might turn his life upside-down for something unknowable, or at least unknown. His own mother, he did not dare tell. She complained when he got a haircut; what would she do when he told her he was getting a child? He'd cross that bridge when he came to it, and the bridge would be shorter then—for the change of having a baby may be great, but the change of expecting him is greater. When he arrives he has already been imagined, but when he is first imagined he is created out of nothing. How smart of God or the accident of biology to give pregnant mothers forty weeks to clear some space. And not just mothers; many's the husband who gained as much weight as his burgeoning wife (and never lost it). Even expecting an adoption, a prospective parent does internal clearing. Space formerly ceded to the rest of the universe must be reannexed so there will be room for the baby when he comes.

Andy weighed himself: nothing yet.

And this was week two.

TWENTY-FOUR

There would only be three. On March 9 a call miraculously made its way past the erratic school switchboard to Andy's office. A boy had been born the previous Friday; did Andy want him? The agency gave him one day—oh, make it two—to decide.

In scribbled notes on sheet after sheet of yellow legal paper, Andy recorded what he could of that phone call, and of the many hasty ones that followed as he sought information that might help him choose. Filled with improbable abbreviations and illegible or now incomprehensible asides, the notes nevertheless make a clear map of his journey; the first entry is simply "non-optimal" (a social worker's euphemism for the circumstances surrounding the birth) and the last is a list of motels he might stay in should his answer be yes. In between, the tone veers constantly, as Andy's mood must have veered as well, from elation to terror to confusion to paralysis—and only a few hours left. Sometimes he seems to be writing a purely medical synopsis: Concepción's drug use and other ailments, her boyfriend's hair color and stature, the

newborn baby's weight and tremors. But other times, with the
phone crooked in his neck and his hand thus restricted to only a
few words per line, he seems to be writing modern poetry, with all
its eccentric enjambments and minimal punctuation:

> Smiles
> when you
> talk to
> him—
> eyes follow
> you
> when you
> move

Adoption gives you choices that biology reserves for itself, but
in doing so it also exacts a price. Where there is choice you must
choose. The panic underlying Andy's crabbed notations is the
panic of having to make a decision without knowledge—like the
nightmare of showing up for a test unprepared. Biological parents
do not know, either, if the child they give birth to will be a source
of a lifetime of heartache or joy. But they don't get to say "No, I'll
wait for the next one." Andy, on the other hand, was allowed to
say no; in fact, if he did not say anything else very soon (it was getting to be Friday) no would be his answer by default. The ironies
piled up. After years of struggle to choose the life he wanted, he
now resented that the choice was so difficult. And yet the difficulty of the choice was what gave him the choice in the first
place. Other prospective adoptive parents—more traditional parents, who'd been waiting much longer—had already wrangled
with themselves and declined.

It came down to this: Was the shaking, as some people Andy
consulted suggested, a possible precursor to neurological problems, obsessive-compulsive syndrome, attention deficit disorder?
Friends who had more or less supported his baby quest now
quailed, told adoption disaster stories they had previously with-
held, and begged Andy to wait. And yet, aside from the tremors,
the boy seemed perfectly healthy; he had scored well on all his
neonatal tests, was HIV-negative, and showed no signs of drugs in

his own blood. He had eaten well at the hospital, and even better in the home of an elderly couple who took him in while he awaited placement. Andy spoke to the wife, who told him that the boy was slightly fussy but delightful and handsome (if nearly bald): a strong little boy—and suddenly Andy began to think he was Erez. *That's Erez down there waiting for me, calling for me: He wants me to come and get him.* Was this the cedar in the nursery, tiny as yet, trembling in the wind? And then, the foster mother said, the trembling seemed to begin to subside. Perhaps the boy, in his first few days, had merely been throwing off his birth mother's burdens, as a dog throws off his bathwater. Only now, looking back on Andy's notes, do I see a scrawled notation neither he nor I ever noticed before: Concepción, her medical history relates, was allergic to (of all things) cedar.

Andy said yes.

It was Friday. Over the weekend he booked his flights, made his first pilgrimage to Toys "R" Us, and scrounged clothes from friends whose children had outgrown them. Elliot helped him clean the apartment. On Monday he took a day off from work to put together the additional eleven thousand five hundred dollars (much of it borrowed from his brother) he would have to mail overnight to the agency; the cost of the adoption, including medical expenses for mother and child, would eventually total about twenty-one thousand. On Tuesday he therefore made reservations at the cheapest convenient lodging he could find: two nights at thirty-nine dollars each (plus tax); as others have a hospital bracelet, we have a motel's MasterCard receipt. Later that day, Andy packed his bag (he'd be leaving from work Wednesday afternoon) and spoke one more time to the foster mother, who would now start calling the little boy Erez. *I'm coming to get you tomorrow*, thought Andy. *You are my child.* But there was one more thing left to do.

TWENTY-FIVE

Andy walked the three blocks through the Brooklyn dusk to his mother's apartment—perhaps the last time he would be able to make even so short a trip so freely. Over a dinner prepared by Madame Raton (Janet was past cooking now, and let her Haitian housekeeper do it), mother and son chatted mildly about Aunt Irene's failing health, the tenant who still owed last month's rent, the latest absurd memo from the Board of Education. Afterward, Andy cleared the dishes, made coffee, and set out baked apples (heavy on cinnamon and raisins) for dessert.

"You already know that I've been thinking for a while about becoming a parent," he started. "Well, it's finally happening. I'm adopting a little boy. He was born a week ago Friday and I'm going down to pick him up tomorrow afternoon. I'll leave work at one and my flight is at four. I'll be back Friday. *We'll* be back Friday. His name is going to be Erez Luís—the middle name after Daddy."

He had thought this last detail would appease her, for in death Lewis had somewhat recovered his tarnished reputation.

But Janet sneered. "What kind of name is that? Erez?"

"It's Hebrew, it's a popular name in Israel, and it means cedar tree."

Apparently trumped, Janet hung back a moment, staring at Andy across the syrupy remains of their baked apples.

Andy was bristling with adrenaline. In some ways this confrontation was reminiscent of—was the culmination of—the fights he'd had with his parents twenty-five years ago, when as a teenager he felt they presented him with a Hobson's choice of being exactly what they wanted or not being anything at all. But he was no longer fighting (he told himself now); the purpose of the current conversation was merely to get his mother to absorb this important information. He didn't *want* anything from her, or didn't let himself think he did. Later, he would admit that he hoped he could get her to share his joy and be a grandmother for his child. Common sense and experience told him not to expect it; he was prepared not to have what other new parents took for granted, and instead be faced with a wounded dragon who would resist to the end, because it gave her a last shard of power. But maybe . . .

"How can you do this?" she said. "You *can't* do this."

"Yes I can, and I am. I'm going to take a child-care leave until the end of this school year, and then take a sabbatical next year so I won't have to go back to work until he's eighteen months old."

"But what do you know about parenting?"

"What did *you* know?" Andy threw back. Then he relented. "I'm reading books and talking about it with friends who have kids."

"And you're going to walk the carriage right out on the Promenade?" she asked, as if he were going to wear a big frilly dress on Rosh Hashanah.

"Yes, sometimes. Why do you mention it?"

Janet didn't answer, and tried a different tack. "How are you paying for this?"

"I'm planning on using money," Andy answered sarcastically.

"How much money?"

"None of your business. Don't worry about it. I'll take care of it."

"But is it already set? When you get down there and see this child, do you have to take it?" One of Janet's sisters had, many years earlier, given back a child she and her husband had set out to adopt.

"If it really seems like there's something wrong I suppose I wouldn't have to take him, but I doubt that will happen. I had a pediatrician here who talked to the pediatrician there and the baby has a clean bill of health."

The lie seemed too little to worry about, and in any case, for all Andy knew, Erez's neonatal trembling, however troubling, could have been the least of it. Concepción seemed to have plenty of problems even without the illegal drugs; her screen had come back positive not only for cocaine and marijuana but for a prescription antidepressant. She had herpes, ulcers, and, at the site of a broken bone, arthritis. She'd once been a heavy drinker, too, and (surely a good sign) now attended meetings of Alcoholics Anonymous—though cocaine use is not traditionally one of the twelve steps. Even allowing for the "happy-go-lucky" boyfriend (it was, admittedly, hard to see how he fit in) it didn't take much imagination to paint the picture and predict the child: depressed, addictive, caught in a cycle of violence. And yet if you painted

Andy's picture from the available facts of his heritage you'd probably get as much wrong as right. In a way, it was a comfort to realize that even for a child raised by his biological parents the
influence of the genetic and emotional inheritance, however
powerful, was equivocal and unknowable.

"And you're going to walk the carriage right out on the Promenade?" she asked again.

Andy shook his head sadly, then moved on to another difficult
topic. "I'm having the bris next Wednesday," he said.

"Bris!"

"Of course a bris. I want him to be circumcised—he will be a
Jew."

"And you're inviting the *family*?"

"Yes."

"Who's going to *do* it?" she asked, as if no one sane would ever
consent.

"I have a mohel—a mohelet, they call her. She's a convert to
Judaism, she's English and also a plastic surgeon."

"How did you find *her*?"

"The rabbi at the gay synagogue told us about her."

"And what is Elliot's role in this?" She didn't mind Elliot.

"As you know, he's moving out. He's interested in what's going
on, he'll help me, I'm sure, but the boy will be my child, alone."

"Well, it may be your child," she said with finality, "but it's not
going to be my grandchild."

Andy got up. "This is your big opportunity," he said. "You didn't
get to spend the kind of time you would have liked with your
other grandkids because they live in Detroit and nobody trusted
you anyway. This is your chance. *I'm* giving you a chance. You
can act like a grandmother or you can act like some kind of batty
old nut. You decide."

But Janet couldn't muster any expression of hope or goodwill.
She looked stricken, horrified, abandoned.

"I have to finish packing," Andy said. As he reached down to
kiss her good-bye, she reached up to touch his face.

That we are shaped by our parents—either into or out of their
likenesses—cannot be denied. But our parents are not one thing,

and keep changing shape themselves. It was, after all, Janet who had by example taught Andy how a person could cobble reality to her own last. And yet in the moment of his mastering that lesson, he graduated. *That was the wrong lesson!* she seemed to say. But it was too late, and what choice did that leave her?

She must have asked herself that question as Madame Raton cleaned the dessert plates and helped her to bed. The next day, just before one in the afternoon, as Andy was gathering his coat and luggage, she called him at school.

"How many people are you going to have for the bris, so I know how many to cater for?" Janet asked.

Andy laughed to himself. "I guess a few dozen."

"I have to know exactly."

"I'll call you when I get to the motel."

And that was it. The forty years' war was over at last. He had won, in his way, and would have, for the rest of her life, a mother.

Now for a son. He shrugged on his shoulder bag, turned off the lights, walked to the 3 train at Eastern Parkway, and . . .

. . . *and took the subway train to the bus and the bus to a plane, and the plane took me far away to another state, where a woman who was able to grow you inside her but could not take care of you was looking for a daddy to love you for the rest of your life. And I was that daddy. And I took you back to the plane to the bus and the bus to the subway—well, actually, this time, we took a cab—and brought you here to Brooklyn to be my son forever.*

II

The
Tear Beat

ONE

At a party given by colleagues on the occasion of her retirement, my mother made a haunting remark. This came after various speakers had painted her as a Cassandra of Academe, "condemned" (as she'd often put it) "to talk about real things." That she was so condemned was in part the sentence of her job; for more than twenty-five years she had been on the faculty of the University of Pennsylvania as a teacher and family therapist, lecturing undergraduates on the basic plumbing of sex and trying to keep wives from throwing their husbands out the window. It wasn't just that the work encouraged a kind of contrarian, cut-the-bullshit attitude (though that helped) but that it often demanded emergency insight, usually from left field. She called this "breaking set" — looking for an answer beyond the apparent parameters of the problem—and was famous for it. But her frankness, her perverseness, the pleasure she took in unexpectedness had all preceded the job; it was part of her personality to puncture even her own balloons and to say the uncomfortably true thing.

She began, that day, after thanking everyone who had spoken, by reporting a new insight. Being condemned to talk about real things, she said, carried with it the less attractive corollary of being condemned to *listen* to real things, too. Counseling couples, supervising trainees, administering programs, and negotiating with the university, she had listened to many all-too-real things over the years and now found, at sixty-seven, that she had heard enough. Her retirement was therefore not a blow, she said, but a relief, however hard it was to leave behind her comfortable patterns and agreeable perks. Indeed, since she had stopped coming to the office regularly a few months before, something strange had happened: Early in the mornings, in the new home she and my father had recently moved to, she woke up, heard nothing but birds and, instead of rising for another day filled with fifty-minute anguishes, turned over and went back to sleep. Only the birds chirped on. Lest people wonder, or worry, what she meant, she drew this conclusion: "I've never been so content in my life."

True to form, she had chosen to leave her colleagues with a quirky, equivocal message. It seemed to suggest that she had saved herself by leaving the very ship on which they were doomed to remain, or that the steady currents that had so far made their passage thereon smooth might someday shift underneath them without warning. As she resumed her seat, they clapped for her in the hearty, arrhythmic way I understood to signify both affection and bewilderment, which is pretty much how they'd always received her. But the remark didn't haunt me because it was equivocal or because it produced an equivocal response; it haunted me because it seemed untrue. Contentedness was a concept seldom associated with my mother. Not that she lacked reasons to be grateful. After two trying years of cancer and chemotherapy, she was healthy again; her hair had grown back, strangely improved. She had plenty of money and a beautiful home. Even the caterer had honored her, with unexpectedly good hors d'oeuvres. But if, counting her blessings, she found them numerous, she was the kind of woman who weighed them, too. Was her recovery too complete to trust? Was her wealth too tied up in her husband's arcane schemes and syndicates? Was the leather divan set at too sharp an angle to the pale green walls? She had always been restless, up at night with ideas (often successful) for improving the lives and living rooms around her—which, in a way, were much the same thing. So: grateful, sure; but content?

Driving home to New York that night, the fluty sound of juvenile snores accompanying us as we talked, Andy asked if *I* was content, but I couldn't even figure out how to view the question properly. So much had happened in the three years since I'd met him—so much of it seeming to contradict the previous thirty-seven—that I felt as if he were asking me about someone we both knew only vaguely. "If things would just stay the same for a few minutes, maybe I could decide," I said.

"Don't trust patterns," Andy replied; it was a phrase my mother had taped to the refrigerator when my brother and I were infants, and it wasn't a fashion tip.

The next morning, my fortieth birthday as it happened, I called my mother as she was waking up. "Mom," I said, "I would love to believe—nothing would make me happier than to believe—that what you said at the party was true. That you've never been so content in your life. But *is* it true? I have to ask."

"Oh, it's totally true," she answered immediately. "It's just not saying much."

We both started laughing. *There* was the mother I knew.

TWO

Don't trust patterns. When she taped this phrase to the refrigerator, my mother must have been telling herself not to depend on things that change. The minute you count on the baby to eat carrots, he will start heaving them onto the floor; as soon as you get used to waking at midnight, he will snore, perversely, straight through to three. Food and sleep were the first seducers, and thus the first betrayers, but there were many more to come—and it was better, at least for the Depression child of Jewish immigrants, not to hope too much or become too content, lest the shock of loss (and what was change but a kind of loss?) be too upsetting. This applied not just to schedules but to ambitions, and so involved a classic paradox. A child taught not to startle the horses is thereby taught that he is startling. Or, to put it another way, the heirloom hidden deep in the closet knows itself to be more of a treasure than the one displayed in a brightly lit breakfront. Why else would so much effort have been expended in hiding it somewhere no thief would think to look?

For in my mother's heart, no less than in *her* mother's heart, the Cossacks were always coming. They had quite a distance to ride, now that the family had relocated to suburban Philadelphia, but

Cossacks were hardy and apparently single-minded. To find us again they had mastered not only time travel (I was born in 1958) but the black art of metamorphosis, appearing at will as street thugs, as IRS agents, as Lord & Taylor salesgirls who refused to exchange a hardly-used-even-twice bathing suit. Later they pushed drugs on innocent teenagers, recruited for cults, distracted Ivy League premed students from their chemistry homework with hopeless dreams of success in the theater. In all cases their aim was to rob you of your hard-won life, its rightful and sometimes wrongful assumptions, its routines and emoluments and retirement savings. You spent a lot of time attempting to outmaneuver them, but they were never far away; they lived in the perpetually next town called Yennemsvelt and would not die. Even in her extreme old age, when she could remember little else, my grandmother's eyes unclouded if asked about her childhood in Dubno, on the shifting Polish-Russian frontier, and the heathen on horses who had chased her thence.

She might have thanked them; what befell the Jews of Eastern Europe thirty years later made the Cossacks look like equestriennes. At least my grandmother got to America, albeit with false papers (provided, she always said, by a "travel agent") that left her permanently anxious about her citizenship. She never applied for a passport or registered to vote, afraid that such presumptuous gestures might attract the interest of an immigration official still obsessed, decades later, with the questionable circumstances of her arrival. It was best, she felt, to operate beneath the radar of any bureaucracy—a policy that may have made sense in Dubno but had strange repercussions here. When my mother discovered, upon applying for *her* first passport, that her name was not Sally (as she had always been told) but Shirley, the tale that unfolded was straight out of Kafka. Aunt Bessie, it seems, had suggested the name Sally but had made an untoward comment in the hospital about the baby's crossed eyes; my grandmother retaliated by banishing her and putting Shirley on the birth certificate. Later, when Bessie apologized, my grandmother restored the child's rightful name, but not on paper. At age forty-five, my mother therefore had to provide the state of Pennsylvania with an affidavit, from someone who had known her all her life, saying that Sally and Shirley were in fact one woman—even though (another wrinkle) their birthdays were not, strictly speaking, the same. Whom could she ask? Her father was dead, she had no siblings, and her mother, now seventy-seven but still cautious, refused. So she went to her uncle Leon instead, but alas, he told her, his name wasn't Leon.

If my grandmother, as she aged, forgot so much, perhaps it was because there was too much to remember. She lived several more lives than most of us do. The girl born in 1898 not only saw the paroxysms of our century but saw them symmetrically undone: Russian Revolution to Soviet breakup. Born under gaslight, she died under energy-saving fluorescents; in between, she watched her mother make candy in the shtetl, rode steerage into New York harbor, ran a drugstore in Philadelphia, learned to drive on the Main Line when widowed, got contact lenses at ninety-one, and never figured out Call Waiting. Was it not her right to forget it all?

Or almost all. In the nursing home as she died, a few weeks shy of ninety-nine, she barely recognized Sally *or* Shirley, but she remembered the one thing everyone remembered, all the old Jews, crumpled in their beds, listening for the final horsemen, and crying out over and over, room after room, as you hiked down the gleaming, disinfected halls: "Mama! Mama! Where are you, Mama?"

THREE

But this is not about dying mothers. This is not about drug addiction, amnesia, anorexia, cults, or suicide. I was never "incested," abandoned, or even hit. I am not a flesh-eater or a recovering self-mutilator or an adherent of Lyndon LaRouche. I have never been abducted by spies. I am not my own daughter by a previous marriage. These things didn't happen in my life. They did happen around me; they were the meteors that landed (apparently quite often) in everyone's hypergreen backyard but mine. Conversions were popular in Penn Valley: Lila Weinstock became a Moonie,

Richie Wolf a Hare Krishna, Suzan Brownstein (most obtusely) a white-bread Presbyterian, if only until her marriage dissolved. Steve Cohn converted more literally, taking (it seemed inevitable) the new name of Eydie when he emerged from surgery in a wraparound skirt. Dropouts, overdoses, Jewish Afros—all the plagues of suburbia hailed down upon the land, conking little heads into dizzy thoughts. Adult heads, too. Divorces, sports cars, sudden hairpieces, embezzlements, facelifts, lecherous dentists: the stuff of a million comic novels, if only the events were more comic and more novel. Every week brought pain to some family; you could see the survivors of the meteor standing stunned around the crater where Johnny not minutes before had been playing, and what was he now? An alien? An emptiness? Quick, call the gardener to infill the depression.

If the heavy weather missed us only by inches, it missed us nevertheless. Oh, I didn't practice my oboe as much as I probably should have, and my father grew an unfortunate mustache in 1972. My brother, apparently defying his heritage, biked his way one blistering summer through the Yukon and Alaska. But this was as far as the meteorology of our world ever took us; Tony returned, with hypertrophied calves, in time for his next semester at Penn. Nothing very untoward ever happened amid the glass walls and teak floors of the International Style renovation on Greentree Lane, except insofar as an International Style renovation on Greentree Lane, which was otherwise made up of cookie-cutter ranches, was untoward per se. The neighbors hated it, until they copied it, but they never understood that the trick of being exposed was to become invisible: People who live in glass houses shouldn't throw fits. In my house the rebellion was always interior to a fault.

So I write this memoir in defiance of the form, without asylums and drunken kisses. Certainly it is not about the trauma of growing up gay, which would have qualified in some other yards as the worst suburban catastrophe of all; in my yard my gayness, however meteoric, was not particularly unwelcome. Nor is it about the accident I suffered in fourth grade, gruesome and telling though it was: When a friend with whom I had planned to "do math" failed to show up at the appointed tree during recess, I joined a soccer game instead, without remembering to remove the pencil I had stuffed in my right front pants pocket. What happened next I now see as if from a security camera, in the perpetual present of slow motion: I trip over the ball and fall to the ground, feeling something sharp plunge deep inside me. Unable to unbend I freeze in a crouch. "I'm going to die of lead poisoning," I cry, until a friend (now, inevitably, a doctor) reminds me that pencils are made of graphite. That takes care of one problem, and emergency surgery takes care of the pencil, which missed my appendix, my femoral artery, and everything else in the area by millimeters. But what will take care of the pain of the boy whose dying wish (for so he moans over and over while awaiting the ambulance) is "Don't tell my parents!" I do not want them upset.

No, if a meteor landed on me (and it would have had to crash through the plates of Thermoseal) its whole violence amounted to this: a tap in the direction of abstraction and complexity. Since I had always tended that way, even a tap was enough to push me over the line. I had been pierced by a pencil, and its point was impossible to miss: One finds meaning only by finding words. The most freakish mark this has left upon me (aside from the caterpillar scar up my belly) is a taste for wordplay, a Kabbalistic mania for deducing significance from accidents of mere orthography: "meteor" is an anagram of "emoter," but also of "remote." The most salient mark is the perversity of what I am writing now, a memoir with few bad memories, no axes to grind (or only small ones), and even a happy ending. Still, my apologia is less for that ending than for this new beginning, which finds me reaching as far back in the chain of connection as I can, one hundred years before I met Andy, once upon a time.

FOUR

Avram Shmuel Zoldag, born in a shtetl near Nyírbátor, Hungary, refused to go with his parents and many younger siblings when they set out for America in 1901. America, he told them, was the golem, the monster: an irreligious land, obsessed with mammon, incompatible with Jewish law. Hungary wasn't exactly an Eden for Jews, but Avram wanted to continue his studies at the yeshiva—he was bookish; perhaps he hoped to become a rabbi—and he convinced his family to emigrate without him. He was eleven.

Over the course of a long lifetime, Samuel A. Green (as the boy was later restyled) must have managed to make his peace with the monster. He came to America a few years after that first refusal, learned its ways quickly, and in 1934 founded the first federal savings and loan in Pennsylvania, in his mother's kitchen on Point Breeze Avenue. Mammon stopped bothering him somehow, for he did not abjure his wealth when it materialized; as the business prospered, he moved his wife and two boys from Philadelphia to a large Victorian house in the leafy suburb of Drexel Hill. He took his family on vacations to Florida and Atlantic City, and his wife on wide travels (though never back to Eastern Europe). But he was not demented (in the manner popularized by members of the next generation of immigrant Jews) with the love of money for its own sake; in any case, savings and loans, as opposed to banks, are owned by depositors and thus do not create huge wealth for their founders. Much of what excess there was he gave away. Acres of Israel were made green with his cash, not to mention the campuses of the colleges his five grandsons eventually attended.

And so his funeral, in 1979, was packed with hundreds of respectful mourners, only in part because he held the mortgages on many of their homes. It was also because he represented several beloved archetypes rolled up in one: pillar of the community; immigrant made good; generous patron; advice-spouting sage. All true, and yet he was something else as well: a bully. Eldest son and early paterfamilias (his father was killed by a Brooklyn trolley in 1920), he was perpetually indulged; his stubbornness and cleverness were assumed to be wisdom, and his success forced people around him into strange, sentimental attitudes. Or, behind his back, unsentimental: His sisters called him Jesus Christ to mock his lordly self-regard.

It was not his self-regard that bothered me; his many benefactions had earned him the right to admire his reflection. What bothered me was his lack of regard for others. Those who did not huddle on his good side, in the proper obeisant postures, were apt to find themselves in his cold, cold shadow as he passed dispensing money and epigrams. Even those in the sunlight might feel they were supernumeraries in the opera of his goodness. To them, he seemed fierce and crotchety and (despite his high moral tone) unfair; did he like me best because I, his youngest grandchild, was fierce and crotchety and unfair, too? Or perhaps he was relieved to be seen for what he was. On a bookshelf in his study sat a little iron "Tammany" bank, cast in the form of a corpulent plutocrat bursting from his waistcoat and smugly mustachioed. When you placed a penny in his upraised hand, it dropped into an opening at his breast pocket, and his round head nodded with satisfaction. In my dreams my grandfather's actual face has been replaced with the one on this highly collectible *objet*.

Though the real man gave us money instead of taking it, he was hard to visit; how much harder he must have been to live with. His frail wife, Theresa, who wore white cat's-eye glasses, unraveled over the years. For a wealthy woman, she had a miser's habits; when she died I found a terrifying collection of worthless junk in her closet, thousands of tiny nothings in her vanity table (a little vanity, to be sure), and plastic bags filled with pins, sequins, beads, soap shavings, used tape, broken buckles. It was as if her husband was so large she had taken recourse in the minuscule. Perhaps she wanted to disappear entirely; she had, in late middle age, taken up magic as a hobby, and attempted to practice it upon us. But she could never whip up any delight in that house. At seders she sometimes played the piano with her tiny feet; "Try to Remember" was a particular favorite—perhaps because, at least in the key of C, it required no black keys. But you wondered, to your horror, how long she had practiced, and how she had come up with the idea in the first place. Her lighthearted notions kept coming to nothing, as did her recipes, which began (I liked to joke): "Preheat oven to four thousand degrees." You could have fired the crockery with the rib roast, if only it *were* a rib roast. Though she was born in the United States (and was unduly proud of it), Theresa tried to cook *à la hongrois* for her husband, which meant serving exactly those parts of animals that other people got rich just to avoid ever having to think about again. My father says that it wasn't until he married and moved out that he realized he'd had indigestion for twenty-four years straight.

He was their second son: a fact and a fate. Where his brother was robust, he was sickly. Where his brother was prized, he was tolerated. Where his brother expected the world, he expected little, and each was rewarded accordingly. My father, it's true, boldly rejected the family business to become—the rebel!—an optometrist. But when glasses proved insufficiently lucrative (perhaps because he donated his services to local prisons), he sheepishly returned to the billfold, as his father never let him forget.

FIVE

But my father had already made a mistake far graver than optometry: He had engaged himself to my mother. Sam and Theresa did not like the girl their Rodney told them he was going to marry. She was from the wrong side of the tracks—from the wrong line altogether; her parents (both immigrants) had only recently moved to the suburbs from an apartment above their store in a Catholic, working-class neighborhood of North Philadelphia. It was bad enough that she was not Hungarian and had not been nominated by someone in the family; they had hoped to interest Rodney in a dull second cousin fresh off the boat. But Sally Swartz had other liabilities—as a Green operative, dispatched to investigate, soon discovered. Her family was not just poor but virtually Communist. Her mother's father had been a union organizer and, even worse, an atheist; it was said that, on Yom Kippur, he deliberately sat in the vast front window of the Broad Street Horn & Hardart so that fasting Jews on their way to synagogue would be forced to see him there—eating pork.

Not that the Greens had so very much to be proud of. Sam at least was wealthy and clever, but below him in the family tree things dropped off considerably. The sisters were smart but (being women of that era) frustrated; the brothers, well, less so. One way or another, my grandfather would support them for the rest of his life, and even after. Still, in newsletters and holiday toasts, the sprawling family promoted its story of brilliance and harmony as if the saga were holy writ. Inconvenient characters were simply curtained off behind scrims of denial: the widower who refused to raise his infant son, the possible homosexual, the burlesque queen who couldn't seem to keep her top on. When, decades later, I first heard of her—and how she rubbed her breasts with ice to keep her nipples perky—I liked to imagine she might be one of the performers still billed in newspaper ads for Philadelphia's last surviving strip club, the Troc, like Clara Net ("a reedy sweetie") or Lynn Oleum ("she'll floor you"). The very idea of a Jewish ecdysiast must have horrified the Greens, but for me the only difficulty was dreaming up her name. Tish Above, I finally decided: "But wait till you see what's below!"

Anna and Harry Swartz, on the other hand, were reflexively modest, silent in their ambitions. Sally was their only child, and a late one at that. She was lonely and serious and pretty and efficient—an odd combination. She smoked and drew still lifes and managed the cash register while imagining houses lovelier than the three-room flat upstairs. Her fantasies were kept in check by the family fear of discovery; when she dreamed up a new name for herself in her teens, it was a middle name only, and Lydia at that. If she was the unacknowledged princess in a story, that was the ideal thing to be, for acknowledgment was danger. Still, each fall her parents sent her with a credit card (or coin, as they called it) to the elegant Tribout shop at Wanamaker's for the best new dresses, and for tea sandwiches in the cafeteria after. They sent her to Philadelphia's best public high school, despite the complex trolley connections it took to get there, and then to the University of Pennsylvania. To the Greens, such indulgence of a girl was not only wasteful but uppity. She was studying *architecture!*

But their disdain came too late. The blind date—an accident, my father substituting for a sick friend—had taken place in July 1950: *Guys and Dolls* at a theater in New Hope. Soon thereafter the pair were engaged. It's not hard to imagine why. My father would have been genial and modest, so unlike the bluff, ambitious princelings Sally had spent time with before. For his part, Rodney probably found it both dangerous and exciting to come under the immense scrutiny of my mother's brown eyes; he had been virtually ignored his whole life until then. When someone looked at you that way, even if you didn't know why, you could almost believe there was something to see.

They were married less than a year later. In a formal portrait from their honeymoon in Miami Beach, my father stands and my mother sits before a shimmering backdrop, he with his pale suit and elaborately peaked handkerchief, she with her short bangs and embroidered organdy blouse; the two of them looking straight ahead, not at each other, quizzical but calm, near but not touching, together and apart, as they always would be.

SIX

They were children. They knew nothing. The psychological acuity my mother would later acquire was barely nascent now at twenty; she had no words for what she surmised, nor nerve to utter them if she did. My father at twenty-four had never made dinner for himself. Now they would make a home and a family— but weren't they a family already? At any rate, having a child was the one thing my mother could do to attempt to satisfy the Greens.

She failed at first; she had a miscarriage. Wasn't she too skinny? They mistrusted her, as if the miscarriage were a repudiation. But they'd already mistrusted her. My father, upon instruction from *his* father, had held his hand over part of the tax form while asking her to sign their first joint return.

"What's that you're covering?" she asked.

"I'm not supposed to show you."

He showed her.

It wasn't even much: some income from real estate sheltered in his name. But a little knowledge was a little power, dangerous in itself and dangerous in implication. She began to think.

The next pregnancy succeeded; my brother was born in December 1954. But Tony (actually Anthony Paul—two saints!) arrived with a mysterious condition that kept him from digesting almost everything he was fed. Months of diarrhea and terror finally ended when a doctor suggested abandoning cow's milk in favor of a formula made from powdered bananas. Tony instantaneously thrived, but as my mother's fear receded like floodwaters, a dense mud was discovered to have settled over her life. She could hardly rise from it; beyond her housewifely duties, always faithfully executed, she spent much of the day in bed. No one spoke of it or would have known what words to use; today we might describe hormonal changes, we might point to statistics, we might invoke comforting Latinate words like "postpartum." Yet all this would be to ignore the obvious. Like millions of women for whom institutionalized feminism came too late, my mother was alert enough to see the jaws of the trap shutting upon her, but not light-foot enough to move. Did she go to college—and finish it, too, even after getting married—merely for *this?* It seemed as if she had landed a job she barely remembered applying for; the job featured impossible hours, a pittance for pay, and no hope of promotion. Slides of the Baths of Caracalla, like the ones projected at the Louis Kahn lectures she'd so recently attended, were strangely unincluded.

Instead of architecture, she had a house: a three-bedroom ranch, with an option to convert the garage to a den, in a development cleared from piny woods in the near hills of Philadelphia's otherwise posh Main Line. The lot, the highest on Greentree Lane, was just a bald crest of dirt and a foundation when she chose it, but she'd at least known how to read the plans and could imagine what the radio towers of the city, visible at right angles to the horizon, would look like from a picture window. Elsewhere on the semicircle, other Ethnic Lite young couples—second-generation Jews, Armenians, Germans—were buying their first houses, too. Soon the great bales of sod were rolled out and the pachysandra was planted. Inside, the sheet-vinyl floors got pasted down and the bedroom set reassembled. A neighborhood sprang up from nothing, as had the individual lives within it.

So she had a place to live. She had a son, now fully healthy, if somewhat small, perhaps from her smoking. She had a kind and handsome husband, adequate help, and her whole life ahead of her. But what was a life? Something merely to fill up, like her bridal Royal Worcester "Bacchanal" teacup? Or something to contain, like the pachysandra soon overtaking everything? Or something to raise in joy and difficulty: like an orchid, or a child?

A child. If you did not think about having one before you had it, he moved almost too fast to take in. At two, Tony had already uttered his first sentence—"Get your feet off, Daddy"—and where had she been looking? She tried to concentrate. You could hope to appease the in-laws with a baby, you could surely please your husband; later you gave the child to himself and to the world, if the world was interested. But in the moment of conception, at least, you had to want to make something perfect for yourself, and you had to know that's what you were doing. Otherwise . . . life was so short.

She got out of bed. She quit smoking. She helped out in my father's optometry office and counted the months.

SEVEN

I was born in June 1958, a smiley blob. As if to make up for the Italian Catholic sacrilege of "Anthony Paul," my mother named me from the deepest core of the Old Testament. In keeping with family tradition, there was nevertheless confusion about my identity. My birth certificate shows me to lack, like my mother, a middle name; the Hebrew circumcision document, the *brit milah*, makes up for this with two. In any case, the names don't match. In Hebrew I'm Isaac, among other things. A teacher once translated the ancient syllables for me: "He will laugh and explode."

Though probably an inaccurate rendering, it was insightful. Even in my own earliest memories, I was a happy boy with a very short fuse—a fuse leading not just to anger but to every large emotion. Unlike some children, who placidly take the shape of the forms set out for them, I was always trying to reform the forms. I seem to have been born with far too many unshakable tastes. Not just in food, though of course I was impossibly finicky; I had the same digestive disorder as my brother, which later proved a useful defense against my paternal grandmother's unspeakable cuisine. But I was finicky about the world at large, too: its fairness, its orderliness, and even its decor. Luckily I had a talent for satisfying (and promulgating) my tastes; people soon came to rely on me. When my father attended Sunday morning meetings at the synagogue, he hired me out to the office staff, for a fee of twenty-five cents, to reorganize their files. I was six, and delighted. Two years later, when my parents commissioned one of my mother's old classmates to redesign and expand their house in high mid-century International Style, they had no choice but to include me in the process. Drawings and swatches were sent to me at camp, where I solemnly reviewed them on my cot during rest hour.

I returned at the end of that summer to a new life under construction. The attic floor had been peeled off its joists and the joists themselves resected; the living room ceiling now leapt to the roof, where light rushed in from a bank of clerestories. The homely old picture window—gone: knocked out to form the stately entry to a living room as yet only suggested by beams and sills and a concrete slab. The old front door now led to a powder room; the new front door popped up unexpectedly in the back. I raced around in amazement and joy. So much transformation! What was once a pleasant if ordinary ranch was now evolving into something large and worldly and somehow foreign. Certainly it spoke a foreign language: the architectural terms ("cathedral ceiling"; "sequence of volumes"), the materials and manufacturers (Thai teak; Knoll), and especially the designers: Bertoia, Mies, Jack Lenor Larsen, the Eameses, Breuer, Le Corbusier. A baby-sitter carried me on his shoulders one night as he serpentined his way among the bare studs and Medusa wires. I could touch the dangling ceiling fixtures, as yet unconnected, and this was heaven.

But why was I so entranced by transformation? You would have thought I was a sad child learning for the first time how a new life could grow directly out of the old one in some way that was both organic and magical. Could a person grow another life from something inside him, too? And yet I did not want a new life, at least not now, at least not for myself. It was my mother for whom I had ambitions, and my elation must in some way have been hers. The intellectual work of imagining a house had helped thaw something frozen within her; I could hear it beginning to bubble beneath the surface like a spring stiffly moving under ice. In anticipation of a change, she was setting the stage or, better, getting her house in order.

One day the giant windows arrived—seven feet square. Now there was a view! At night, the lights on the radio towers flashed in slow sequence from ground to air, three red dots suggesting elliptically that everything was open-ended. Incompetent or otherwise unpleasing structures could be revamped. The imagination could be brought to bear concretely on reality; reality (assuming it was bribed with enough money) would have to be compliant. A new house was like a child in that way: always incipient, always absorbing, at least until the first pipe burst.

Oh, how I loved the big, square spaces, the way they made me feel small and important! That was the perfect combination for me: little enough to be lithe, strong enough to be heard. I did not ever want to adulterate the mix; puberty, as I watched my brother trudge through its door, seemed so dreary and unesthetic. Instead I wanted to dash among the adults' legs forever and get to the dessert table first. I wanted to be, like Robin, a Boy Wonder. (And didn't Batman send a strange message, with his bulging leotard and swishy cape?) I was so content in my little body that I vowed—after making myself cry over and over by singing "Where Is Love?" from *Oliver!* in my best boy soprano—to make my voice stay high forever. The vow was fruitless, I knew; at the point in the lyric where the singer is offered a choice of two roads—"Who can say where she [he] may hide?"—my voice already cracked.

EIGHT

If my early childhood looks in retrospect like a cliché of pre-gayness, that was not in prospect apparent. I did, after all, have a mad crush on my kindergarten teacher—though, like a hair-dresser, I mooned over her "dirty blond" tresses, a phrase that excited me. I did not lisp or prance. I enjoyed, at least in theory, all sports, especially those (like baseball and billiards) that seemed to express the logical properties of mathematics and physics. I liked to run and swim and kick balls (though not to catch them) even if I was not by any means a jock. Competition on a physical plane vaguely appalled me. It was the same in sports as it had been in decor: What I was drawn to was not so much the content as the process—the map, not the country. I clambered up high trees to look down, from which vantage point the world seemed orderly, rational, and therefore (for so I liked to think) just. The vast wild cherry tree in our backyard contained no error, even when I sat for hours within it. I wasn't so much gay, it seemed, as I was a perfectionist.

Perfectionism in a vivid child can be a scary thing. It has a moral, almost reproachful dimension that in an adult is put down to priggishness. In a child, presumed closer to God, the will toward correctness of line and behavior has an element of the uncanny that makes people edgy. Does he know something beyond his years? Has he seen the world's awkward truths already? I guess, in my own privileged way, I had: For better and worse, I'd been steeped in the unfairness of my father's family toward my mother, and had suffered it the more because it did not touch me directly. In fact, I was favored: Theresa framed my homemade greeting cards and Sam quoted my Thanksgiving poems as if I were Emerson. How intolerable that they should prize me so evidently, but not the person I (as it were) represented.

And yet it's always nice to be prized—and paid: Even on my brother's birthdays, twenty-dollar bills got stuffed in my pockets. If I could do nothing about this unfairness, or the way I benefited from it, I could at least shape myself against it; transferred and generalized, my pain over my grandparents' injustice became a horror of all things crude, and I a pint-sized Savonarola. Woe to him who in my earshot polluted the air with racial prejudice, impoliteness, or "dirty" language—including, for some reason, the name "Jesus," which I couldn't bear to hear spoken. Perhaps it was too much like mine.

Instead of Jesus in our house, we had a more secular icon of social justice; our dining room was dominated by the dour visage of
labor firebrand Eugene Debs, in a vast Baskin woodcut that em-
phasized his resemblance to a biblical sage. Hard to cheat or even
wangle with that face overseeing you. Is it surprising that in the
game of Cops and Robbers, not wishing to take sides in a conflict
I lacked information to judge, I played the role of the friendly gas
station attendant? (My brother and his friends ignored me.) I
railed against my grandparents' casual use of the Yiddish word
shvartzeh to describe the black help, and my grandfather's use of
the word "girl"—or worse, "girlie"—for anyone deemed unworthy of a name. (When the phone rang: "Hey, girlie, get the ma-
chine.") Our own *shvartzeh* "girls" I loved fiercely and
defensively: Ruby, Cathy, Mary, Dorothy: ample or attenuated,
sentimental or tart. I once glimpsed Mary taking off her wig—I
hadn't even understood that the short, straight brown shag was
not her own hair—and was shocked to see that the cornrows beneath it were totally gray. She winked, as if letting me in on the
secret: She was an old woman, still doing floors! And I felt there
was something wrong when Cathy, showing me where her skin
had paled beneath a bandage, said: "See, we're all of us white underneath."

The world, mysteriously, had many bifurcations, all idiotic and
eventually invidious. I did not understand patriotism or what was
so bad about intermarriage (constantly railed against from the
pulpit) or why most women were addressed in public as if they
were generic nonentities. ("This is my wife," my father would say.
"Sally," my mother would add, testily.) The differences between
men and women particularly intrigued and infuriated me. My
mother, I noticed, stayed at home; my father left at dawn and
returned at dusk, often with mud on his boots from some god-
forsaken housing development on (as my mother put it) another
planet. A child of the suburbs could spend his daylight hours
without seeing anyone male except the art teacher—and wasn't
he . . . funny?

However much fathers were touted as potentates, for a child it
was almost exclusively his mother who ran the world. She miti-

gated the father's punishments, inveigled his dispensations. Who, every evening, marshaled the schedules, categorized the grocery lists, and patched together the car pools? After every bar mitzvah, who directed the parade of husbands marching to the parking lot with purloined centerpieces? In the suburbs every boy, including Papa, was a mama's boy. And yet Mama had no independent power. Perhaps I expressed something of the circularity of this paradox, not to mention of sexuality itself, when at three I reported home from Hebrew school that the first man and woman were named Odd and Even.

NINE

Even I knew this was odd. Why was I so attuned to paradoxes, and to the promiscuous language that gave them voice? I had, it might now be said, a case of attention *surplus* disorder: I noticed too much, concentrated too deeply. Not surprisingly, considering the world, I cried quite often as a result, without feeling particularly sad. I developed an elegiac tone—strange in an otherwise cheerful boy—and it now seems to me that the source must have been my mother. Had I taken up her abandoned battles (abandoned only temporarily, it turned out) as my own? I seemed, at any rate, to have taken up her fears. My brother and I shared a room (though he was sloppy and I was neat) with pinwheel wallpaper that terrified me at night when the pinwheels mysteriously started spinning. To master my panic, I wrote my name over and over in the air, forward with the right hand, backward with the left, as if to make sure it would not disappear.

I now see how Jewish this is, how virtually Kabbalistic, despite the fact that I never took seriously the religion to which I was so heavily exposed. I was much impressed with the intellectual aspects of Judaism: the vowelless language, the interpretive guile, the moral fixity (though I had different morals). The rest I laughed off. Perhaps this was merely a case of siding with the all-but-atheistic Swartzes; my grandmother Anna did eventually start going to synagogue, but her faith was largely a cultural after-

thought, equal parts chicken soup, mah-jongg, and brisket. (Even
the chicken soup was unorthodox: In her nineties she finally di-
vulged that the delicious secret ingredient was . . . *veal.*) Or perhaps I was laughing at the lunacy of belief: I despised credulity,
which seemed much the same thing. Certainly no one could syn-
thesize for me the paradox of a religion that built a monument of
exegesis upon a foundation of bitter fairy tales. While Hebrew
school teachers meant to puzzle us with Talmudic conundrums
like *Could God make a rock he couldn't lift?* I knew, alas, that he
already had. Indeed, this was his one sympathetic trait! God was
otherwise just another bully—possibly real but best to avoid, even
if he had chosen you.

The triumph of suburban Judaism, as I lived it, was based on
the profoundly un-Jewish notion of blind faith. Our tennis-
playing rabbis did not encourage true introspection but alle-
giance to arbitrarily legislated modes of decorum. In this they
were only imitating the overarching American religion and could
hardly be blamed; they were at the mercy of their congregants,
whose will to assimilate was indivertible. When my parents broke
away from the rigid and exclusionary Judaism of my grandfather,
and the urban synagogue he still attended, they meant to practice
a less formal, more individual kind of faith. But as every parent
learns one way or another, each new life evolves a new orthodoxy.
Children and reform movements get out of hand. The new synagogue my parents helped establish in the leaky greenhouse of a
decrepit Main Line mansion soon became as dense and doctrinaire as the one it had broken away from; eventually the two institutions awkwardly merged. In the meantime, my mother served
on the committee that supervised the design of a vast new sanctuary, and I, as the first child born to the founders since the found-
ing, held the first shovelful of dirt at the 1964 groundbreaking.

Religion is useless to the person it excludes, and this new suburban religion, in its unreality, excluded almost everyone. Certainly I shut it out as soon as I heard its voice used to put women
in their place and to "sympathize" with homosexuals. The huge,
squashing pressure of its ponderous sermons and ten-pound
pound cakes ignored the fact that Jews were individuals, more di-

verse than not. How could a religion that for centuries sought to comfort the outcast (and all Jews were outcasts) now make its goal the glorification of the compliant? This was not a message I had any interest in hearing. I wanted to hear instead those glorious Talmudic paradoxes that illuminated by confounding. The most lasting image from my fourteen years of formal Jewish education involved such a paradox, if a ludicrous one: the rebbetzin—the rabbi's wife—chain-smoking cigarettes and rasping about the evils of marijuana during her bimonthly antidrug rap sessions at Hebrew school, while we students scarfed down the chocolate and vanilla (but not the strawberry) sections of the Neapolitan ice cream cups that were our bribes for listening to her. There she sat, in her miniskirt and white vinyl boots, emitting numinous clouds of smoke like the burning bush. She might seem an example of bad faith incarnate, but I loved her, or pitied her, caught in her traps, and she died of lung cancer, of course.

TEN

What the rebbetzin most effectively warned us about was the tragedy of growing up smart and underused—a warning I needed as little as I needed the one about drugs. Against that latter scourge I was vaccinated, perhaps too well; a mind-bending high was exactly my notion of terror. Why would I want my mind bent, when it was all I had that was perfect? The terror was indiscriminate, though: One morning I took a double dose of the delicious cherry fluoride pills recommended by our family dentist; horrified at my violation of pharmaceutical propriety, I hid behind the kitchen door until my father found me there and took my tearful confession.

So I was not to become the first fluoride-crazed child murderer on Greentree Lane. But I did become a kind of junkie for disappointment. As my mother struggled to find some destination for her life—beyond us, beyond marriage, beyond the redesign of her house and synagogue—I began to notice how virtually every other mother in the neighborhood was engaged at one battlefield or another in the same war. They all professed a sense of accomplishment in their kids, which even in the mother of our future transsexual was obviously genuine. But if it was genuine it was not unmitigated, and this ambivalence was what I locked on to. These women had wanted children, to be sure, or knew no other possibility than to want them, but having a child and being a parent are two vastly different things. Your years were marked with pride but your days with disappointment, and your hours were a litany of bitter carping (among those strained beyond their capacity) or of finagling, coddling, scooching, distracting, and constant compromise among the others.

I think I had already divined that this ambivalence about parenting was a choppy translation of ambivalence about marriage, which was itself a bowdlerization of life's existential farce. Doors slammed in your face constantly, and the ones you did manage to get through led more often than not to the wrong rooms. In this sense mothers, abandoned to their children—without (for half their days) male or even much adult female company—were in the same boat as most childless women of the time. But I didn't care about childless women; the only ones I knew were on television, and how vile I found The Honeymooners, with its mechanical geysers of sulfur and steam! I preferred the diffracted family dramas playing nightly at theaters everywhere near me, in every picture window. Each house on my block offered a different spin on the story: the imported Appalachian wife cowed by her fast, intemperate brood; the former sexpot watching balefully as her Lolita squirmed on the menfolks' laps; the kindly slob who could not understand why local kids refused milk and cookies at her chaotic, pigsty house.

The more subtle the sacrifice, the more compelling the story. I watched one day as a neighboring mother gave her eight-year-old daughter a block-stamping kit, complete with tools, bright paints, and glossy paper. Little Minnie did not exactly embody her mother's ideal of graceful femininity; she was hearty and lurching and perhaps a bit dim. "Slowly, now," warned Mrs. B., but Minnie ripped open the box, unscrewed the paints, and immediately started smearing them all over the special paper. "No, Minnie, no—no, honey—that's not what you're supposed to do with them, sweetie—you see, you make stamps, it's not finger paint. . . ." but Minnie would not be swayed. It was too late: She was already happy.

I didn't know then what fathers did, but I knew that mothers sacrificed; they bled their stores of happiness into the children they loved. The stronger or more fortunate paradoxically thrived on the letting. They beamed while taking tickets at the May Day Carnival, and put fifty thousand jolly miles on their Estate Wagons without ever leaving a ten-mile radius. They grew plump. The other mothers became anemic and desiccated, liable to crack. They took drugs. In either case the bulk of their parenthood was all too soon over—and then what? They had been lifted like leaves from the surface of the sea, and dropped back down after five or fifteen years. My beloved next-door neighbor, the Appalachian wife, packed the last of her four children off to college, divorced her husband, and moved back to the mountains. She still—but just barely—retained her accent.

Well, surely suburban motherhood wasn't as Bergmanesque as all that; we see what we look for. But if I was truffling for rue it was not because that was all I experienced: It was the *confusing* part of what I experienced, and needed explication. The rest I knew. I was secure. Indeed, what kept me buoyant about all the sadness I sniffed out in the neighborhood was the faith that my own mother, when returned to the water from her child-raising flight, would not sink from the weight of having loved me.

ELEVEN

I hope it was just a coincidence that the year I got pierced with a pencil during a game of soccer was the same year my mother began her new career. Both involved the same local hospital, and both were accidents, or at least unintentional. Mine was an oversight: I forgot to empty my pockets before playing. My mother's, she says, was a clerical error.

She meant to sign up for banjo class at night school: a horrible notion, but there it is. The banjo's bright and plangent sound had always moved her, and furthermore she was under the impression that my father, with his fluffy new Jewish Afro, looked like the country music star Mac Davis. Now that I was nine and my brother almost thirteen, she felt it was time to resume her life, but despite discussions with those few of her friends who had kept up careers—one a lawyer, another an academic—she feared she was too old to start on a path that might lead to some similarly professional profession. While waiting for clarity on the issue, she would indulge one of her periodic kooky, artistic whims, which over time produced an atticful of baskets, beadwork, macramé, ceramics, oil paints, pastels, and skeins of would-be sweaters. She did them all well—too well, really. Now it would be banjo.

Somehow her registration card got misrouted, and the class she showed up for did not feature "O Susanna" but the Kinsey Report and cunnilingus. It was a sex education class, part of a program developed by a local hospital to train teachers in all aspects of what was delicately called (this being 1967) "family life education." "All aspects" pretty much meant sex and drugs; the hospital did not have a music division. Nevertheless, my mother stayed on—for the banjo story was of course a cover, as even a moment's reflection would have revealed. (How could a registration card for a night school class run by the Lower Merion School District get switched with one for a professional development course run by Lankenau Hospital?) The ruse was designed to make my mother's eyebrow-raising choice of curriculum seem unintentional; for the same reason, over the next few years, she told her mother that the classes she was taking (and soon enough teaching) were classes on how to be a teacher. When my grandmother wondered what *kind* of teacher, my mother without hesitation said, "English."

Well, she did take to it like a native speaker; within a few months of her first Tuesday night class she was addressing Girl Scout troops on the supposed joy of becoming a woman. For PTA groups she made drug presentations, which included the burning of a synthetic tablet that was said to smell like marijuana. After a little more training she was sent to speak to kindergarten classes about "what makes a family" and to sixth-graders about testicles and contraception. She must have been good, for she was soon in demand, making rotations through thirty school districts, including, all too often, my own. Soon, too, she was being harassed and threatened by members of the John Birch Society, who accosted her in parking lots, after lectures, on her way to her car. Eventually the threats became scary enough that my father started accompanying her to evening engagements, standing at the back of gyms and auditoriums like a diva's bodyguard.

I don't know how she approached the subject with other kids, since she carefully arranged that our paths would not cross, but I do know how she had approached it with me, many years earlier, when I'd first asked questions. She already had liberal ideas and was totally matter-of-fact and comprehensive, at least as far as the standard stuff went, starting with *When a mommy and daddy love each other very much* and moving on to *Insert Tab A into Slot B.* On the other hand, when in 1968 my parents saw the original New York production of *Hair* and loved it enough to buy the album, I realized there were things *beyond* the standard stuff else why would my fifth-grade chorus teacher have omitted from her medley of the show's greatest hits that lovely number "Sodomy":

> Sodomy, fellatio, cunnilingus, pederasty.
> Father, why do these words sound so nasty?

It was rare for me to come across four words in a row I couldn't define. "What's sodomy, Mom?" I asked one night between forkfuls of spaghetti. She looked at me and then at my father. "Rodney?" she said brightly.

The handoff produced a mild if unenlightening answer— "Why, unnatural intercourse," he said, as my brother snorted— and though we calmly returned to our pasta I nevertheless understood that I had ventured into the part of sex that was dangerous and real and had nothing to do with babies. In any case, if the answer was unenlightening, I would not remain unenlightened for long.

TWELVE

That was the year I learned to cook, or at least to defrost. My mother started working toward her master's degree, attending evening and afternoon classes while continuing to teach during the day. To make her week less onerous, and to make sure the rest of us ate when she would not be home, on Sundays she prepared a dozen hamburgers, six chicken breasts, and two quarts of tomato sauce, which she taught me how to bring back to life. It pained her not to have fresh meals on the table, just as she could not bear to leave the beds unmade, but the truth was that she was happy, and therefore so was I. I could make my own bed.

But could I lie in it? In 1968 I finally got a bedroom of my own—designed, of course, to my specifications, including a charming woodcut and a black fake-fur spread. In one corner was my weather station (I updated the glass-covered map every morning) and in another the bench where I whittled my oboe reeds. Is there a better definition than this very picture of the word "dweeb"? As my mother had moved further into the world, I had started retracting, it seems; my accident had caused not just the skin around my vast scar but my very heart to pucker. Recovering in my new bed near a window, I could watch my neighborhood friends as they cut through backyards on their tiny sportive missions and understand that I would never play soccer again or climb trees; it would be years before I exercised at all without the most forceful coercion. I had been severed from my body, or perhaps it would be better to say that my physical being escaped from itself through the puncture hole made by the yellow pencil; in any case, I would never again feel safely contained in my skin the way I had for the delicious ten years of my childhood.

When soon I began to sense the rumble of sex it therefore seemed like something happening in another clime—there, under that high-pressure system near the Gulf of Mexico. Not that I was in the dark; I was something of an expert, really, or as much of an expert as one can be about a foreign place as yet unvisited. I believed I understood that place from books, just as I believed I understood London from reading *Oliver Twist*. But these were different kinds of books. In my parents' library, not far from the Philip Roth novels and Civil War tomes, a veritable bibliography of sex started accumulating on the shelves: everything from medical monographs to explicit how-to guides. It would be hard to say which fascinated and which repelled me more. In one book—*Show Me!*—beautiful Nordic men and women made love in the impossibly gauzy glow of the camera light; their unscarred children touched themselves and each other with shameless abandon. In another book—the terrifying *Sex Errors of the Body*—a series of black-and-white photographs depicted boys with breasts, girls with beards, hermaphrodite monkeys and long-donged preteens. There they all stood with their deformities and wonders, arms splayed back against a height chart as if they were criminals, naked but for an obscuring black dot—not over their genitals, but their faces.

If I didn't look like these medical monstrosities, I didn't look like the ripply boys in *Show Me!* either. And I certainly didn't feel like the girl-obsessed adolescents described with such enthusiastic sympathy in treacly books like *Between Parent and Teenager* and *From Boy to Man*. No, it was the girls I felt I understood, at least in their longings. I quickly learned what this was called: I had looked it up often under "H" and "G," had read in my mother's psychiatric texts the current thinking and statistics on the subject. And though some books described my "condition" with sympathy, not one was enthusiastic. None told me—as virtually all of them told everyone else—to celebrate my awakening sexuality, but at best to endure it in hopes of a miraculous alteration down the road.

I did not feel that I required miraculous alteration, at least not in terms of whom I might desire; instead, I worried that I would never be free enough to enjoy (with whatever kind of partner) the activities that these books insistently portrayed as the deepest expression of humanity. Knowing the words for every possible act did not explain to me why I might ever want to perform them; though I was an expert, I was by no means expert, and no amount

of candid information, it turns out, saves you from having to puzzle out for yourself the codes and consternations of love. Like the
weather I studied and even predicted, the internal pressure of desire was vast and chaotic, but unlike atmospheric pressures, it was
unreadable on instruments, unmappable on glass.

THIRTEEN

So I stuck to the facts. At age twelve, in the dead of night in a
cabin in a clearing, I set my bunkmates straight about venereal
disease and toilet seats, about how pregnancy happens, about
what was going on inside our bodies—and inside the bodies of the
girls across the lake. They listened intently as I shared my knowledge of tubes and tubules, sperm and spirochetes: the biology of
love and disaster, without the love, or the disaster. What I only
learned years later was that while I was delivering the theoretical
news, my chums were compiling a huge body of empirical data. In
the woods or behind the cabin or locked in the stinking lavatory
stalls, the boys were all having sex with each other, and loving it, despite their bare and hairless pubescence. Well, it *was* an arts camp.

How did they know that they wanted what they wanted? I am
mystified still. I had assumed that being gay (if that's what they
were) was a kind of twisting *away* from the body; that homosexual
desire, lacking the putative excuse of procreation, was at best a
kind of mathematical abstraction: $x + x = 0$. It was a sex error of
the *mind*; not a moral error, as some would have it, but certainly
a frustration and a puzzle. Later I would come to understand that
this abstraction, which most gay adolescents tend to feel as an
alienation from society, was for me the result of an alienation
from my body. Consequently, it would not have made much difference if the person I fell in love with had been my busty oboe
teacher; I could not have put my failed body into the picture long
enough to do anything about it. My recourse was to conceive of
my sexuality, at least in the years before there was any physical evidence of it, as an extension of my love for my parents, because it
was only as a child that I had been perfect.

As it happened I first fell in love not with an oboe teacher but with a counselor—this is a cliché among gay people, but there you have it. In fact there were several, none older than twenty, all kind, all hearty, all comfortable in their skin. The one who played the bass fiddle was the one who moved me most; he embraced me when the summer ended in much the same way he embraced the burly wooden shoulders of his mournful double bass. My feelings for him were both carnal and chaste: erotic in intensity but spiritual in content. I dreamed of sleeping curled up with him or even somehow curled inside him, but more like a fetus than a phallus. It would all be so clean. He was already engaged to be married and wrote frequent love letters home to his girl; quite soon he learned that I could produce, even better than he could, the adoring phrases and purple touches that gave deepest voice to his longings. So I dictated his letters. The words came easily, of course, since they were only my words for him transplanted; as I painted a picture of their life together, I imagined myself as part of their marriage. In me he would have both a child and a lover— it didn't make sense, but it didn't have to.

Elfin Cyrano that I was (though it wasn't Roxane who interested me), I relished the opportunity to voice feelings otherwise unspeakable. I did not delude myself that anything would happen. Several years would pass before I discovered that men who have feelings for other men could live those feelings out; they need not forever talk through a screen. Despite—or really because of—all my reading, I had imbibed more than the usual draught of the poisonous idea that homosexuals were narcissists if not pedophiles, doomed to be lonely and childless. I didn't believe it, but the only gay people I knew were a few boys at school who were classic fairies, decoupaging their notebooks and frosting their hair. They were roundly abused, as in time I would be, for what reasons I never understood. Could everyone simply read into my longings? Or into my supposed frailty?

But the books I had read, with their mild bigotry, had inoculated me against more virulent strains: a hair of the dogma that bit me. A legacy of my mother's years promoting "family life education" (she had now moved on to the university) was that sex remained a topic in our district's health curriculum—albeit a topic taught by embittered gym teachers with old war wounds. "Okay, today we're going to discuss homosexuality," announced one of these men, a dim-witted but genial lacrosse and football coach. "And we're going to hear from some actual homosexuals. Before they come in I just want to say: These people are clever. They'll have an answer for everything. But I want you to know that I think the whole thing—*and it's just my opinion*—is sick and perverted. Think about if your parents had decided to be homosexuals: You wouldn't even be alive!" This was apparently his *coup de grâce*, for he raised his eyebrows significantly.

I laughed, couldn't help it, and he shot me a glance.

"What's so funny?" he snapped.

"Are you saying homosexuals can't have babies?"

"I'm saying they don't *want* to"—to which I had no comeback.

FOURTEEN

At sixteen, I was pretty much indifferent to babies, never having spent time with them. I didn't fret much about becoming a parent. Someday, I believed, I would be forced to ask whether I wanted children or wanted to be gay, but I had a healthy sense that such questions lay far in the future. For now it was enough to wonder if I would ever have sex—and, more important, at which Ivy League college?

If Yale at the end of the seventies was a great center of sexual learning, I seemed to keep showing up, like a figure in an anxiety dream, at the wrong time with the wrong books in the wrong rooms for the wrong tests. Where was the teacher? Though the campus was crawling with alternative sexualities, and I quickly found a circle of homophilic friends, I remained almost entirely celibate, not for lack of trying. Nevertheless, I was rumored to "run" a stable of homosexual actors, each of whom had to sleep with me to be cast in the plays I directed. If only it were so! But directing seemed to be the one foolproof way of ensuring that no one would do more (or less) than respect me deeply and hold me at bay. I had proved my old gym teacher wrong: I had become a parent. And without making love.

Part den mother, part father confessor, I maintained a brood of intimate friendships, which though they were their own reward frustrated me deeply and confused my family. At any hour my phone might be answered by anyone of any gender. My parents, I knew, were beginning to wonder: Did I have a *special* friend? Oh, at least a thousand, it seemed; if only one would notice me! On campus I sometimes wore a pink triangle pin—though with my long overcoat, my reddish beard and the dark, round glasses I affected, I looked more like Trotsky than anything suggested by the word "gay." I was as out as a person could be, short of the senior who called himself Shirley, and yet at home I remained tight-lipped. It was such a bother, coming out: The closet may be a tiny space, but its thousand doors must each be opened, laboriously and one at a time. I would later realize that this burden, however peculiar, was not unique. Gay or straight, male or female, we must all come out: Come out, come out, wherever you are. Because only when you're out is it possible for anyone to see you.

It does not seem likely that there were ever parents who could be expected to accept such news as I had to deliver with more grace and equanimity. My mother's course in human sexuality was by now the most popular class at Penn, perhaps because of the dirty movies; even today, people at parties, upon learning whose son I am, are apt to say things like "My God, everything I know about sex I learned from your mother!" My father, I knew, whatever he might feel, would never raise an objection; my sex life (like everyone else's) was, he believed, none of his business. And by now my brother had made it clear he was aiming to marry and have a family, so all seemed safe on the passing-down-the-genes front. There was only one problem: I had nothing to say.

It was a political nicety that delayed me. I did not want to tell my family that I was simply gay, which seemed at the time a meaningless category, ripe for confusion: a club too undiscriminating for me to join. Rather, I wanted to tell them that I loved somebody, and that the somebody happened to be male. It took several years, and my move to New York City, to produce such a person; even so, I'm afraid he was a bit of a shill. I fell in love with him almost entirely (and just barely long enough) to have someone to discuss at Thanksgiving that year, in my parents' den.

Oh, how I nattered! Gay theory, social construction versus essentialism, the outlaw role of the artist in society. It was really too much to ask my parents to listen to this *and* pay for graduate school. Finally, I got to the point and described the man, an Australian actor, who lived in a strange East Village apartment that had been retrofitted (I realized one morning, looking up at a stained-glass Star of David high above his dingy bed) into the shell of an old synagogue.

"Australian?" my mother asked.

"Yes, from Sydney."

"Then . . . he's not Jewish?"

My parents had been sitting quietly, as was their habit, on the love seat covered in a swirling velvet by Jack Lenor Larsen. My mother had her legs in my father's lap, and he rubbed her feet, as he had done forever, to the point where you were surprised there were any feet left.

"Sally," he said, "don't be ridiculous."

"But why? Why shouldn't I want the same thing I would have wanted?"

"If you're going to break the mold, just break it."

After they had argued the point for a while, they turned back to me. "Son," said my father, "we will always love you."

"Of course," added my mother, trying to smile. "It's only—it's just that . . . I don't know how to say it. Wouldn't you have liked to have a child?"

FIFTEEN

By a process I don't yet fully understand, but which apparently involves love, marriage, and mysterious incantations, my brother's wife became pregnant in the fall of 1986. My parents rejoiced, as did I; though they had been as good as their word when I first came out—supportive and accepting and carefully inquisitive—

the birth of a grandchild was sure to ease whatever remained of their sense of potential loss in me.

So this thing created by Tony and Mary (who had married two years earlier) became the subject of intense scrutiny long before it was born. Chromosome spreads, ultrasound movies, measurements, kicks: All were shared and interpreted at length. At home in New York I eagerly awaited each month's photocopy of Little Miss Embryo, and then her successor, Little Miss Fetus. I watched her progress from something that looked like an algebra problem to something you might expect to find in an undersea documentary. Ah, we all sighed on a tangle of phone lines, the miracle of life. The miracle of human conception and growth. What we didn't discuss was the other miracle, the much more subtle one happening outside the womb.

People behaved in bizarre new ways. My brother began returning his calls and, one day, even cleared away the fungal tide of his desk. My mother started coming home early from work, distracted, glazed. "Look what I got," she'd tell my father, caressing the bales of pink yarn she had bought. "I'm actually knitting booties!" And my father, not to be outdone, retrieved from the attic his router and lathe. "I'm making a Colonial-style infant's chair," he announced.

Wondrous nature, the child was completed before the chair. On May 20, 1987, baby Aviva was born. However altered everyone had been by the mere anticipation of her, it was nothing compared with what would happen now. All eyes turned on the six-pound dab of life in Mary's arms: a perfect dab, unparalleled. The world had never seen one such. If she appeared a little odd, had a wild, immense, full head of hair, this was character, this was charm. "She looks like a monkey," my mother burbled. "But I mean that only in the best sense of the word."

She'd been delivered by cesarean section—an operation whose goriness was fully documented in Polaroid pictures. What couldn't be documented was another operation, gorier still, by which everyone around her was transplanted into a new generation. My parents became grandparents. My sibling became a father. And me? Up until that moment, *I* had been the baby:

youngest, quickest, closest to the ground. Now I'd been booted upstairs. I was an uncle.

"Uncle"—the word fairly reeks with unpleasant connotations. "Dutch uncle." "Say uncle." "Uncle Vanya." "Uncle Tom." The message is various, but entirely negative. You picture a submissive yet overbearing coward. Try to get your picture from television instead and you don't fare much better. There's Uncle Joe from *Petticoat Junction*, Uncle Charley from *My Three Sons*, Uncle Fester, Uncle Tonoose, *Bewitched*'s flaming Uncle Arthur— deviants all, and ripe for committing sex offenses against the minors in their homes.

I could imagine how these creepy uncles got that way. In my own family, we couldn't manage a five-minute discussion of the news or the weather before our attention was turned, as if magnetically, to little Aviva: her cough, her toes. We, who formerly had looked in whatever direction our own roads lay, now looked back, almost fearfully, to that tiny place from which we had each once started. In doing so, we inadvertently saw how much of our journey was already complete. My grandmother shrugged to find herself ninety; my parents blinked and swallowed hard at the heart of middle age. Even my formerly childish brother, so recently thirty, was suddenly being accorded by friends and strangers the full respect due adults, just because he had married and bred.

I was also—though differently—changed. On a twigless branch of the family tree, merely an uncle, I would never achieve that kind of adulthood; I'd just keep aging. My hair might fall out, my gums might retreat to the bone and beyond, but all it would make me was old. Without a child you were always a child: a hanger-on, an exile, a zero. But for a gay man, even a gay man living in Greenwich Village, this sensation of superfluity was by no means novel. How often I'd felt it at the bank, at the laundry, where I'd impersonate maturity but feel weightless, invisible. Somehow I wasn't a proper adult. In doctors' offices, I found myself skimming the latest issue of *Highlights for Children*. Automatic doors in supermarkets refused to admit me. Even the man behind the counter at my favorite bakery seemed unaware that a human lived inside my parka. He tossed me my change as if I were a tollbooth.

SIXTEEN

Everything conspires against the single, childless man. Each new living thing in the world each day—berries, babies, crocuses in spring—says: *You are alone, and not getting younger.* Some gay men I knew reacted to this sense of betrayal by rejecting the world of children entirely, like a club they proudly refused to join because it refused to admit them. Others seemed to blame children for their own unfortunate childhoods, and offered quasi-political defenses (since defenses were apparently necessary) of sex without procreation. They were thus involved, it seemed to me, in a process of *anticreation.* Of course, the great majority of gay men pitched in to the intergenerational effort with vigor, as uncles or teachers or pediatricians, but rarely without the feeling that they were immigrant workers on narrow visas, like Turks in Germany.

I wondered what kind of uncle I would be, but I had been a quasi-uncle already. When I was twenty I worked as a summer intern with a magazine editor who was sexy and ursine and sad and garrulous. His wife—I was shocked to learn he even had one— was as sly and minimalist as he was immoderate; while he made big improvisatory stews for dinner, she devised tiny *pots de crème* for dessert. Nine months after I met them she gave birth to twin boys, whom I loved and photographed and (when we were eventually all in New York) took to the playground. Later, I wrote an exquisite recommendation (my finest work up to that point) to help get one of them into preschool—horrified though I was that being selected to smear Play-Doh into your hair now required testimonials. Once they were in school, however, the twins were even more lost to me than they were to their parents.

It had been a grim if entirely natural letdown, and so it was with some trepidation that I went to meet my niece. I made my way through the cryptic halls of the maternity ward (it was the same hospital I'd been taken to twenty years earlier) and came upon, in Room 521, the wriggling, squinting, scaly-footed creature. Mary said, "Look, Aviva, here's your uncle," and handed her over to me as she rose. "Would you hold her? I need to get washed."

"Sure," I said. Mary waddled to the bathroom, Tony wheeling the IV on its tall pole behind her.

Left alone, I stared at the baby, who did indeed—but only in the best sense of the word—look like a monkey. Her expression was one of silent omniscience. She stared without blinking and followed my gaze. Like the man at the bakery she seemed to sum me up in a glance, but for her the sum was not zero. "Aviva," I murmured, "my little palindrome!" She smiled as if approving of something, but then the smile froze and she started to wail.

"Could you change her, please?" Mary called from the sink.

Change her? I thought. *I hardly know her.* Yet somehow I remembered how to untape the diaper and put on a new one, how to straighten the inscrutable shirt and restore the chimplike smile to her face. When her parents returned, I was beaming with satisfaction. See, I could change her. And she could change me.

I had forgotten that part. The way you feed them but they feed you. A child might push you closer to the edge of the cliff without throwing out a line by which to save you, but there were compensations. The line was, in any case, your own responsibility, baby or no. Thus, on vacation with my family at the New Jersey shore, I volunteered to give Aviva her bottle each midnight. I crept into the talc-scented room, loath to disturb such an idyllic sleep. It seemed almost cruel: to wake her, to force upon her a bottle instead of the breast she preferred, to make her drink through her yawns and then, when she finally seemed about to open her button eyes fully, to thrust her into the lonely crib, with nothing to accompany her back to her dreams but the metallic chirping of a doll that played, at a tempo too lugubrious for any adult to bear, "Thank Heaven for Little Girls." It seemed cruel, yes, but how often do we get to choose how love will be offered?

One day the next winter, Aviva was enjoying a tour of the Village, cinched facing forward in a sack on my chest. It pleased me that people kept stopping to make her giggle, to touch her simian hair or just watch. But I felt guilty taking credit—that was the phrase that popped into my mind—for a child not my own. Dutifully I always said, "This is my niece. I'm only the uncle." Still, when we arrived at the bakery, I forgot for a moment that she wasn't "mine." Back aching from her meager weight, I stooped to examine a loaf of semolina. "One of these, please?" I asked as Aviva peered around.

The man behind the counter looked up and did not see through me anymore, but smiled. My niece had made me real, first to myself, and then to anyone who happened to be watching—real, because I loved her.

SEVENTEEN

In Margery Williams's classic story, a velveteen rabbit, made real at last by a child's true love, stays real forever. I, on the other hand, reverted to my usual state of suspended animation the moment Aviva, strapped in the back of her parents' Volvo, disappeared down MacDougal Street en route to the Holland Tunnel. When I finally gave up on waving, I climbed the stairs to my little apartment, cleaned up the mess of the two-day visit, and—despite the din of life outside the window—fell asleep on the unmade bed within seconds.

How did full-time parents do it? To visit a child—spend a few hours, sing a lullaby, and leave—was a pleasurable encounter, full and sufficient; to live with a child at close quarters was a nightmare. However much I enjoyed Aviva, I did not envy Tony and Mary, who looked like raccoons from lack of sleep. But sleep was the least of it. More disorienting was what happened awake: the chaotic shifting of perspective from the familiar world outside the home to the mysterious playpen within it. It was not, after all, as if Tony and Mary had suddenly been relieved of their regular lives. They both had interesting, demanding jobs: she as a second-grade teacher, he as some sort of biotechnology wizard. But no one had taught, nor could any wizard conjure, a way to make having a child anything less than cosmically disruptive. Which, presumably, was the point.

I did not want to have my life permanently disrupted; it had taken so long to rupt it in the first place. When I woke up from my nap I was relieved to find my world restored, my compass reoriented in its familiar direction. There were, I told myself (just as I had been told too often, under different circumstances), many kinds of love, and this was the kind I had to offer: the kind at one remove. Wasn't that, finally, the real definition of "uncle"? One remove. I was content to let Aviva vomit mostly in her parents' house instead of mine, to let them worry about her vaccination schedule. And while I would surely give her gifts from time to time, and descend from glamorous New York to speak to her elementary school classes about writing, I would not need to save for her college education, or for the prize Beanie Baby she might so desperately want.

Was it selfish to preserve my limited resources for my own priorities? Sometimes it seemed as if gay men were despised and envied because they did not, as a rule, dig themselves into thirty-year financial sinkholes by having children; they could afford thirty-year mortgages as a result, and on nicer homes with nicer appointments. For myself, the lack of a child would mean, among other things, the freedom to do more of what I wanted in life: to write an ill-paying novel, say, instead of becoming a lawyer. I would not have to factor in a mountain of debt to Zany Brainy and Baby Gap. If that made me somehow weightless, so be it; children seemed to like me for it. I came without strings and tensions and burdens, all of which a child instantly divines. Cranky babies calmed in my arms, causing people to say, "You'd be such a good father." But they didn't understand: My weightlessness was my strength. My pleasure, too. Parents, I'd realized, are quickly forced to temper their joy, to mix it with worry and call it something else. But I got to have it again and again, unalloyed, as long as I gave it back to its owner.

And yet, the next time I went shopping for bread I was once again an invisible man. Was it only the presumption of heterosexuality that had entitled me to a baker's smile? This made me somewhat defiant; I said thank you too brightly as I handed him my dollar. But I was in fact uncomfortable with defiance as a modus vivendi. As I had discovered while writing about AIDS activism, defiance was almost always an untenable stance for more than the short run. To live in defiance was a hopeless egg-and-spoon race: You either concentrated on your gait, and thus dropped the egg, or concentrated on the egg and thus stumbled, breaking a tooth—and the egg too. Was the egg worth it? With AIDS, obviously yes. With me it was less clear. For the most part, I was content to be who I was, even without bakery smiles, even having to read preachers' constant imprecations against me; but sometimes I wondered if being gay and choosing to be childless was the fruit of self-knowledge or the punishment for it.

The paradox reminded me of a joke—well, really a parable— that my mother had told me. Sadie is walking down Collins Avenue in Miami Beach when suddenly she spots her old friend Esther emerging from a fancy store, followed at a distance by an ancient man with giant ears, no hair, ten shopping bags, and a hacking cough. "Esther!" shouts Sadie. "I haven't seen you since your beloved Sidney died; what is it, darling, twenty years now? But you look just marvelous! Such beautiful clothes! And that ring, my God, is it fifty carats?"—for Esther is wearing a diamond the size of a peach pit. "It's called the Rabinowitz diamond," whispers Esther significantly, "and it comes with a curse!" "What's the curse?" Sadie asks, making the sign of the evil eye. Esther tips her head toward the old man hobbling slowly toward them. "*Rabinowitz*," she says.

EIGHTEEN

At the heart of the story of the Rabinowitz diamond, "chosen" people—not just Jews but all long-suffering types—will recognize the theme of anxiety over God's dubious honors. Naturally the theme is expressed as irony: The curse is the source of the blessing; the blessing a perpetual monument to the curse. A more sanguine reading might put it this way: If the brilliant jewel comes with a price, at least the price gets you a brilliant jewel. The deeper truth about humanity is that the jewel doesn't have to be so brilliant. Even the most bedraggled souls, when hypothetically offered the chance to exchange their lives for someone else's, generally refuse. Oh, they'll take the money, of course, but nothing will persuade them to relinquish the personality that their lack of money produced in the first place. The thing that deforms us, forms us—and so, for the most part, if we're being honest, we like our curses and our crosses. I did, at least. If being gay had its disadvantages, those disadvantages led to advantages, and the advantages had come to seem so advantageous I could not imagine my life without them.

In drawing this conclusion I found I had a surprising ally: my parents. Though they had at first grieved (for the most part privately) over the presumed loss of potential grandchildren, and wondered (if only reflexively) whether they had done something "wrong," circumstances had long since assuaged them. There were, of course, Tony and Mary's kids: Aviva soon had a little brother, Max. But there was also a secret advantage to my childlessness that no one had anticipated. I was available. I had the energy to clean out their attic and the eye to rearrange their furniture and the time to do it over and over. A lover, when I had one, only doubled the available manpower. And when I lost one, what better place to recover than home? It was little more than an hour by train from New York to Philadelphia; really, I could bring my laundry. The train *from* Philadelphia seemed even swifter. Certainly my parents took it often, showing up for a day in the city: a show, a nice dinner, and home again with a bag of bagels from the shop on Sixth Avenue. I was never too busy to spend these days with them, or to see the latest Sondheim on their American Express card.

And so they quickly took up my gayness as an opportunity; they gave money to antibias organizations and enjoyed meeting my "interesting" friends. It sometimes seemed as if my life in Greenwich Village was even more fulfilling to them than it was to me. The city had long occupied some hallowed place in their imaginations. My father basked in the corned-beef aura of a mostly mythical Lower East Side; my mother, on Friday afternoons when she had no clients, slid herself beneath the bedspread, let her head stick over the edge of the mattress, and skimmed *The New Yorker* for motes of sophistication. If it was inevitable that, for my own reasons, I should move to the city (I had subscribed to *New York* since I was eleven), perhaps it was inevitable for their reasons, too. Our reasons, in any case, overlapped. I had not yet heard of the designated daughter—and would have rejected the term if I had—but I *was*, in a way, the designated dandy, with my chic insomnia and bohemian digs. Is it too embarrassing to reveal that, for a time, my mother and I both had our hair cut at the same Upper East Side salon, my rate discounted in deference to hers?

Any child may have the taste, but only an unencumbered child will have the freedom to attend to his parents' dreams in the process of attending to his own. At an age when many of my friends preferred to see their families only as swiftly as sailors on shore leave, I gladly spent a summer month or more with mine every year, down the shore or up the mountains (as they say in Philadelphia), reassembling day by day the configurations of my childhood. Each morning spent in these generic rented houses began, as it always had, with the din of my father at his coffee grinder, and each night ended with the ice cream dishes stacked in the sink. All was as it had been in high school, although my brother and his family showed up only on weekends; there was nothing to interrupt the endless stasis of our lives, except what might wait behind the horizon. We did not look.

Well, I peeked. Is it just my shadow, or does the story of the Rabinowitz diamond adumbrate a fear of dying alone? My mother's mother, long a widow, hoped to outwit that fate by preempting it; she asked to be poisoned and put out in a Hefty bag at the first sign of incapacity. "I don't want any bother," she'd say, but she did not get her wish. My mother, on the other hand, has made it clear that she wants *total* bother: She has stipulated a "Do Resuscitate" order and instructed us to keep her alive using any and all extraordinary measures. Now that my brother has his own family to tend, the responsibility for my mother's immortality appears to fall on me; but I have always felt I bore the burden of ensuring her happiness anyway, and thus my father's. Age merely ups the ante. For my parents had not only grown comfortable with my being gay, and even delighted; they had also, I realized, grown dependent upon it. Without children myself, I would always be their child.

NINETEEN

If adulthood and parenthood are, for most of us, synonymous, that may be because most of us were raised by parents. Almost all the adults we knew when we were young had families—and, as far as we were concerned, that is *all* they had. The marriage, the mortgage, the professional machinations were matters sequestered behind the Oz curtain, and what was left in front of it was us; happily we believed we were not just the center but the whole of their lives. We defined them: If children were what adults took care of, then adults were those people (and only those people!) who took care of children. Oh, sure, there was the occasional unmarried great-uncle, but great-aunts spoke of his condition with the sad sympathy otherwise reserved for teenagers with acne, as if being childless were a developmental mishap. He proved the rule, as did my brother, who never seemed much of a grown-up to me until the day Aviva was born, at which point society suddenly conferred upon him the respect it reserves for those who have "chosen" adulthood. That he was no less (or more) childish on that day than he had been the day before was irrelevant. He was now a parent, and therefore no longer a child.

Formulated this way, adulthood becomes a tricky concept for those who don't procreate, or who wait longer and longer to do so. For gay men especially—but for more and more heterosexual women, too—the question of what forms a mature identity has been left, since the first days of the sexual revolution, unanswered. And often unasked. Throughout my twenties I contented myself to observe the obvious: No matter how much I doted on my niece and nephew, no matter how many godchildren I might walk to school, I felt more like them than like their parents, and I startled when the classroom door shut me out. The world did not confer its accreditation easily; however many babies I diapered and dandled, I was still, in my own eyes, a child. Only later did I realize that this observation implied a challenge: I was going to have to create some idea of adulthood without the idea of parenthood to give it form—or not become an adult at all.

Not becoming a real adult, by which I mean a traditional adult, remains a viable option for gay men; they can become faux adults instead. Banished from the precincts of Dreft and Kwell—as I have come to call the five-year landscape defined at one horizon by baby laundry detergent and at the other by toddler lice shampoo—some gay men who remain single make a kind of life's work out of adolescence, their days filled with gossip, crushes, self-beautification. Others cultivate an eerily parallel world to the world of families, in essence adopting each other as children. And others become drones, working so much that they have no time for anyone, including themselves, which seems to be the point.

A sad truth about life before prime-time lesbians—or my life anyway—is that it lacked, for want of a better term, relevant role models. It wasn't until my mid-twenties that I met an older gay man who was out and comfortable and seemed like an adult. At the time, I was working as a music coordinator on Broadway shows, making sure the right songs got sung in the right keys every night. Backstage at the Broadhurst was not the most likely place to find functioning adults of any stripe. There were hundreds of gay men in that world, of course: from the unreconstructed fairies of the chorus, with their lewd jokes and camp attitudes, to the marquee talent who were gay but "discreet"—surely their prerogative. But they could not help me.

Eventually I happened to get hired by a silver-haired composer who was open and modest and successful in his art; without my having to frame the question (or even knowing what it was) he said to me unpatronizingly one day as we marked up a score: "Life won't always have to be such a production number. It takes longer for us because of the way things are, but it doesn't mean we don't get there. It took me until I was fifty to figure out what I really needed, but not long after I did, I found it." He was now happily married for life, he told me, without even putting the word "married" in quotes. Touched as I was, fifty seemed impossibly far away to me then.

In any case his words were soon drowned in the melodrama of backstage life, and in the melodrama of my own. I gave up the theater, which though desperately fun was like living in a nursery school twenty-four hours a day. Back at home, as I stared at my keyboard—the computer now, not the piano—I wondered what kind of life I could have. Surely not the footloose life of the flitty chorus boys; I was rather at pains to differentiate myself from them. ("Do you know why gay men grow mustaches?" one asked me. "To hide the stretch marks." I shaved mine off.) But I did not have enough money to collect fine china, and no amount of bench-pressing had ever made me look like a proper homosexual. As my new work began to absorb all of my time I found, to my horror, that even my housekeeping was becoming subgay. The bed was unmade, sometimes for days; my spice rack no longer made sense. What kind of perfectionist was I?

TWENTY

I had no dog, no garden or Roseville, and barely ever a lover near enough to impose himself on my neatly made bed. No garden, no mad obsession with needlework or frequent-flier schemes to keep me busy during family hour. But I *did* have a mania. Every night for years, when any sane person would long since have been dreaming, I watched back-to-back reruns of *The Mary Tyler Moore Show*, with my old friend Meg on the other end of the telephone line, anticipating together the punch lines we knew by heart and laughing harder for the foreknowledge. I could not fall asleep without the familiar squall, without the nattering nanny of television watching over me in its bland, impartial way. But our choice of shows was no accident, either, for the theme of the series was that a single person could make a kind of family out of her work, and could become an adult by treating herself like one.

As I reached my thirties, this was an ever more comforting message, for by then I realized that if I was to become some sort of adult it would be no sort I had been trained to recognize. Like Mary Richards, like the vast majority of singles I knew, both straight and gay (and like more and more married people, too), I had unknowingly entered into an alternative contract with the world—a contract that paid me a living wage of respectability in return for exorbitant amounts of labor. Work was by now my only child, and I fretted over it in much the same anxious, proud way my mother, it seems, had fretted over me.

We had all been like that, my crowd, in our twenties. But more and more of us were carrying it over into another decade: a series renewed a few seasons too long. I had a boyfriend, call him John, who under normal circumstances worked seven days a week until nine; when his supervisor was fired he virtually stopped leaving the office at all. He spoke of his irrational devotion in the same way we speak of the needs of a difficult child: "What choice do I have?" John was extreme—probably he'd be a workaholic even if he were rich and married—but all my friends, most of whom were magazine editors or writers, worked fiendishly hard. True, it was fun, like putting on a show: *Hey, I'll stay up all night sewing costumes!* Except that the minute the show opened, the next show had to be built from scratch. Every month. Or every week.

No wonder Mary Richards was on the Pill. None of the women I knew would have dreamed of having a baby while in her twenties; where would she deliver it, in the copy room? And there was the slight hitch of finding a suitable father. But one by one, as the clock struck thirty, they started craving and agonizing—and here two roads diverged in the wood. Some got married and quickly pregnant, including Meg, thus ending our marathons. The others hesitantly set off down the path we gay men were on, and kept looking back. Mightn't there be an unmarked trail to switch them back to the road more traveled? Or would they have to buy Tampax straight through to menopause and withstand the patronization of their aunts?

We gay men shared with them the queasy feeling that we were, despite the terms of the alternative contract, still seen as Lost Boys and Peter Pans: uncertain of gender, clinging to childhood. But at least we men had signed willingly; it was a way to stabilize our position in the world. The women had mostly signed under duress; it was a way to destabilize theirs. Despite liberation, cultural support for spinsterhood was scarce; feminism—never fully internalized, and garbled by its backlash—had only come to add to their burdens. Their mothers need only have given birth to a baby to feel they had discharged their cultural duty; my friends were supposed to have the careers of wise crones and the sex lives of Lolitas. *Plus* the baby.

Gay culture, on the other hand, at least as represented to those of us at its Manhattan epicenter, asked little of its adherents except that they not grow old. They should certainly, for a start, stop dying. And they should be careful about how they were seen. Children (and old people) were to be avoided like unflattering light. They threw off the curve. Without the two extremes around, those of us in the middle would never age, or at least the day on which the signs of aging became obvious could be forestalled almost indefinitely. Which is why most sixty-year-old gay men look like straight men at forty. That virtually all eighty-year-olds nevertheless look identically ancient turned out to be a nicety many gay men would not get to consider.

TWENTY-ONE

It was not some moral superiority that spared me, but only the accident of my prudishness. I had lived more like a priest than like Priapus; the unsafest thing I did in bed was eat poppy-seed bagels—*My dear, what a mess!* I nevertheless took the HIV test repeatedly, and was glad, for the first time in my life, to fail. Or do I mean pass? For the disease proved metaphorically infectious even when you did not have it.

Does it seem like a dreadful detour to take a quick ride through AIDS? What could be more unwanted in a story about babies—healthy babies, of course—than a story of blood and semen and pain? Of course they are really the same story; it is only recently that the two ends of life have been so rigidly segregated, both from us and from each other. We tend to think of childbirth now as sterile and safe, whereas HIV infection is dark and microbial. But in the hospital there is much that binds them: the test, then the wait, then the momentous arrival. Outside the hospital, too. For gay men did not (however much they tried to pretend) spring fully formed from their own imaginations. Each as he died was still someone's son.

My friend Mark died in 1994; had he lived a little longer, he might have lived much longer. But he was infected early, before he could have known what precautions to take. Not that he would have taken them, necessarily. A copy editor, he was punctilious about his commas and colons, less so about his sexual partners. The possibility of pleasure was all he required, and pleasure came readily to him, for he was square-jawed, tall, all cheekbones and sideburns. Even ill, he was astonishing to look at; his mother, as he died, whispered the words of Psalm 139 in his ear: "I am fearfully and wonderfully made." Was it the fear she spoke of that had made him so rangy and restless? At his desk, when I first met him, he kept lists of restaurants and movies and men, each a little brick of possibility on his scratchpad; he got around to most of them. But his punctiliousness was not based (as mine was) on the dread of omitting something; it was based on the anticipation of some new pleasure that only punctiliousness could unearth. He was a librarian of enthusiasms, and whatever he knew he shared; he was nearly transparent, and what you could see inside was as neat as his penmanship. Consequently, he was the ideal friend; but in love, he lacked the gift of adhesion. Men passed through his life like so much copy: He made his inscrutable marks upon them and passed them along. They left but one mark upon him.

The key metaphor for Mark was connection, not roots. Those bricks on his scratchpad were parts of a bridge, or parts of many bridges he built in all directions and charged no toll upon. How many people did he point toward jobs? How many sublets fill? He did his share of matchmaking, too, though you couldn't call him a yenta. He made the introduction and then withdrew; sometimes love ensued, sometimes disaster, sometimes, God help me, both. He had arranged my introduction to John and, in his last months, endured the woeful tale of our breakup. He was sorry for my pain, of course, but not quite sympathetic. He knew from wide-ranging personal experience that you cannot—should not—force anything to fit. The bridge was beautiful in itself; the destination irrelevant.

A bridge is fearfully and wonderfully made. It suspends disbelief. It says: Despite your fear, you will not fall. It shows you so by not itself falling. But though people cross over, and on occasion jump off, they do not much remain. Bridges connect and stand alone. Mark hoped to have been crushed with one great love; failing that, he made himself lovable to as many people as possible. Was it his loss? Well, if so, he was rarely alone enough to feel it. In any case, it was his friends' gain. Mark took us over a river; and if he has crossed beyond reaching now, he is still a bridge—a bridge that says (he would have objected to the idea of a bridge speaking): Need less, love more, rise, span. Look everywhere, invite surprise. Don't insist on knowing the destination; sometimes go just where the road does.

TWENTY-TWO

Though the cast was exaggeratedly manly—decked out in leather jackets and chest-enhancing T-shirts—I always saw the fight against AIDS as a drama of adolescence. Not in the petulance of its activists (though of course there was plenty of that) but in their heartbreaking earnestness. Members of groups like ACT UP attempted to live out the egalitarian democratic ideals they'd learned in junior high school history: inclusion, debate, consensus, action. No matter that the virus was not a tax bill to be finagled, or that eighteenth-century New England methods didn't always survive transplantation into twentieth-century Greenwich Village. They did their best and made a difference. Were their neat crewcuts not meant to show that they were good boys, too? Gay men may have resisted the process of aging, capped tooth and manicured nail, but that did not mean they would just lie down for a beautiful, early death.

Constitutionally unfit for activism, I served as a witness to the disease instead—a paid witness, but still. I wrote dozens of long, grueling articles about AIDS. I scribbled on the sidelines at demonstrations, toured hospital wards and vaccine labs, discreetly handed tissues to kind, heartbroken mothers. My brother helped me understand the science; Mark helped me understand the sex. The emotions I had no trouble understanding on my own: the pain of invisibility, the betrayal of the body. Even so, except for the journalism, I kept my distance; in the novel I wrote—set in gay New York in the eighties—I avoided the subject like, well, the plague. It was not clear to me that AIDS could be satisfactorily dealt with in fiction, any more than it could be in life. It was too catastrophic and too minute all at once; it threw off your sense of scale.

But if the disease was a tragedy, it was also a bandwagon. Not just for those of us who profited from it literally: the writers, the hospitals, the enamel trinket–makers. It was also a bandwagon for the so-called community, galvanizing fund-raising, eliciting (for the first time ever) widespread sympathy, creating an identity based not on sex but service. Many gay men (and their straight and lesbian cohorts) found their lives transformed for the better by the catastrophe: They shed useless illusions, learned to treasure their friends, set out to repair or let go of the damage society (they felt) had done them in the first place. For those who remained uninfected, there was nothing like a cold look at mortality to kick-start a career: Chronically out-of-work actors became social workers. Burnt-out screenwriters became Jeremiahs. But even those too sick to restyle their résumés—and I talked with hundreds in that shaky boat, every last one of whom is now dead—could speak convincingly (if shockingly) of a trade-off: clarity in exchange for health.

A fatal disease is not the ideal way to become fully human. And with AIDS in the gay community, there was another twist of the knife. Historically, medical and political disasters have usually led to renewals; after the decimations of World War II, for instance, the French instituted a national policy of patriotic sex and repopulation. Now, however, even if unprotected sex were feasible, no amount of state-endorsed sodomy was going to bring about a gay-baby boom. That job, despite the right wing's protestations, was largely the responsibility of heterosexuals—who, when they realized what business they were in, often disowned the product. For a time it therefore seemed as if AIDS would cripple not just the current gay generations but the short institutional memory that might nurture new ones; there would be nothing left in the future for homosexuals but a return to closets and florist shops. For some gay men (including Andy, as I would later discover) the devastation of AIDS was directly linked to their thoughts about becoming parents—not in order to produce gay children per se but to replace, in whatever form, the great lost souls they had known. For others, the epidemic shut off all thoughts of progeny, spiritual or otherwise, as too painful—which may be part of the reason why agencies for gay youth could never raise the kind of money that AIDS service providers did. In any case, the disaster did not focus most people's attention so much on children as on parents: the mild fathers and sheltering mothers belatedly coming around, or not.

TWENTY-THREE

Of course, I knew that territory. In my journalism I had long since found myself drawn by invisible threads to stories about bereaved mothers, rescued babies, gay teens struggling to inhabit themselves. When asked by fellow journalists what my beat was, I ruefully told them "the tear beat," as if it were a *Times* bureau in Asia. Wherever someone was weeping over a child in trouble I flew, cupping my hands and then stealing away with my precious plunder. Often, of course, the tears would be over AIDS itself: I made a specialty of mothers who, literally or figuratively, held up placards that said I LOVE MY HIV-POSITIVE BOY. One of my first published articles was about Helen DeFiglia, the mother of choreographer Michael Bennett, who when her son died in 1987 took up AIDS as a cause, dancing as a hobby, and "Bennett" as a new last name. She seemed to be trying to reproduce in herself the boy she had produced, and lost, in the first place.

An extreme story like this inevitably raises weird Oedipal specters: a mother so in love with her child, she attempts to usurp his life (or death). But any intense relationship between a mother and son, especially if the son is gay, is liable to seem perverse in our society. Partly this is the unfortunate legacy of denatured Freudianism: all those overbearing mothers collaborating with ineffectual husbands to produce their homosexual offspring. (Why, then, do they have heterosexual offspring as well?) And partly it's just misogyny—the bond between a woman and a gay man being only slightly less threatening to straight male dominance than lesbianism, and without the thrill. Still, like any stereotype, the image of a mother like Helen DeFiglia cuts at least one slice of truth: She does seek solace in loving her son. What the stereotype fails to catch, however, is the possible corollary: The son is much loved.

This is the saga of the radiant child, burnished by hope and glazed with tears. And the saga of the pietà. AIDS intensified but by no means invented it; a child could disappear as easily into life as into death. I wrote the story again and again, in various guises. There was the Navy mother whose gay son was murdered by shipmates who stomped on him like horses. There was the Connecticut mother whose idealistic daughter was jailed while doing relief work in El Salvador. There was the elegant mother whose successful son had bought her a beautiful house in the woods—but was she happy? I sat with them all: in eerie kitchens where the kettle boiled dry, in noisy dens where only the phone was mute. There were never any fathers around; they were dead or drunk or had long since decamped. That was part of the saga, too.

This repeated note of absence echoed uncomfortably in me. Though my own father has been a model of steady, if vague, benevolence, and has slept apart from my mother fewer than a dozen nights in forty-seven years (not counting hospital stays), I feel that I know him at one remove, like a photograph so fragile it must be kept in a safe. The photograph has been described to me, of course: It shows a handsome, kindly, stubborn man, loyal to a fault and hopelessly unselfish. But I have never seen it for more than a second. This is not just a matter of personality, though my father has had every reason in life to keep himself aloof. Nor is it a matter of the terrible hours a man of his generation spent working, for mothers now spend as many. Sadly I came to the conclusion that what I was feeling was the inherent unfairness of fatherhood: that you would be forced to the periphery, if you did not go of your own accord. It is often remarked how children are

robbed in this way of their fathers, but less often how their fathers
are robbed of them. Mothers are robbed of their children too—
I'd now become an expert on that—but at least they had them
once.

TWENTY-FOUR

*Once upon a time there was a kingdom that had no salt. It was
landlocked, so there was no sea to provide it, and not even the elders
remembered anymore the location of the caves from which the crys-
tals had, in ancient times, been mined. Salt, however, was crucial
to the people's health; without it they fell into stuporous trances,
and no work (or too much work) got done. Those who were wealthy
enough imported their supply, at great expense, from realms beyond the desert; but the trading routes were dangerous, lined with
bones and thieves. Everyone else made do by swallowing their tears,
except that—and here was the heart of the problem—most of them,
once they were older than five, could not remember how to cry.*

*In this kingdom, a certain kind of child was therefore prized. He
was called a crybaby—not because he cried so much himself (he
did) but because he was able to get others to do so. A baby thought
to possess this power was a source of pride to his family, for the custom of the kingdom was that, in return for his services, he would be
paid a tithe from any tears he elicited. A very talented crybaby
could net a vial a day, which he brought home to be sealed under
wax in blue glass goblets until needed.*

*But if he was a source of pride, he was also a source of worry; he
had always to be protected from the threat of kidnapping, for there
was such a black market in tears. It was necessary to send him to expensive schools, run by a faculty of aged basset hounds, to learn the
secret methods. Nor was the crybaby especially easy to live with. He
had overly firm opinions. He ate peculiarly. He doubted himself
and was sure of himself at exactly the wrong moments, and so was
impossible to comfort. In short, he was odd and arrogant and
glowed with intent, which many admired but most shied away
from. People are afraid of the radiant child. And so is the child himself.*

One crybaby or another was always being hailed as especially effective. His teachers would admire his particular style in poking his stick, or insinuating his needle, or patting a mother's hair just behind her ears—mothers' tears were deemed the most potent. His skills were so great that eventually the elders, in consultation with the faculty of bassets, would send him on a dangerous journey. Provided with only a faded map and a sad book about a spider, the boy was sent off into the desert in search of the ancient salt mines. "Follow your heart," his mother would tell him. "And the vultures," would say his father.

For many years no one knew what happened to these boys, for none of them ever returned. Until . . .

One night, a mother was awakened by a noise in her kitchen. There, having a glass of milk, sat her son.

"Did you find the mines?" she breathlessly asked.

"Yes," he said, "but they were empty."

"Oh. But did you find anything else?"

"Yes: the boys—I call them boys, for none has aged—living in the empty caves."

"But how do they survive?"

"They make each other cry with their stories and swallow each other's tears."

"And why did you, alone among them, choose to return?"

"No: They all returned, just as I have, to see their mothers. They stayed one night but then went back to the empty caves. And there they remained. If you never knew, it was only because none of the mothers dared to speak of it. Perhaps that way it still seemed possible—"

"I will speak of it," said his mother defiantly, but then stopped cold. "Will you go back?"

He looked at her, and started crying. By force of habit, he drew out a vial to catch the drops.

TWENTY-FIVE

If Mark was a bridge, leaping from one place to another, I was a root. He had moved dozens of times, with equanimity, even a month before he died; I still lived in the same apartment I had rented, fresh from college, in 1980. (My parents won the prize, however: They lived in their first house for forty-two years.) I could not rise and span as he did, much as I admired him for it, and now his death immobilized me further. My recent breakup had not helped matters; when I tried to get out of bed each morning, it was as if a great bear in my soul was refusing to lift its head. I had plenty of assignments that should have pulled me out the door, but I was as tired of honing other people's grief as I was of honing my own.

Like my mother after having her children—but in my case with work instead of with kids—I had met the first goals I'd set for myself (minus the Peace Prize and federal judgeship) and now sank back stymied. I lived in Manhattan. I had written a novel, well enough received. I had learned to make my own *pots de crème*, just in time to abjure the indulgence. I had even appeared on *Jeopardy!* and won six thousand dollars. Surely, I was no longer a child. I had seen a friend buried (scattered, really); if the death of a contemporary didn't make you an adult, what ever would? I was thirty-six, the same age as my mother when she signed up for banjo class . . . no, that was too weird. I did begin piano lessons, playing two-part Bach fugues at half tempo, but my teacher suddenly moved to Europe after our sixth lesson, so I never sped up. And what was the point of a fugue at half tempo? I asked myself significantly.

I started dreaming about white picket fences and quiet country houses and tomatoes tied to tall stakes. I was not much in the mood to date, but I let it be known I might consider coffee with someone whose house in Sagaponack sat empty all winter, the Jacuzzi unplugged. A nice banker, perhaps? Of course, when I did go out I was so grim that my dates didn't know what to make of me. Perhaps it was not such a good idea to break the ice by revealing that I was wearing a shirt I'd taken from Mark's apartment after he died, and how his other friends were all schlepping around in his sweaters, a ragtag army in surplus uniforms. "If death," I intoned, "is to be the new skeleton in our closets, we have little choice but to make it feel at home." A real turn-on.

It was true, though, which is why Mark had loved the AIDS quilt and even those bitty, flop-eared ribbons that everyone else derided. Like the ancient Greeks, they made fate domestic if it must be inexorable: an act of drawing, spinning, and cutting the thread of life. We gay men, at our best, honor what is delicate in us, so that even in grief we somehow refuse to harden completely.

So I didn't quite harden. I sat and thought. I spent more time with Max and Aviva. John pointed out—we remained close, despite almost everyone's advice—that I talked constantly about my niece and nephew, and always seemed to feel better around them. "You've written so much and so often about children, don't you think you want some of your own?" he asked. But no. My work had only warned me off; I did not want to cause more sadness, especially my own. It had taken me this long to shake off the orthodoxies of the world I was born to; what a blessed relief! I visited my family not on the High Holidays but when I actually wanted to be with them, and that turned out to be more often. I wrote my own commandments and lived by them; I chose and fulfilled my own obligations. Why would I want now, when I was finally free, to indenture myself to the most tyrannical master of all?

Still the question hovered, vibrating slightly, like the ceramic figurines in my fish tank. This was not the kind of fish tank with fish in it, mind you, but an aquatic diorama built by a friend—the mother of the twins, in fact. In it, pink cherubs, suspended on invisible strings, wobbled amid bubbles and tall vegetation; they seemed to be chasing the pale blue seahorses, which in turn seemed to be chasing the cherubs. To me, the scene represented the idea of babies at the moment of conception, when they first imagined what it would be like to hitch a ride on a seahorse and gallop out of the water. Of course, the tank burst a seal one day while I was on a business trip; it leaked until empty and ruined my stereo.

Ah, well; I went back to work. I was Mary Richards, and so be it. All I asked in return was a neat, efficient life with not too much dirt at the edge of the rug and, if not a shelf full of Roseville in the country, a few unbroken things. I understood that a world so fine and clean and safe could never withstand a live-in child, or a live-in parent for that matter. This seemed a shame, but approaching forty I believed I had finally come to understand the truth about myself: I wanted a house, not a household. The never abandoned yet never fully faced notion of becoming a parent had seeped out of my heart through broken seals when I wasn't looking; good riddance! I would not have a child.

And then I met Andy.

III

Éminence
Mauve

ONE

"I'm dying, I guess," said the still familiar and oddly jovial voice on the phone. "But I'm in a great play! Will you come and see it?"

I hadn't heard a word from Trip in almost twenty years. Back in high school, we had been friends if not intimates: members of the same circle, a few degrees apart. I had directed him in musicals and eaten at his house but we'd never, for instance, discussed our crushes—perhaps because they were on the same men. The difference was, Trip could probably have *had* those men. He was campy enough to signal his interest and pretty enough to make it worth signaling: tall, giraffe-lashed, wonderfully made. Reimagining him over the phone as we spoke, I was reminded of Mark, except that Trip had never given up acting (as Mark did when he became a copy editor) and had at last found a great love, only to lose it. His mate, with whom he had shared a charming Victorian house in Montauk, at the easternmost tip of Long Island, had died of AIDS not long before. Now Trip was ailing, too. Still, as he put it, he wasn't dead yet; he had landed the leading role in a production of a play called *Pterodactyls*, which was running for a few performances at Southampton College over the next few weeks. "I haven't seen you in so long, and who knows if I ever will again. And, plus, it'll be fun," he said, changing gears almost audibly. "My parents will be there."

Now, *that's* fun: going to see a play about a gay man with AIDS who confronts his pickled Main Line parents with the fact of his disease and how he got it—while sitting next to the pickled Main Line parents of the gay man with AIDS who is playing the role of the gay man with AIDS. It was just up my alley. I rented a car.

Well, I was looking for something to occupy myself those spring weekends in 1995. Two years after my breakup with John, I was not only unattached but apparently unattachable; my grim work took up most of my time, and my grim countenance soured the remainder. In that regard, I was in the same boat as most of my female friends—except that I, a supposedly gay man, had more expected of me. My upstairs neighbor, the actress Mercedes Ruehl, whom I called "the star above," tried to help: She would knock on my door when she knew I was entertaining a date and stop in for five minutes to help me along by scattering fairy dust around the apartment. "Mmm, that smells good, Jesse's such a good cook, and he's got the best taste, I mean look at that sofa!" My dates adored her—and left after dessert.

"Ah, well," Mercedes would murmur, putting on her Zen face. "When the pupil is ready, the teacher appears." Easy for her to say; willowy yet womanly, Mercedes apparently had a more desirable campus than I did, for teachers who were eager to instruct her lined up nightly outside our building, baying.

You don't expect to hear Latin from an actress whose most famous movie line is "Just give me the fucking ticket, dickhead," but when I first met Mercedes, climbing the stairs to her new apartment, she was talking a dead language. "A *locus amoenus*," she said. "You know what I mean: a pleasant place. That's what I intend to make." She was describing her plan to renovate the derelict concrete courtyard behind our house into a verdant wonderland. A few months later she had done it; her transformative powers were prodigious, as her career had proved. On the other hand, like me, she seemed to be stepping carefully around a big hole in her life; it wasn't until later that I would learn what the emptiness was.

As it turned out, Mercedes had known Trip's late partner, an actor turned real estate agent, and had spoken at his funeral. She bade me farewell as I sped off for the Hamptons the next Saturday morning, where I had arranged to stay the weekend with friends. These friends, a Mutt and Jeff couple, had promised to throw a little party in the afternoon, after which I would see *Pterodactyls*. A change of scene, I told myself, would do me good.

It was awful, of course: every line a torture. I kept my eyes fixed rigidly on the inane stage doings, lest I accidentally witness the much more compelling drama playing out on Trip's parents' faces. That would be a drama too perverted to watch—the perversity of life forcing parents to outlive their child. When the play finally ended, about ten lifetimes later, Trip and his family wisely hightailed it to a bar.

"You look well," I told him, and it was true, though he raised an eyebrow as if he knew better. Driving away, I kept examining Mercedes's maxim: *When the pupil is ready, the teacher appears.* Could even the readiest pupil ever be prepared for death? In any case, death found Trip before the year was out.

Fickle human, though, I was smiling as I drove away from the bar. Earlier that day, I had met . . . a teacher.

TWO

A handsome man was getting out of a beat-up car as I watched from the kitchen window. I was standing at the refrigerator, refilling a pitcher of lemonade, when I heard the noise of tires on gravel. Elsewhere in the house, Ken and Stuart, my Long Island friends, were hosting their Saturday afternoon party; the dining room table was sagging under the weight of serving dishes. Near their little dock on the water, the grill was billowing smoke. But I forgot them, and my lemonade mission, for the next few minutes. The man emerging from the car was, at least superficially, what I would have called my type, except that I could only identify my type in retrospect, by particular example. This man was one. He had oval wire-rimmed glasses and a trim Vandyke that made him seem both intellectual and sexy, as if he attended museum lectures and yet knew how to dance. As he opened the front passenger door of his car to release a goofy, shaggy mutt, about the size of a coffee table, I thought to myself: *Ah, good to animals.* Then the man walked to the back door and reached inside. *A gift for our hosts?* I wondered, as he fiddled with what seemed, from a distance, to be a bright, heavy package. *A very large, squirming gift for our hosts?* No, it turned out, a baby.

First impressions are definitive, except when they're not, and the details of this one would turn out to be meaningful later. I saw Andy before I saw the baby. Though Ken and Stuart had told me about a friend of theirs who'd adopted, I did not put together until thirty seconds later that this was that friend. Even when I saw him carrying the little boy, I thought for a moment that he must be some straight guy, divorced or going stag—so strong is the presumption against gay parenting. Eventually I understood who he was; I finished refilling the lemonade and made my way through the party, not quite casually, to meet the new guest. Guests.

Andy (I learned as we spent the afternoon rudely ignoring everyone else) had adopted Erez, over virtually everyone's warnings and objections, when the boy was only three weeks old; he was now just shy of fourteen months. His hair, of which there had been virtually none at birth, had grown long enough to produce a few stray curls, and his ears had grown large enough to receive messages from Telstar. He was completely expressive, which made him charismatic, even though he so far spoke fewer than a half-dozen words: "Dada" for Andy, "dibee" for dog, "Abba" for Elliot—Andy's ex-lover-to-be. Though Elliot had recently moved out of Andy's apartment, his status was still murky at best.

"We thought we'd try dating again," said Andy, "but it isn't working."

"And what is Elliot to Erez—his other father?" I asked.

"No. No. Definitely not. More like an uncle."

"But Erez calls him Abba?" "Abba" is Hebrew for father.

"It's just a name Elliot taught him. Erez doesn't know what it means."

"No," I said mildly. "But Elliot must."

We were standing on a little dock jutting out into Three Mile Harbor. Erez had only recently learned to walk, so we took turns holding him; I did not for a second worry that he would be uncomfortable in my arms and so, of course, he wasn't. He fit. He looked at my face or alternately rested in the hollow of my neck. He was ripe and fragrant, like an August tomato.

He was not just charismatic, I realized, but like all happy babies a faith healer. I knew I was smiling. His needs were very deep but narrow, and so fulfillable. I felt my congenital grimness starting to slough off me, like dead skin—let it! There was no danger of its not growing back. In the meantime, for a few minutes, the exfoliation would produce a glow that made me (I knew) more attractive, at least to myself and presumably to others. When I kissed the top of Erez's head, whom else was I kissing?

I found Andy attractive even aside from Erez: a little bit tough, with his leather jacket and Brooklyn accent and the mark of Abel upon him. But Erez, like a magnet, flipped Andy's polarities—that is, the child brought forward in his father exactly those qualities usually turned inward. Seen that way, the jacket and the scar were actually signs that Andy was in part undefended and soft: available, like Erez, to a stranger's tender interest. But would I make myself available to his? I didn't see how I could.

Still, we each kept maneuvering around our obvious attraction. When a long pause opened up between us, we looked at each other frankly across it. Then our noses started twitching.

"Diaper?" I said, and Andy nodded.

We took Erez back to the lawn; I laid him down without hesitation and proceeded to change him.

"You sure know your way around a baby," said Andy.

But not an adult, I thought.

THREE

We said our hope-to-see-you-agains, but on my part, at least, the hope was not an expectation. Certainly I would not contact Andy, however much we'd hit it off. I couldn't consider taking things further until the ex-lover-to-be was conclusively ex—or so I told Ken, later that afternoon, when he offered to act as a go-between. "Call me old-fashioned, I don't date married men," I said, "no matter how almost-unmarried they are. And when there's a child involved, you've got to be doubly careful." What an odd thing for me to be saying after almost two decades as an openly gay man—and yet, when was there *not* a child involved? I drove to Trip's play and then back to the city and returned my bright red rental car. It had all been a lark, a weekend trip to fantasyland, wherein one could play with a baby and flirt with a daddy and come back to one's life unharmed and unhandled.

Though as promised I did not call, I did keep thinking about father and son. I wondered what it would be like to touch Andy, what he would look like without his clothes. Erez I'd already touched and seen. These thoughts, and the accompanying illustrations, did not sit well together in my imagination; they were like two superb flavors you would not wish to mix. Erez was caviar: a bright, translucent egg of intensity. Andy was chocolate: a warm, velvet blanket to get lost under. The lascivious thoughts on the one hand kept getting crowded out by the no less tactile (but nonerotic) thoughts on the other—and then vice versa. I didn't know which it was proper to focus on (or if neither was fair game) but both made me happy. And then I remembered I would not see them again.

Should I revisit my refusal to date a "married" man? It was not just an ethical but a practical stance. Relationships founded on someone's pain often foundered that way too: Live by the sword, die by the sword. On the other hand, it seemed unfair to hold a gay man to such bright-line standards. One of the injustices hidden behind the lack of gay marriage is the attendant lack of gay divorce. As a result of it, homosexual couples rarely know when they are definitively apart any more than they know when they are definitively together. To patch over the latter uncertainty, they tend to choose anniversaries somewhat at random: our first sighting, our first date, our first sex, our first shared key. But since these milestones are rarely solemnized it is almost impossible to deconsecrate them cleanly.

Of course there *are* gay weddings, of no legal standing; I have attended some and found them wanting. They are usually too earnest and at the same time too campy, with their readings from Sappho and Whitman, their highly alternative clergy, and their terrifying, handmade vows. *The ladies do protest too much, methinks.* Such ceremonies tend to raise more questions than they answer: If marriage and fidelity (as some theorists argue) are patriarchal-heterosexist prisons, had not homosexuals, in being excluded, somehow been spared as well?

Perhaps so. But for me, to proscribe or even finesse fidelity because of the inequities of marriage was to throw the baby out with the bathwater. I wanted—if not a wedding—a honeymoon, a proper morally binding contract, a free-and-clear partner, plus a nice set of Calphalon.

Ethics being what they are, I might have called Andy anyway had I not begun working just at the time on an article that shed uncomfortable if oblique light on the subject. The piece was about "walkers": a dying breed of urban gay man who, many nights during the social season, would escort a fancy lady to a ball or an auction or a charity dinner, gossip brightly, dance if need be, redeem her sable, and cart her home. In their old-fashioned, fussy discretion, in their docile acceptance of second-rate status, walkers were often ridiculed as some sort of Aunt Toms; while this was unfair (they got a lot out of the deal as well), it was true that the contract was innately unbalanced. No newfangled gay man would deign to accept such a role, whatever its emoluments, for you cannot get what you want in life (I wrote) by trading your exquisite élan "for a deathbed visit from Nancy Reagan, for a free lunch at Mortimer's, for Pat Buckley's kiss." The whiff of patronization in such arrangements was nicely expressed in a synonym for "walker," derived from his usefulness in filling out boy-girl seating arrangements when so many girls were perforce unaccompanied: "extra man." Place-filling, necessary—and disposable.

Somehow it seemed to me that to date a person who was otherwise engaged, even if only minimally, was to court the same fate; I did not want to be anybody's extra man. Though of course, as far as Erez was concerned, wouldn't I be anyway?

I called Brooklyn information to get Andy's number. I wrote it down, then threw it out.

FOUR

A value not deeply held has a narrow jurisdiction. When Andy eventually called to ask me out, all I needed to hear in order to say yes was that he and Elliot were "not together." I did not further explore what the state of affairs was between them, though I knew from my own experience that there were many shades of gray between *together* and *apart*. It was *apart* enough for me, for now, that they had their own apartments.

Our first date, on a Friday in June, was somehow the more exhilarating for being somewhat haunted. Not only by the specter of exes. Andy had come directly from a memorial service for a friend who had recently died of AIDS; as we stood in line at the Astor Place Starbucks, passing time before a late movie, a wraith from my past—Mark's roommate—wandered in. It seemed impossible (and rude) to ignore all the ghosts floating about, so when Andy and I sat down to talk, our conversation revolved around Erez's first, and our friends' last, months. In the presumable middle of our lives, we sipped our coffees (well, mine was hot chocolate) and kept company with the two extremes.

"Tell me about your life as a father," I said.

Andy began at the beginning. His mother, he told me, had done as she promised and put on a nice circumcision party. Despite her fears, all the relatives came, and none seemed troubled, or less than jubilant, about Andy's becoming a father. Aside from everything else, the boy was so pretty—hairless but pretty. Crying but pretty. He *did* cry a lot; for a few months, Andy worried there might still be something wrong with him. Not that he trembled anymore; the trembling had ceased before he was two weeks old. But how long, and in what secret ways, might prenatal drug use affect the resultant child? No one seemed to know for sure; no more than they knew, really, how long (and if) *anything* affected a child. Andy at forty-four, one might argue, was still living with the results of his parents' *post*natal drinking. In any case, Erez passed each milestone exactly on schedule, or a little early. So did Andy. He learned right on time how to mix the formula, change the diaper, bathe the baby in a plastic basin. Still, he worried over his child, and over himself, as only a newborn parent can.

And yet he was ecstatic. At this point, the huge encumbrance of a tiny life still seemed like a liberation. There was, of course, the literal freedom of time off from work: He had, as planned, taken a six-week family leave when Erez first arrived in Brooklyn;

immediately thereafter came his summer vacation, and then his long sabbatical. He would not return to work until September, at which point Erez would be eighteen months old. The terms of his sabbatical did require him to use the time for professional "enrichment"; at a nearby college, Andy attended evening classes (while a baby-sitter watched Erez sleep) in Spanish and French and computers and music. During the day he lived the life of a father at leisure: He visited the aunties, went shopping with Erez strapped to his chest, took weekend trips to the house on Long Island, and pushed the pram along the Promenade.

But his sense of liberation was more profound than the joy a pretty baby offered. There was also the liberation of becoming more fully himself. With Erez to take care of, his life all at once made sense, as at that moment when stereoscopic images, formerly out of focus, suddenly merge and snap into place. The wasted energy of doubleness, of misalignment, is now available for better uses; the color is brighter and the world is dimensional. This was Andy as a father, not a sketch of himself but the real thing. Erez's full and immediate bonding brought the point home: *You are everything*, it seemed to say, *and you are sufficient.* Consequently, when people were confused about Andy's "situation," he was delighted, eager, hot to explain. "How's Mom doing?" said a fellow father sympathetically as he sat next to Andy and the month-old Erez on a bench one day. "I wouldn't know," Andy replied. "I adopted him as a single man." Though this was a bit aggressive, his benchmate didn't quail—but then, Andy had not said "a single gay man."

Even Janet came around, which was also, for Andy, a liberation—from the lifelong prison of her disappointment. She had begun, for once, to approve of something her son had done without her approval. That the approval had come so late was a shame; with her health deteriorating, she could not enact it with any vigor. She did give Andy money to help with the baby-sitting and started referring to Erez as a grandson. Sometimes she sat in her easy chair and putted a ball at the boy with her cane. But she couldn't hold him, he was such a dense, squirming package. Instead she looked at her son's son and smiled, albeit with a glaze of wariness; perhaps it was her old fear come true, that the baby withdrew its store of life from her dwindling savings. But at least she smiled.

At which point in his narration Andy smiled too, and tapped his watch. "We should go, I suppose." But we didn't get up.

"You're happy," I said, somewhat amazed.

"Pretty much."

"Good for you." I collected our paper cups for the garbage. The movie was terrible, but we didn't mind; halfway through, I took his hand.

FIVE

Janet died a week later. Andy was fairly sure, he told me, that her death and our dating were unrelated, though he did find a recent *New York Times Magazine* on her nightstand, with a story of mine on its cover. If he sounded surprisingly upbeat—did I want to come to the funeral?—he was not a mourning person; and, after all, Janet had been threatening to do this for years. How much different would his life be anyway? He would not have someone to argue with on the phone every day, or be evasive with at night. And yet, when Erez stood up in his crib all smiley on the morning after Janet died, Andy broke down like a baby himself, just held his son and wept.

What finally provoked the tears was his realization that Erez, even as he was beginning to say the word "Grandma," would not in fact have one. He already did not have a mother. And for all that Janet had done to undermine Andy's confidence, she had been a kind of immovable landmark, in reference to which he could always chart his position. Even being a father was defined, in part, by being her son. How would he know what *not* to teach the boy? For his values came from his mother, directly or by opposition; without her, he believed, he was inadequate to pass them on. "The advantage of being taught good values by a controlling and overbearing person," he wrote in his eulogy, "is that you learn them. The disadvantage is that you feel trapped, and your most defiant rebellions turn pallid because you never really do anything your mother taught you was wrong. I was only half joking in the sixties when I said the reason I didn't join the Weathermen was that my mother wouldn't let me."

He handed me the neatly typed eulogy on our next date. It was the first in a series of thousands of pieces of paper that would pass between us over the next few years, as others might pass love notes. I took it as such. Clearly, I could not know Andy without knowing Janet, and this was the beginning of her reconstruction—a reconstruction that at times came to seem a bit too successful. Sometimes I would feel I was living with her; other times (especially when Andy got angry) I would feel I *was* her. In any case, I found I identified with his potent distillation of her philosophy: "People are more important than things. Individuals are more important than groups or institutions. Don't give your life to any idea, or even art, unless you also hang on to your day job." Only the last of which I had violated.

For the rescheduled second date I ventured, as if on safari, to Andy's neighborhood. Though Brooklyn Heights was only four stops away on the A train—no more than ten minutes—it had always seemed another world. Did it not, after all, have a different area code? A different lineup of cable channels? The East River, however many tunnels and bridges traversed it, remained for me psychologically impassable. As a result, I had only visited the so-called Borough of Churches two or three times in fifteen years, and then with much groaning. Brooklyn was everything I thought I wanted to avoid: the place people moved when they first came to New York if they could not afford Manhattan, or where they got sucked back again when at last they gave up their dreams. This was pure snobbery, of course, but not just *my* snobbery; even Andy called Manhattan "the city," as if Brooklyn were not the city's largest borough but instead part of dread New Jersey.

Of course Andy had grown up in Brooklyn, which meant he hadn't "settled" for it, so that was okay. And I had to admit it was awfully lovely: a little like Cambridge, a little like Georgetown, but mostly just like Manhattan except sane. Approaching Andy's address I passed trees, and stately stoops on handsome five-story brownstones, and wrought-iron gates recently painted, and gardens and brass and everywhere kids. Including Erez, now standing and waiting, next to Andy, outside their house.

They had just returned from Friday-night services at a nearby synagogue, where a prayer had been offered for Janet's soul. Andy did not want to go in just yet. It was an exquisite summer evening, and so we walked along the Promenade; the Manhattan skyline looked just like its postcard, backlit by the sun hanging low over Upper New York Bay. Erez wanted to be on his feet, to run ahead, and it was totally safe so we let him; when he got tired he sat in the stroller and promptly closed his big button eyes.

Why did everyone beam at us? It was not my experience that gay men elicited warm fuzzy feelings from strangers, even in Metropolis. Was Brooklyn that friendly? Were our clothes so appealing? But no, it was Erez. We were two lucky guys at the periphery of a cute baby's halo; it disguised who we were, or shielded us. In any case, we were no longer gay—and this was only our second date.

SIX

Several years later, when Erez's speech was fluent and flavorful but not always accurate, he asked me if I planned to abstain from food on Yom Kippur. "Are you going fast?" he said. "Do you like to go fast?" At four, speed was his organizing principle. If someone woke up in the morning before him, he'd say, "You cheated! You slept faster than me!" So it was not surprising that he would take advantage of an accident of language to merge the subject of food (which was also highly rated) into his overarching, favorite theme. Speed was a hunger, and hunger a speed.

Do you like to go fast? had traditionally been a question associated less with gay men than with chain-smoking high school girls, but it was a question I was nevertheless asking myself on my second date with Andy. I found it hard to answer. "Fast" was perhaps not the word I'd have used to describe my sexual style; "lurching" was more like it. I had moved seldom but precipitously, often knocking things down as I fell. More recently, though AIDS was encouraging some men to adopt a *carpe virem* attitude, the atmosphere of disease only made me more uneasy. This was a Chinese finger torture, for the more I abstained the more I craved, but the craving was a kind of pleasure, and satisfied itself. Having sex began to seem like having a car: a luxury sometimes, an inconvenience other times—and hey, what's the deal with parallel parking? It's so hard to do well that you feel, when you do it at all, unreasonably triumphant. Better to take the subway.

But Andy knew exactly how to maneuver his beat-up car, and I had the feeling that any step toward greater intimacy between us would inevitably result in mad acceleration. Not just because I was attracted to him (though that was a factor) but because of Erez. A baby drastically increases the density of intimacy, which is one reason parents at playgrounds are so much more social than other groups of strangers. (When their children know each other's names and play so hotly, how long can they remain aloof?) Dating a parent intensifies the feeling. You might not be fondling each other yet, but you *are* fondling the child, who is a kind of intermediary. An evening of diapers and drool and tears leaves little to the imagination; as soon as you play at parenting with someone, aren't you virtually married?

On the other hand (or is it the same hand?), the fact of Erez militated *against* speed. I had almost never been cavalier in my relationships, but this was clearly going to be a situation in which I would have to be especially cautious. It was one thing to tease an adult with the possibility of a long-term relationship, or even to say you'd give it a shot, but it seemed cruelly unfair to make any representation to a child unless you were prepared to follow through. If you could say "I like the father, but I know for sure I don't want a baby," or "I like the father, but I know for sure I don't want to marry him," you should stop cold and head for the door. While casual sex might be defended, and even on occasion heartily endorsed, there was no excuse for casual parenting. Babies at Erez's age love so quickly and fearlessly if you prove lovable, and they don't understand "*C'est la vie.*"

134 · Jesse Green

So I recused myself that evening from the intimacies of fatherhood—and from the intimacies of adulthood, too. When it was time to put Erez into his crib and read him stories and kiss him good night, I stayed in the living room, thumbing through a copy of *Parents*. And when Andy emerged, blissed out, from that ritual, wondering what I'd like to do next . . . I started lurching.

"I didn't notice it before," I said in what I hoped was a seductive voice, "but you have beautiful red highlights in your hair."

"No, not really."

"Yes you do! Not red, exactly, but a lovely kind of, I don't know, auburn, a kind of coppery glow, like tea?" On I nattered until Andy's face turned, remarkably, the exact color I was trying to describe.

"Thank you," he eventually said. "It's dye."

"Oh. Well, it's nice."

We sat at opposite ends of a green leather sectional sofa, our legs up and slightly touching. My nervousness compelled me to continue flogging this dead horse of a different color. "What would it be normally?" I asked.

"By now, gray, I suppose," said Andy—and I wasn't sure whether he was referring to the agony of this conversation or to the fact that he was eight and a half years older than I.

"I *love* gray," I said, before finally shutting up for a minute, thus giving myself time to switch gears. "Let me be frank. I notice that your bed is in the same room with Erez's crib."

"Oh, once he's asleep," Andy said, "he doesn't wake up for anything. Not that I've ever done anything in there he shouldn't wake up for."

"It's not that I think there's anything wrong, despite Freud, with a baby accidentally glimpsing the *primal scene*, and certainly it wouldn't matter whether the scene was straight or gay. It's just that I don't feel right seeing *myself* in the primal scene. I mean, I hardly *know* him."

Andy laughed. "You don't have to make a life decision," he said, "in order for us to sleep together."

"Oh, don't I?"

SEVEN

In retrospect, my lurching efforts to slow things down appear to
have been carefully calibrated: strong enough to feel good about,
not strong enough to succeed. I knew perfectly well what I was
doing when I invited Andy for dinner the following Wednesday in
Mercedes's *locus amoenus*. I knew he would stay over, and that
was all it took. By the next morning I was fully embroiled in whatever it was that I was becoming. Our pillow talk was of play
groups and public schools and should Erez have a bar mitzvah.
When Andy kissed me, he did so with such force that I wondered
if he was kissing for two.

It was not just the good stuff embroiling me, though. In order
for Andy to spend the night at my apartment, Erez had to spend
the night at Elliot's. This was not, by now, a novelty; Elliot baby-
sat Erez, in his new apartment, about once a week. So far, the
arrangement had proved mutually beneficial: Erez enjoyed a
change of pace, Andy got an evening off, and Elliot got an
evening on. Elliot, having grown more and more attached to the
son as his attachment to the father frayed, especially welcomed
the opportunity—at least until he paged Andy the next morning
and found he was not at home. We were eating breakfast when
the beeper went off. Is there anything more instantaneously guilt-
inducing than the insistent peep of the baby's proxy while one is
lounging in a robe, eating croissants? Andy quickly dialed Elliot's
number; I tried to busy myself with the jam as the tears leapt
through the receiver: "What if there had been an emergency?
What if I had needed you?" And though Andy calmly reminded
Elliot that he could have paged him at any moment—hadn't he
done so just now?—the problem was not really a possible emergency but a probable slow transformation. It was beginning to
dawn on Elliot that if Andy got serious about someone, that
person might get serious about Erez. And then where would
Elliot be?

He was not wrong to fear being reduced to the role of baby-sitting uncle; Andy wanted to see him as such. Even when they were still a couple, Andy had never intended to be anything but a single parent, no matter how much Elliot eventually joined in. And that was the problem: Elliot joined in. He was eager and coddling and always available, and Erez obviously adored him. He was too good a bargain. Without family nearby to supplement hired help, Andy depended more than most parents on the generosity of interested friends. In order to have a social life, whether a date or just a movie alone, he had to plan and often pay for it, one way or another. And so he had not stopped Elliot from thinking what he wanted to think. He had even been so accommodating as to allow Elliot's name to appear on the birth announcement; it was a big mistake, for it seemed to authorize the ex-lover-to-be's claim as a father. Other friends, who baby-sat without a title, were shocked and confused—as I was, too, when I first saw the card. But what choice did Andy have? It is hard to do hard things cleanly. In a single day, the day Erez came home, his life had changed radically from one of nearly total freedom to one of nearly total constraint. And though he welcomed the change, he could not afford to question whatever help he could muster.

The situation was more complicated for the shadow people: those of us who were not Erez's family but whose lives were altered by him anyway. When I agreed to go on that first date with Andy I did not think I was choosing to admit unending unclarity into my life. Yet here was a man on the other end of my phone, crying his understandable grief. And here was I, trying to start imagining a future in which I was—what? A stepfather? A co–adoptive stepfather? Or just another unidentified orbiting body? That group included various behind-the-scenes friends and family, like the man who'd been Andy's first long-term boyfriend and whom I'd soon christen Chief Wife Number One. Not to mention the clan of Haitian women who had taken turns helping Janet through her last years and were now helping Erez through his first. Did they not love and yet have no claim on the child?

Ah, the child: See what he'd done? Drawn all these people into his orbit? If he was exceptionally loved, it was not just because he was himself exceptional; every baby is exceptional by virtue of being a new human life. But not every baby lands, as Erez did, among people so eagerly looking for something beautiful and healthy and worthwhile to focus their love upon. It may take a village to raise a child, but there are few villages left for children to be raised by—not those kinds of villages we remember, or imagine, with extended multigenerational families, with nosy but dependable neighbors, with teachers and storekeepers and Good Humor men who know where each child belongs. Erez had an affectional village that may have seemed chaotic from the outside but was a blessing from within. You had only to take one look at him to know that, whatever confusion went on around him, he felt secure at its center with his one true father. He held on to Andy as if they were figures at the stationary middle of a merry-go-round: Look at all the amusing people on their painted mounts, revolving, rising, falling, spinning—all of them lovely, all a blur! On Elliot! Wayne! Eliane! Jesse! Betsy! Chauncey! Uncle Frank! Strike up the calliope! And here we two will remain safe together, whoever may dance about.

EIGHT

Andy wisely hired a baby-sitter, a teenaged girl from across the street, the next time we went out. I don't know how we ended up in a downtown gallery, watching a modern-dress Mozart pastiche, but I remember thinking that the farcical doings (trysts and betrayals and a search for something valuable) seemed apt enough. It was called *The Small Jewel Box*.

When all was resolved, in the opera at least, we headed into the foggy night, walking east and then south toward the Brooklyn Bridge. As we passed the Criminal Courts Building, we saw a crew filming what was evidently a commercial for the latest *Batman* movie; a caped figure stood atop each of two bleak obelisks in the mist, while crowds milled about, awestruck, below. We felt, in that way common to all new lovers, removed from the ordinary wonders of the world: Everything was interesting and none of it mattered. We dared, periodically, to hold hands as we walked, but undid them turning each new corner. We forgave ourselves for doing so.

As we approached the bridge, Andy recounted its history: the obsessed engineer, the granite from Maine, the workers who had died of the bends while excavating the footings. He pointed toward the tops of the towers, shrouded in the freak summer mist. It was so thick I could not see where the roadbed landed even as we neared its middle, but I could make out the water below, glinting like knives. I thought of Mark for a moment as we climbed; would he have believed what I was now doing? Crossing through fog into the unknown—or at least into Brooklyn? For it was at the height of the bridge, where Andy and I stopped to kiss, that a compact between us seemed to be ratified. I did not know what its terms were, exactly; I was still too far on the blurry periphery to see where I was headed.

But at least I was partly visible—something that couldn't be said for everyone in the story. As we descended into Brooklyn, Andy told me that Erez's birth mother, the woman he called Concepción, had recently delivered another child. I shivered, as if a ghost had spoken, but she wasn't a ghost, at least not to Andy. Concepción existed in some state that was not quite whole and yet not quite dispersed; she was behind yet not part of the enterprise, everywhere yet nowhere at all. Even so, Andy knew her face from the snapshots she'd had the adoption agency forward. He didn't need to look at them to remember every detail—quite the contrary; they were locked in his safe-deposit box as if they were legal, or illegal, documents. They seemed somehow radioactive, both glow and danger: the proof and the epitaph of her place in the proceedings.

Now she had claimed a place once again, or at any rate tried. "Baby boy, same birth parents, quite premature" was the message the agency tried to leave Andy, for he had indicated (back when Erez was born) that he might want to adopt a sibling if one came along. Unfortunately, the handwritten message was dismembered or misplaced; had Chauncey chewed it? Had Erez himself? In any case, by the time Andy found it and returned the call, the baby had been situated with another family. He may have prospered or may have died; we don't know, and probably never will.

We entered Andy's house in silence. With so many ghosts and quasi-ghosts milling about, not to mention the living shadows, it seemed a crowded place these days. Would there ever be room enough for me? Let's say we did become a couple—I thought about this as Andy paid the baby-sitter and locked the door behind her. Let's even say he wanted me to be some kind of father to his son. Then what? The role had not exactly gone begging: It was occupied by a marquee star, with an eager understudy in the wings. Where would I fit? Would I have any rights? And what obligations?—for I saw my small savings being sucked up by Baby Gap. Would Erez love me? If so, what would happen if Andy someday did not? Would I become another orbiting ex? I did not want to do anything that might end up hurting the baby, but without taking some risks it was impossible to proceed with the father. This made for a difficult courtship.

It wasn't Andy putting up roadblocks. When, a few days later, he invited me to drop by as he packed his mother's apartment— her annotated dictionaries and years of balanced checkbooks— he was all but explicitly inviting me into his life. Nor was it Erez keeping a distance; he turned like a sunflower when I shone upon him, or was it the other way around? Naturally he lunged for his daddy the moment anything went wrong, but as I continued to recuse myself from bathtime and bedtime, I saw that I was the one keeping a distance. Perhaps it was understandable, perhaps it was even smart, but if I wasn't careful I would soon be just another Concepción: there but not there. What went on behind those doors, anyway, with the tears and laughter and coos of contentment? I had to be in the room to find out.

NINE

Back in college, I tortured one of my best friends by describing what he would be like at forty; the idea of being forty was torture enough, but I cruelly embellished the portrait with Suburban

Gothic details. He would have, I told him, a schoolteacher spouse, an adorable child, a receding hairline, and a wood-paneled Estate Wagon. To a twenty-year-old rebel with esthetic aspirations, this was tantamount to saying he would die in a hole with his Shriner's cap on. Not to worry for Michael, though: As it turned out, I was precise but not accurate. At thirty-seven, it looked as if I was the one who'd be ending up with the school-teacher spouse (well, a guidance counselor), the receding hair-line, and (in a way) the adorable child. Whereas Michael, though at least he was almost totally bald, was appearing off-Broadway as an East German transsexual rock diva while moonlighting on guitar with a post-punk band and serially dating leggy blondes.

At least I didn't have the Estate Wagon. I had never owned an automobile, and doubted I ever would. For the price of garaging in New York City, you could buy an extra set of internal organs. If you didn't garage, you were courting theft, not to mention sub-jecting yourself to the insane calculus of New York's parking reg-ulations. Best to rent when you needed a ride: Was that not my grand philosophy? But then, in the week after his mother died, Andy finally traded in what was left of his Lancer and, hocking part of his Board of Education pension, bought a new car. Or *was* it a car? It was a huge gleaming thing, a silver bullet, aerodynamic and all kitted out with velour and cupholders and integrated child seats. Two integrated child seats.

We called the van the Space Station Mir and wondered how it would ever get filled. Andy imagined Boy Scout troops and He-brew school car pools and platters of cupcakes for PTA bake sales. I imagined it just as it was the first time I saw it: clean and empty. God knows, the rest of my life with Andy looked as if it would be messy and full; here was something new, with no history, no mark of other lives upon it. And look: There was even a place to store coins! For all my antisuburban rhetoric I was bourgeois enough to love its luxurious thingness: the way it perfectly accomplished what it was supposed to be. The day Andy brought it home, we just sat in it for a few minutes and sniffed. It would not have that nice, new smell for long.

We'd had six dates in one month by then (if you include packing up Janet's apartment as a date) and had decided to spend our first weekend together at Andy's little house on Long Island. At noon on a Friday in early July, we therefore loaded our luggage into the maw of the space station and set out on our maiden voyage. Erez, strapped into one of the fold-out child seats, sucked on a bottle and looked happily around. Chauncey the dog lay on the floor beside him. As we merged onto the Long Island Expressway, the car's digital compass correctly told us we were heading east: We all but applauded.

I did not take it as an ill omen when Chauncey tried to snatch my biscotti. I already knew that Andy's theory of dog-rearing (if not child-rearing) involved plenty of love and very little food. He seemed to think there was a fixed sum of kibble in a dog's lifetime; feed him less and he would live longer. It is true that Chauncey never got fat and was hale and athletic at nearly fourteen. But it is also true that he was constantly ravenous. His bowl, when put before him, was empty in seconds. The rest of the time he nudged around and begged under the table and sucked up every fallen scrap of Erez's meals like a vacuum cleaner. Andy liked that.

We drove along happily for the first half-hour. Then Erez started to make funny noises. I had heard the term "projectile vomit" before but never witnessed it. I'm sure you could do intricate calculations involving the speed of the car and the force of the retch to determine the maximum curdal displacement. What I can tell you is that pretty much the entire right side of the cabin was covered. And then, hungry Chauncey began to chow down. Erez giggled.

I was stunned but stalwart. After stopping at a roadside market to buy paper towels and Evian (they would not give us anything to clean up with), we wiped down Erez and what we could of the car and set off again with all the windows and the sun roof open. Soon Erez started making odd noises again—this time from the left child seat, the right one having become so encrusted with vomit it would not lock properly. "Oh no!" I shouted, and covered my face. But he did not vomit. How can I describe what happened now? Perhaps all the previous excitement had dislodged

Erez's diaper—or perhaps the devil had possessed his bowels. In any case I looked over my shoulder in horror as a steady stream of brown sludge extruded itself from Erez's shorts. It did not stop. It never stopped. Erez giggled as hungry Chauncey began to chow down.

"I guess the car is christened," said Andy, patting my dead cold hand.

TEN

I guess I was, too. But even if I didn't yet have a sense of what was in store for me, I would very soon, for the morning after our arrival at Andy's house Erez promptly began to teethe. The beautiful child was hot with pain, whimpering and then screaming like a bright red kettle; nothing would soothe him except Andy's shoulder. But what would soothe me? It wasn't just the noise, though that was terrible; it was not knowing—not ever being able to know—what the crying wanted. I stood before the tortured baby, helpless as when a tourist asks directions in an impenetrably foreign language.

A child's miseries, like his colds (as I'd soon learn), are highly contagious, and I proved susceptible. Andy, on the other hand, seemed to be buoyed by Erez's wretchedness, or at least not sunk by it; it gave him a clarity of purpose that was otherwise elusive. His entire life's work in that moment was solely to be a comfort to his son, and there was no one on earth who could do the job better. It wasn't that he knew any magic words to chant; he didn't say much at all, out loud. It's that he remained cheerful and calm, unfazed by the assault of such huge unhappiness. This was part of his imperfectionism: He could tolerate and even thrive on disruption and disarray. Was there a more useful quality for a father to have in moments like this? Whereas I was a zombie, suffering from some sort of empathy disorder: My teeth started hurting. I thought I might cry.

"Don't torture yourself," said Andy. "Why don't you rest? Or look around?"

Rest? There weren't enough earplugs in the world. Somewhat guiltily, I chose option two.

The house was an unpretentious clapboard bungalow on almost an acre of cleared pine woods. You could tell from the sky that water was near, you could hear its faint sipping noises, but you couldn't actually see it for the other houses and trees. Fringing the exterior walls with color were various blowsy, exuberant plantings: hollyhocks, purple iris, Montauk daisy, butterfly bush. Inside, the decor was just as eclectic. Andy had furnished the four main rooms with flea market finds and what I called auntiques— items remaindered from his old-lady friends' attics: an absurd wing chair with a bald-eagle pattern, a chipped enamel breakfast table straight out of Betty Crocker. There was nothing remotely new in the house, including the dishes and flatware and art. On the walls he'd hung many pleasant, bad paintings by a distant relative named Zusse.

I found it sweet and a bit overwhelming. Had I been an ordinary guest I would have looked upon each odd knickknack as an indication of Andy's taste, and thus as a delight. But I was something more than a guest, if something less than a host. There was no way around it: I was auditioning us for a life together. This house (or what it stood for) would be one of the settings of the drama, so I was looking for cues to the dimensions of my possible role. Would the profusion of Andy's many tastes ever leave room enough for mine? Would my precision admit his profusion? This was more than a matter of area rugs. People's habitats, no less than their habits, are central to who they are; marriage, however you choose to decorate it, must be a coherent shelter.

As a single man, I had built a shelter for myself that was quiet enough for me to think in, yet vivid enough to give me thoughts. The motto carved above its door was from Baudelaire: *Luxe, calme et volupté*. It had taken me years to achieve this improbable melding of order and indulgence; all of my life so far, in fact. Was that too long to have spent ridding myself (to the extent I had) of bad faith, bad dogma, and all the received obligations that were doubly intolerable for being received and for being obligations? It is never too long to spend, to feel free. To take one's friends as

they are, or leave them be; to write what one pleases and suffer
the consequences; to be foolish with self-knowledge and brilliant
with self-doubt: to be rampantly and rigorously and exclusively
oneself. In short I had perfected everything possible in my world
except me—but that was all right, because the sturdy house I'd
built was only big enough for one. It would take more than a wolf
to blow it down.

But I'd let the wolf in, and what now?

Don't live alone too long, went the saying. *You might get used to
it.* We were neither of us young. We had spent many years refin-
ing our separate tastes and peccadilloes into separate certainties
and cranks. My certainty was my rootedness, my faith in moral
logic. Andy's certainty was his son, the opposite of logic. I had not
known when we first met that our essential styles would prove so
different; I had seen us both as ironic atheists with broad melancholy streaks. A match made in heaven (if only there were one)—
but perhaps that was just our testosterone talking. In fact, we were
only as similar as any two works in the same language; was that
not partly the source of our attraction? I had never been romanti-
cally interested in men much like myself. What was the point?
You would look through each other at once and come out the
other side. Instead, I'd been drawn to people who knew something different from me; often, it turned out to be too different.
Perhaps Andy and I would strike the right balance: different
enough to keep things sexy, but similar enough to keep the peace.
Luxe, calme et volupté. Certainly our hands believed it, whenever
they interlocked.

ELEVEN

The teething passed quickly, though not before a neighbor,
alarmed by the screaming, dropped by to see what the cause of it
was. I instinctively attempted to recede as I saw her approaching,
but Andy made introductions—in the course of which I found I
had officially been promoted to the position of boyfriend. Did
Meghan lift an eyebrow? She lived across the street and had

known Andy since he bought the house; she therefore presumably knew Elliot, too. In any case she was perfectly warm, and offered, since she was going to town, to pick up a teething ring at the five-and-dime.

When she left, I asked Andy how he thought it went.

"How what went?" he said.

"Well, I mean, do you suppose she's *okay* with me?"

"She's an artist. She was friends with the guys I bought this house from. She volunteers for local AIDS organizations. Of course she's okay."

But that wasn't what I meant.

I had not before met even one of Andy's friends—strange in a relationship quickly speeding past flowers and into Father's Day cards. In part, I dreaded doing so: Friends were the people who did not want you to change. I knew that each of them would be evaluating me—as I would them, but for different reasons. The usual "Is he good enough for our Andy?" would be intensified with "Is he good enough for our Erez?" And on that score I quailed. The certainties of unclehood were useless to me here; invisibility was no longer an asset. Of course I knew how to hold the boy and entertain him with faces and songs and distract him from his unknowable misery, if only briefly, but these were things any smart baby-sitter could do. More would be expected of me if I was to become some kind of parent; if I wasn't to become some kind of parent, what was I doing here?

As long as I was trapped in that paradox I would remain a lame duck, or really its opposite: a pro tem appointee, a man without a mandate. It was not a position that suited me well. I was used to making unilateral decisions and, since I was the only one they applied to, having them carried out. And yet I could not reasonably present myself as anything but a father-in-waiting until—what? Until the law said so? The law was not a generous conversationalist when it came to gay men: It was mostly sullen and unforthcoming.

No, I could not present myself as a father until I was reasonably sure I would stick with Andy, and thus not leave Erez, for all of our sakes. I had seen the results of Elliot's assumption—his sadness, Erez's confusion—and did not wish to make the same mistake. In so doing I ran the risk of making the *opposite* mistake: of not being ready to assume the mantle even when the mantle fit. Would I always insist on being called Erez's father's partner—how ungainly! And yet complicated truths must evolve complicated language if they're to have any language at all.

Most gay parents I had met were known to their children by matched sets of endearments: Mommy and Mama; Papa and Dad. Others took an egalitarian approach: Mama Susan and Mama Jane. Still others chose not to distinguish themselves at all; either (or both) might answer when the child cried out for Poppy. These all seemed like good solutions for couples who were clearly co-parents. But when Andy and I discussed that summer what Erez should call me, we agreed that none of these possibilities made sense, at least not yet. On the other hand, I had always felt that kids who used their parents' first names were overly adultified—or rather, that their parents were insufficiently so. I once knew a ten-year-old boy, I told Andy, who was apt to say to his mother things like "Can we stay up late tonight, Linda?" Linda had seemed to find this intimate and sophisticated, whereas I found it creepy.

"Well, we won't let Erez call you Linda then," said Andy.

In the end, I tried to teach him to call me by my first name, but he couldn't say it: The "J" was too hard. I did, however, insist that we wean him off "Abba" for Elliot. If I was unready to share the word "father" with Andy, I would not have him share it, even in Hebrew, with anyone else.

TWELVE

Was it arrogant of me to establish such boundaries? If so, I didn't see how else to stake my claim. I felt as if I had been given one of those logic puzzles in which you are asked to connect several figures using only a few lines; you despair that there aren't enough lines to do it, until you realize you can draw beyond the box. Success is satisfying but disorienting: The box, once broken, is never whole again.

I was hardly the first to experience this. My mother, over the years, had developed a specialty in working with so-called blended families; television was overrun with them. Many of the ones on television were transracial, adoptive, blended families, just like Andy's, except of course that no one was gay. In any case, "blended" was a term more hopeful than descriptive, suggesting a simple mechanical task and the smoothness of pancake batter. In fact, the process that produced such families resembled more closely some of the other settings on a kitchen appliance: "chop," "whip," "froth," "knead," "fold," "incorporate," "pulverize." Nevertheless, as in ordinary families, the result was always lumpy.

Another word used, especially by gay parents, to describe newfangled households is "alternative"—as if there were an option not to be. It describes my experience even less well than "blended." Choice is the main thing a parent gives up in embracing a child: One big door is opened, but thousands of others are shut. The only alternative I had, and briefly, was not to love Andy, which didn't seem possible; beyond that, my map was reduced to a few obscure roads. I had never liked the concept of alternativity anyway, at least insofar as it suggested second-tier status, or status defined only in relation to supposed normalcy. Alternative lifestyles were faintly malodorous. Alternative realities were delusions. Of course, the word as applied to families was not intended to bear so much meaning; it was just a euphemism for "different." But why not say "different"? Every family is different (even happy ones, despite Tolstoy); saying so levels the playing field.

Not that I was in any position to be doctrinaire. I had always been able to count on the privilege of living my life, however gay, in the main stream of the mainstream. This was a matter of temperament, yes, but also of class and race and cash. Alternativity was distasteful to me in part because I didn't need it; for others less fortunate, it was often a major step up. In New York City, for instance, the Board of Education had created an Alternative High Schools superintendency to serve new immigrants, the chronically ill, juvenile prisoners, kids with no homes—and (as I had written about often) youths so abused for being gay they could not survive anywhere else. Despite periodic objections from civil libertarians (who pointed out that separate is not equal) the alternative system took root. Even so, I understood the pathos of the gay boy who attended the Harvey Milk high school and told me: "This school should not have to be."

I was therefore all the more determined not to be seen by the world as some sort of alternative parent; I worried that I would be alternative enough within my family. This worry was exacerbated by a friend of mine who, in one joyous, tumultuous year, had gone from single career gal grabbing sushi for dinner to burger-broiling soccer mom. Stepmom, that is: Her new husband had joint custody of his two grade-school girls. She told me how things moved horribly fast and yet not fast enough; all her gauges were thrown out of whack. She felt pressure to be fully a wife to her husband but only partly a parent to his children, whom she loved but had not *grown* to love and thus was awkward with. When she miscalculated, she was as likely to be upbraided for presumption ("You're not my mother!") as for deference ("You don't work hard enough to earn their respect"); her double bind was implicit in the name of the job—"step" somehow suggesting both insertion and abstraction. You step into the role but are always a step removed.

Beyond that, every daughter whose father remarries thinks she is Cinderella. In fairy tales especially, stepmothers are vilified; they are seen as rapacious, sexually and otherwise, and tend to get their eyes pecked out. The law is hardly more helpful, as any tabloid trial will demonstrate. But if courts do not automatically recognize a formal relationship between a woman and her husband's children, at least society does. Not so for me. Since I could not marry Andy I could not be Erez's stepfather, by law or custom, even if the term weren't so invidious. The best I could do, some years and much money down the road, would be to apply for a so-called second-parent adoption—recently legalized for gay men in New York State—which would bind me to Erez if not to Andy. The law did not offer enough lines to connect all the figures in the puzzle, but at least (for now) it offered some. In the meantime I would remain a shadowy figure, powerful perhaps but illegitimate: an *éminence mauve*, whispering my thoughts in the cardinal's ear and backing away from the light.

THIRTEEN

Since the cardinal was as liberal with Erez as he was with himself, my whisperings were frequently about setting limits and creating patterns. As I discovered that first night in the country, Erez rarely went to bed without a struggle. He had once been successfully trained, Andy told me, according to the precepts of sleep guru Richard Ferber, whose immensely popular book on the subject was both adored and reviled—often by the same people. Adored, because the method it outlined usually worked: Babies who had been Ferberized "went down" without much fuss and stayed asleep, or at least stayed calm, throughout the night. Reviled, because the conditioning process was sheer torture for the days or weeks it took to imprint, during which time parents were instructed to resist, for longer and longer increments, the child's pathetic cries. Erez's conditioning had been allowed to lapse, so that he once again was going to bed whenever and wherever his eyes happened to shut, and waking up several times each night in need of laborious (if delicious) comforting.

Over the course of the summer, we Ferberized him again— which is to say, we Ferberized ourselves. We set a bedtime, developed a calm, enjoyable ritual of bath and books leading up to it, closed the door, and held our breath. We learned, as did he, to tolerate the separation; in so doing we seemed to give him a way of predicting (and thus feeling secure in) his world. On those occasions when he did howl in protest, I felt like an evil stepmother. But what was the alternative? Opponents of Ferberization suggested that the baby should sleep in the parents' bed; that way, when he woke up in the night, he could nurse on demand. Even if Erez had still been an infant, my breasts weren't up to it. Besides, he was now seventeen months old. I knew couples who slept with their children well into toddlerhood—what were humans but upright cave bears, chromosomally primed to sleep in piles? More power to them. I, on the other hand, a newcomer to the cave, wanted a corner of adult privacy. As it was, with the crib in Andy's room, he and I had to make love elsewhere: potentially fun in summer or when feeling athletic, less so when cold and bone-weary.

Most couples get at least nine months, if not a few years, to explore one another in peace. A spouse who's attentive can quickly learn the ins and outs of his partner's body and all the likeliest buttons to press. By the time the baby comes along (if it does) the parents are expert enough to size their needs to the brief time left them between feedings and cleanings and cartings and jags; if the needs are too great, they forgive themselves the overage. But for us, there was a child in the picture before we ever took off our clothes. I had only thirty seconds, when I first spotted Andy getting out of his car, to see him as a man before I saw him as a father. Thank God for the thirty seconds! Ever since then, even when we hired a baby-sitter so that we could go to a movie, Erez has been with us one way or another. The pager might peep at any moment; our guilt might peep for leaving him home. When we actually found time to make love, he hovered around us like an aura as we stripped: Out of our pockets rained undersized Legos, contraband candies, glintings of foil and bottle liners. Our shirts as they fell were blotched with burp stains; the smell of diaper rash ointment stuck to our busy fingers.

As far as lovemaking went, we could manage awhile without a room of our own. The same could not be said for sleep, which I needed at least as often. Already Andy's snoring and his demoralizing ability to drop off in five seconds made it hard for me to relax. With Erez in the room I never would. *Is he breathing? Is he, God forbid, waking?* I combed the silence all through the night for clues to our safety and happiness.

Making the best of a bed situation, we moved ourselves into the guest room. Mornings we lifted Erez from his crib and brought him in to romp and snuggle. Sometimes he fell asleep again, flattened between us, just as the cave bear advocates desired; it *was* awfully nice, for ten minutes or so. If we were Jesse Helms's worst nightmare, so be it. At least we were not mine.

FOURTEEN

Once upon a time there was a much-loved king whose land was so small and castle so large there was nothing to rule except his household. That was enough, though—almost too much—for there were vassals and ministers and gentlemen of the garter and women whose function remained obscure but seemed to involve hot kettles and quilts. Beyond these hirelings and functionaries the king had only one true subject: one person, that is, who was not on the payroll. And he was the heir to the throne.

One day an outsider appeared at the moat and, finding the guard station completely unmanned, walked directly over the drawbridge. "Your front door's open," he told the king, who saw him at once.

"So that's why all these people are here!" said the king. "They come and go so frequently I can hardly count them. What do you think we should do about it?"

"For a start, close the drawbridge," said the outsider.

The cables were old and swollen; once the bridge was finally lifted, it stuck in place and no one could budge it. Not that many were left to try: The operation had been performed on Saturday night, when only a few of the most essential people were home at the castle. The rest were locked out; come Monday morning, they started looking for work in another kingdom.

Though the castle staff was thus depleted, things inside strangely improved. It gradually became clearer who was who among the few that remained, and what their jobs were. The king saw that the outsider might be helpful in other ways and so asked him to stay. "What inducements might persuade you?" he asked.

"Other than the fact that the drawbridge is broken?"

"Other than that."

"None," said the outsider. "I will stay because I want to."

"You like it here."

"But I wouldn't quarrel with nicer towels."

"Done," said the king, except there was no one to do it—the seamstress being one of those who had disappeared across the moat.

"And one more thing. I'd like a name."

"What, have you none?"

"I had a name on the other side, but I've forgotten what it was."

"I'll think on the matter."

"And what will you call me until you've thought?"

"It won't be necessary to call you anything. I shan't leave your side."

And so the outsider came to live at the king's right hand, advising him on matters both foreign and domestic. On the foreign front he remained discreet; he read dispatches but did not sign them. Hoping to speak without being overheard, he brought his mouth as close as he could to the king's kind face. On the domestic front, he was more forthcoming. "Let us undertake an inspection of the castle," he said one day, and so he and the king lurched down dark halls and up cryptic stairways, bearing an old ring of keys so vast it had to be worn around both their waists. After much trial and error they managed to open each of the hundreds of doors they found; some of the rooms were empty, some full to overflowing, some with bad smells and some beautifully furnished beneath dust covers. If it was too much to absorb on a first inspection, at least all the keys got labeled.

But something did not add up properly: There was one more door than there were keys. Amazingly, it was a door the outsider had seen quite often, situated at the back of the king's bedchamber.

"What is in there?" he asked.

"My son," said the king.

"And where is the key? It isn't noted on my chart."

"I do not wish to say just yet; you understand my caution. Let us play with him out here and in time you'll know the answer, or not."

"Is this a riddle? I'm good at riddles."

"No," said the king. *"It's more like a test."*

"Well, then, here's a riddle for you instead. What has three legs in the morning, three legs at midday, and three legs in the evening?"

The king smiled. *"I know that one."*

FIFTEEN

I quickly took my first baby steps. I told Andy I would like to give Erez his bath some evenings. On those occasions, I might choose his pajamas; some mornings, I picked out his day clothes as well. It soon became an unremarked event if I prepared the bottles or answered a cry; even at night, Erez allowed me to comfort him, and I returned the favor. In a way Andy and I had become one organism—if not yet in terms of each other, then at least in terms of Erez. Andy still did the lion's share of the work; this was, after all, his summer vacation, whereas I was constantly scrambling to finish (and all too often scrambling to start) various complicated assignments. It was not just a lack of sleep and an unfamiliar desk that threw me off. It was also the noisy fun going on in the next room. "Close the door if you want," Andy said. But I didn't want to.

I loved the noisy fun, it turned out. I was envious when it went on without me. Nevertheless, I was disappointed to find I could stand it only for very brief stretches. I'd hoped I would turn out to be the kind of parent who let a child's shifting tempos prevail as we slopped all day from one thing to another. But I couldn't do it. I needed more structure, and time to myself. Andy, on the other hand, had developed an almost infinite tolerance for the vagueness of those summer days, filling them like a magician with walks and playgrounds and swims and ice creams and toys and books and Dr. Seuss. I couldn't keep up; I got headaches by three in the afternoon. But even lying down with a washcloth over my face I was beginning to feel a bit like a father, in the house at least.

In public I was still recessive. When we visited friends, Andy usually carried Erez, who was shy at first in such situations; I hovered a step behind. Window shopping, I only pushed the stroller briefly before remanding it to Andy. I was somewhat shy of the neighbors, too; when the older woman whose garden adjoined Andy's chatted with him about privet and beach plums, I waved from the front door but did not come forward. I needn't have been so careful, though: No one cared. Surely the couple whose purebred German short-haired pointer came each day to play with Chauncey—despite Chauncey's unorthodox parentage—would not blink an eye at Erez's. Or only blink once. Even the rabbi who lived next door had nothing but pleasantries for us; he and his wife baby-sat on occasion.

Of course, our acquaintanceship was self-selecting. The kinds of people drawn to the east end of Long Island are generally open-minded. Andy's particular town had the further advantage of being less heartlessly chic than the famous oceanside resorts nearby; I called the place Least Hampton. Some of its residents descended from old New England whalers and were basically libertarian; others were artists and artists manqué who had moved here for the light and lifestyle. The summer people, most from Manhattan, found us boring if they found us at all. We had virtually no way of meeting the sleek young couples and well-groomed gay men who filled the bistros and barreled down side streets in their open-top sport utility vehicles. And what could we do with them anyway—invite them for drinks and bathtime? Sometimes we encountered a clutch of buff bodies at the beach; they took one look at us with our diaper bag, smiled condescendingly, and moved their umbrella.

If this was hostility, it was open and mild. The kinds of meaningful disapproval we faced were always more subtle. Teenaged girls, however pleasant their baby-sitting experience, might suddenly prove "unavailable" (their mothers would tell us) when contacted for a return engagement. Newspaper-reading playground dads might move abruptly to distant benches when our situation became clear to them. Waiting in the checkout line at a toy store one day, I watched another family—a mother and two toddlers—watching us. I could see the mother go through the various calculations as Erez pranced from Andy to me and back again, clearly at home with each of us. Shamefully, I tried to ignore him; what I couldn't ignore was how the mother's eyes hardened even as her children's widened. Did she scowl at me?

Painful as such moments seemed, I'm not even sure they were real; Andy has no recollection of the mother's reaction, nor of most hostilities I think I have witnessed. He tends to see opportunities where I see danger: Perhaps the mother *learned* something in noting how happy Erez was with us. And the truth is, even in my paranoid worldview, hostility is far less common than curiosity and even fascination. I began to realize that some people seemed to enjoy using us as a way of surprising themselves with their openness. The gruff contractor who often did work at Andy's house brought his little twin daughters for a visit one day; when one of them asked who Erez was, he explained that the boy was "Andy and Jesse's son"—a phrase that took him aback as he uttered it. Then he smiled and decided not to correct himself. Was he pleased with himself? In any case, I would see it over and over that summer: As hearts trump clubs, fatherhood trumps gayness.

SIXTEEN

Every parent of an even halfway pretty child is familiar with the freely offered smiles, the googly faces, the random compliments that the child and thus his family receive wherever he goes. But what most parents may never know is how unusual, even unheard of, this kindly attention is for gay men. In public situations that might have been uncomfortable for Andy and me if we'd been merely lovers, Erez's presence seems to alter the equation radically. Even in the heart of Greenwich Village, it can feel dangerous for us to hold hands; we and our friends have been scowled at, spat at, screamed at, hit. But if our hands are connected only indirectly, through Erez's, we might as well be royalty. We are no longer homosexuals but parents, leaving people who might otherwise be inclined toward disapproval in a state of confusion over their warm feelings—and leaving us with the uncomfortable sensation that bright little Erez has become our shield, protecting us as much as we protect him.

An uncomfortable sensation, yes, but thrilling. To be so welcomed! To be so admired! When on occasion I took Erez out by myself, it was as if a secret, parallel world of heterosexual privilege and bonhomie was suddenly opened to me. Men who ordinarily would keep their distance suddenly winked at me as a comrade. "Giving mom the morning off?" a chummy father said to me at the playground. The moms themselves watched wistfully as I dizzied myself at the merry-go-round: a perfect father. "Your wife is lucky," one said to me as I mopped my brow. "Is she Asian?" She was reading, I suppose, into Erez's eyes.

"No, Hispanic," I stuttered. "I mean—oh, it's a long story."

When Andy and I were together with Erez, it was more difficult for people to preserve a presumption of our heterosexuality. They tried, though; you could almost hear their mental gears clicking. Typically, they concluded that Andy and I were divorcé pals or that we were brothers (though we look nothing alike) or even, amazingly, that *Erez* and I were brothers through some cutting-edge process of remarriage and cryogenics. When our homosexuality was a stated, unavoidable fact, some people still went to comical (if unconscious) lengths to finesse it. "Who does he look like more?" a new acquaintance wondered aloud, studying us quite seriously. "I think he looks like both of you!"

Apparently, a child could wipe away not only sexual preference but the very laws of biology. I was familiar with this phenomenon in the straight world; once a couple had a baby they were pardoned the indelicacy of having had sex in the first place. But for a gay couple to be similarly pardoned was a much more exotic and piquant sensation. At least at first. Later, it began to seem costly and dangerous, like the Japanese fish that, despite being poisonous, was just then all the rage in Manhattan. For Andy and me, the forgiveness was ultimately as indigestible as the fish. Not only because each of us, having spent decades adapting ourselves to the stress of being openly gay, had come to enjoy the adaptation, but because it seemed unfair to Erez. I had always held (some would say I pontificated) that children should not be props or dodges for their parents. I understood that we are all to some extent our parents' best means of expressing themselves, of squeezing themselves into the future. We represent (literally) their aspirations and ideals—even, somehow, when we reject them. They are proud of us if we do good things, especially if we do the same good things they did or wanted to do: If we have chil-

dren. If we go into the family business. If we dress nicely according to their lights.

But there is also a less legitimate kind of parental influence: a
Diane Arbus world of children pressed into service as mouth-
pieces for specific, often political, agendas. I'm not sure which I
find more disturbing: those tiny T-shirts that say I'M A PRO-CHOICE
BABY or the ones that say THANK GOD MY MOMMY'S PRO-LIFE.
Along the parade route of a gay rights march in Washington one
year I saw a man holding up a boy who in turn was holding up a
sign that read GOD HATES FAGS. I was only slightly more comfortable with the toddlers I saw bearing homemade sandwich
boards—homemade, yes, but not by the toddlers—that said
I LOVE MY LESBIAN MOMS in a faux-naïf hand. This sort of thing,
however good the cause, had always seemed to me to be too blatant a usurpation of a child's discrete selfhood. The teenaged
mothers Andy counsels at school are no less misguided when they
offer this implacable defense of their parenting: "I wanted something of my own to love."

A child is not something of one's own; in different ways, Andy
and I both knew that from our families. You don't have to be a
perpetual pageant runner-up or a frustrated former high school
jock to misshape your child toward your own interrupted fate.
Every parent in some way hands down his lovingly maintained
grindstone, but a child should be free to choose his own axes. It
would not be fair to Erez to turn him into a placard that said, in
effect, MY DADDIES ARE GAY—let alone into a placard that said
they aren't. Nor, however fascinating, was it fair to ourselves. Had
we dismantled one closet just to build another?

SEVENTEEN

My brand-new seersucker suit seemed the very thing for a late-
afternoon cocktail party at a gallery in Most Hampton. The party,
a benefit for the local gay organization, was the first and only
dressy event Andy and I would be attending all summer, and certainly the first time we'd be venturing out as a family in a crowd

of homosexuals. After months of nothing but shorts and T-shirts, all helplessly plastered with baby emissions, I suddenly found myself deeply committed to the idea of wearing something clean. Perhaps I should have known better; Andy had wisely chosen a pale green linen blazer not in its first youth.

We looked awfully good, I thought: decent enough specimens (if you didn't peek beneath the clothing) of *Homo americanus* circa 1995. We did get lots of those sidelong glances I had always been told were common at gay gatherings. It soon became apparent, however, that the glances were not directed at our natty outfits and were not entirely appreciative. Oh, the lesbians liked us: They came rushing forward, volunteering to baby-sit while virtually opening their blouses. Erez smiled at them flirtatiously and took turns in their arms, while they detailed their own experiences of adoption or insemination or fierce, unfulfilled longing.

While Andy proselytized them obliviously, I saw how Erez's appearance had sent shock waves pulsing from canapé to cocktail. Among the younger men, it seemed that the presence of a giggling baby jangled the erotic energy they were attempting to cultivate. Some turned their backs to block out the interference; others looked over with sour expressions that suggested we were about as welcome as a chaperone at a prom. When we laid Erez down on the grass to change him, one gleaming gym-bunny actually squinched up his nose. Older men, on the other hand, looked balefully at the boy as he held our hands, perhaps envious of an opportunity that had largely been denied them. One sixtyish gent, fussily patting Erez's head for a moment, laughed off his embarrassment by saying, "In my day we could have been arrested!" I was not sure whether he thought it was such a good idea for gay men to be around children even now.

I had always dismissed the pedophilia canard by asserting flatly that gay men have no physical interest in children. But now that I was spending so much time with Erez, I knew that there is, in fact, a physical relationship of incredible intensity between a child and the adults who care for him. In its least problematic form, this can be as simple as the sensation of warmth that wafts from a sleeping baby toward its parent. Rather more often than was called for, I would stand over Erez's crib to watch him sleep, curled and solid in his footed one-piece pajamas, his tummy stretching and contracting. At such moments it was almost more than I could do to restrain myself from waking him, just so I could bring him closer, feel his touch again, let his hot cheek seek its natural place in the pocket of my neck.

But children are not merely physical, they are sensual, and blissfully immodest. Erez is never so happy as after his bath, when he is permitted to run through the house stark naked. I am, unfortunately, less immodest, and have sometimes heard in my head the resentful voice of prudery instructing me to cover the boy up and teach him to be afraid of his body, as I am afraid of mine. As a result, I must steel myself against imagined criticism merely to perform the ordinary—and yet extraordinarily intimate—parental duties of diaper and lotion, soap and sponge. There are things I do routinely to Erez that, if done to Andy, would constitute foreplay: massaging him with skin cream, making raspberry kisses on his belly until he convulses with laughter. And he demands these attentions with all the ardor of a lover accustomed to getting his way.

I will not even speak of suppositories.

What now seemed perverse to me was that gay men would *not* have a healthy physical interest in children. It seemed a form of self-denial, or vengeance: *Childhood was not kind to me, so now that I am an adult I will not look upon it.* Or maybe it was a sad piece of wisdom: *I cannot make you happier than I managed to make myself.*

It was not that I wanted these handsome young men to have children; I think the world would be better served if homosexuals and especially heterosexuals became parents only when they felt they must. But (for my own sake as well as theirs) I did not want gay men to feel that having a child was a violation of the hallowed principles of liberation. Sadly, what I began to learn at that cocktail party was that fatherhood trumped gayness for everyone: If we were no longer gay to straight people, we were no longer gay to most gay people, either. I suddenly felt like the South American Indian in full jungle regalia who once sat near me at a Waldorf-

Astoria rain forest benefit. He and his tribe were the beneficiaries of the good works financed by the other guests, but no one could speak to him, or even face him directly. He was too much an emblem of how far the world had come, and of how much it had lost in the process.

EIGHTEEN

The other thing I learned at the Most Hampton party was not to wear a brand-new suit when the baby you're holding likes to eat strawberries. A baby's handprints are all but indelible. Though Andy and the dry cleaner insist that the jacket is now as good as new, I still see the little red amoebiform blobs, faintly pulsing, behind the blue-and-white stripes on the shoulder and yoke. Ah well, let it be *my* tattoo.

One way or another, a child marks you forever. I had always thought it a bit sentimental when new parents described the arrival of their firstborn as the most moving event in their lives. Now I was beginning to understand what they meant. I was not around for Erez's birth, but he was around for my birth as a father—and what a difficult labor it was! In any case our first months together showed me that the use of the word "moving" was not sentimental but brutally concrete. Having a child alters every relationship, shifts every certainty, *moves* every last thing in your life—the more so when your life has been shaped around the likelihood of being childless. That I no longer recognized my clothing was the least of it. I no longer recognized myself.

There was more of me not to recognize. With so much of the day spent getting food into, off, or out of Erez, I found myself grazing continuously; sometimes I ate some scrap or noodle right off his high chair, or his face—no better than Chauncey. And Andy liked to cook. Not neat little book-learned meals like the kind I deployed, but big gutsy improvisations with whole fishes and chocolate sauces and dozens of pots piling up in the sink. My breakfast for years had been half a bagel and a glass of orange juice; Andy was in heaven serving pancakes and cocoa and homemade biscuits. Slowly but inexorably my waistline expanded: my pregnancy pounds at last. Having been overweight as an adolescent (my bar mitzvah outfit came from the euphemistic Husky department), I had as an adult kept myself to a trio of nice round—no, flat—numbers: six feet, one hundred fifty pounds, thirty inches. Well, I'm still six feet.

My vocabulary began expanding, too. Words I had rarely heard before June I now spoke regularly, if not unself-consciously: "onesie," "croupy," "amoxicillin." Even old, familiar words took on new meanings: "Honey, you melted the nipples again!" In that sense, my vocabulary was not only expanding but contracting; Andy and I might go hours without uttering a thought that was not centered on infant digestion. But perhaps that's not so; my sense of hours (and of days, and of decades) was warping too. When Erez cried, a minute was an eternity. On the other hand, an eternity was a minute. We had been some sort of proto-family for just one hot summer speck of time, but we were already glued, it seemed, for good. One night I sat bolt upright from sleep wondering how old Andy and I would be when Erez graduated from college: sixty-six and fifty-seven.

And who would send him? Janet had mellowed just in time to embrace her new grandson before she died, but not in time to encumber him (as she had encumbered her biological grandchildren) with a college fund. Andy himself was scarily overextended; he would have to dig himself out of debt—the car, the house, the very adoption—before he could consider saving for the future. Let no one fool you: The major change a child causes in your life is financial. If your contract with the world is, like Andy's, to be paid well but spend it all, you have cause to worry upon becoming a parent. No current will support your swift little raft when a child's hefty needs are balanced upon it. You will sink like a rock.

And what of my contract? I was paid less well but, in essence, permitted to do what I liked: a fair enough trade-off. If my modest expenses were met each year with little to spare, at least I met them. I cleared my full credit card balance each month. It had seemed important, in a banking family, to be self-sufficient even as a writer—especially as a writer—and so I was proud not to take money from my parents. But pride falleth before a goal, and if I was someday to be a real father I was going to have to pay for it. Is that not what fathers did? And all they did?

NINETEEN

Back in February, before I met Andy, my parents, as usual, had made a down payment on a large summer rental—this year, deferring to my mother's dread of humidity, in Pennsylvania's Pocono Mountains. The size of the house was something of a gamble, as it was unclear whether my brother would be available: He had virtually no vacation time during the five-week lease, and his kids might well be going to day camp. I, of course, was nothing if not available, or at least so we all thought back in February. Now that I'd met Andy, things had become more complicated. My parents were counting on me to keep them company in that big house; part of the reason they made these summer plans each year was to give me some luxury I could not otherwise afford. On the other hand, I did not want to separate from Andy and Erez now that we were so deep in the process of joining together. Where should I go? Sometimes the decision seemed dreadful: family of origin, family of destination. Other times the choice seemed as unworthy of dread as a choice between chocolates. In the end, sweet-tooth Solomon, I bit both: I decided I would go back and forth. And Andy decided that he and Erez, despite the complexity of the arrangements it would entail, would join me for a few days in the mountains. They had not yet met my parents.

In the weekend before Andy's arrival, while I grew increasingly excited and tense, my mother busied herself with solving what she saw as a problem. The owner of the house had provided all sorts of useless amenities, or useless to us, at least: a party-sized icemaker, an advanced Nintendo system. But he had left only four passes to the nearby swim club. The two adult passes had already been filled out in my parents' names, the two children's passes in the names of my niece and nephew. A teenager at a gate-house had the job of collecting an entrance fee from bathers who lacked the laminated badge, but my parents, who had spent a for-tune on the house without hesitation, could not countenance what they saw as a waste and a rip-off. My mother therefore con-cocted a scheme to defraud the club by having Andy and me present ourselves as Sally and Rodney; Erez could go as my nephew, Max. That Andy might not be very credible as Sally was a complication the real Sally had anticipated; she advised him to say it was short for Salvador—a cousin from Cuba! Perhaps Andy's accent was unconvincing; in any case, we were caught. Mortified, we paid the ten bucks, which my mother immediately refunded.

It was a peculiar but not false introduction to my parents. Look-ing at them (and myself with them) in the light of Andy's expec-tations, I for the first time began to see how odd we were. He had arrived in the woods on a Sunday night imagining a big warm house stuffed with cousins warmed by a roaring fire, with Mo-nopoly games and jigsaw puzzles laid out half-finished, with old songs and hard cider and marshmallows ready for roasting. But we were not that family. What games we played were finished and reboxed. The fireplace was fallow. Our three spare lives glided in parallel, but we had our own agendas. It was easy enough to say we did not indulge in false camaraderie, or in garrulousness for the sake of filling empty air—and this was so. But it was also so (I began to notice) that we were glazed with melancholy. We looked upon the world with disappointed love, but did not let it touch us directly, lest we become infected.

Of course, my parents were perfectly friendly. My father asked Andy how much coffee he liked to drink in the morning; my mother surveyed and accommodated his tastes in food. Together they laughed at what I called Erez's charismantics. But they were not quite the warm, welcoming people I had advertised them to be. Andy saw how their enjoyment of Erez was shallow and per-functory, as if they were watching a rerun of *Seinfeld*. They would barely touch him. And I saw how they kept their distance from Andy, conversing properly but deliberately, as if on stilts. I couldn't understand it. Andy was easygoing, handsome, stable, kind, enthusiastic, smart, funny, well-informed. He was deferential and acerbic. And hadn't I finally brought home a nice Jewish boy?

But not Jewish in any way my parents were used to. After the Salvador fiasco, Andy and I swam at a nearby lake instead of the pool; it was free and quiet and featured a crescent of beach. Erez in his tiny trunks splashed happily and collected pebbles and made friends with other kids. Andy chatted with their families and then napped in the sun while I read, over and over, the same sentence of Henry James. After a while my mother arrived bearing a bag of refreshments she had thoughtfully prepared. She was smiling with her own goodwill as she approached, but then her eyes suddenly swerved and locked on the upper part of Andy's right arm. I had warned her about his tattoo, but still she flinched to see—if not the live baby now standing wet in front of her, the ink baby pricked into Andy's skin.

TWENTY

My mother had never known a person (other than a member of what she called the Auschwitz crowd) who had a tattoo. To her it signified someone low-class, probably uncultured, perhaps a sailor. At any rate, not Jewish. It made her sad, she told me later, that Andy had felt the need to mark himself thus; wasn't the earring enough decoration? She did not even have pierced ears, she pointed out; Judaism respected the body too much to permit its disfigurement. Except of course (I snidely retorted) in the case of cutting off a piece of a newborn boy's penis.

My mother and I had fought off and on since I was fifteen, in the way only people who are very much alike can go at it for hours. Twenty-two years later, this would prove to be our last real fight, not because the matter at hand was clearly resolved but because the beast somehow, finally, swallowed its tail. When I accused her of being cold to Andy, she simply did not disagree. "You have to understand I don't warm up fast," she said. "And I'm not used to this. Him and the baby and the whole idea. It scares me."

"What scares you? That I might be happy?"

Andy was upstairs, napping with Erez. My father was riding his bike in the woods, undoubtedly getting lost. My mother and I sat in the den, she crying submissively, I haughty and hurt.

"I want you to be happy, but I've seen how crushed you can get when people fail you. Two years ago when you broke up with John you were in so much pain I could hardly stand it. To see you like that, it was like I had lost someone in my *own* life. I still can't forgive him, though I know you have."

"And why would you assume Andy would fail me?"

"I don't know; people do. And with a child involved things get locked in very quickly. Who will you be if things don't go well? I sometimes think about Elliot"—I had told my parents the whole history—"and how sad he must feel that he somehow lost that child even if it was never his. And I am very concerned about you having to constantly negotiate decisions from a powerless position. I've seen it over and over in my work: You will have no ground to stand on."

"But Andy won't be that way."

She raised her eyebrows. "I'm sure he's very kind. But I don't know him. He's not like your other friends."

From my parents' perspective, my other friends had exciting vocations, even if they'd utterly failed in pursuing them; they were glib and sparkly and knew famous people, or were famous people themselves. They were fun to talk to at dinners and parties, as they were still busy flapping around in their lives. Andy, on the other hand, had already been an educator for more than twenty-five years. He came with a full set of mismatched accoutrements: a child, a house, a housekeeper, an earring, a mortgage, an ex, an automobile. My friends were mostly quick-change artists; their dreams had not yet narrowed down to one bright beam. They were still unencumbered, as I had been. They might always be unencumbered.

Perhaps my parents, who had become beneficiaries if not exactly boosters of my gayness, feared losing the advantages they'd so gracefully trained themselves to accept. If I had a real partner—and a child!—I would no longer be theirs for the asking. This was painful to me as well, but I would have the compensation of Andy and Erez. What compensation would my parents have? My father had already told me directly that he doubted he could ever consider himself a grandfather to a child adopted by his son's lover; he regretted his narrowness but saw no way around it. My mother now told me that seeing me with Erez, far from elating her, had made her enormously sad. Why had I not chosen to get a child of my own?

"But I have, in a way."

"Your own flesh and blood. Like through a surrogate. I know it's selfish and probably wrong, but I can't help feeling: A piece of me that is in you has ended." She did not say, "a piece of your father."

For if Andy and I were vastly different, we were no less different than my parents. It was, of course, a major part of the attraction in both cases, and therefore part of my mother's concern. Though Andy was (she admitted) an excellent houseguest, she had seen that he was not particular, not finicky, not attuned to nuances of neatness or, for that matter, subtleties of emotion. While this was useful, even admirable, in some ways, she knew it would always be a source of tension between us, for he was too old and I too bossy to change. The next day, while Andy was packing the car (we were leaving together for New York), she saw me carefully remaking the bed he had already—thoughtfully if imprecisely— straightened. A bed was one thing; it could be stripped if need be. But how do you remake a life?

TWENTY-ONE

We drove off into the sunrise, Andy and I holding hands when we could, Erez babbling behind us. He was the only one talking, at least at first; the monumental if impassive beauty of the country-side, the rifts and sweeps of the Delaware Water Gap as we crossed it, seemed to put mere human disappointment into geo-logical perspective. Are the hills still hurt by the river, which once cut them down? Is the river still cowed by the hills, which tower above it?

I would return to the Poconos twice more that summer, but I

already knew it was the last year my family—my birth family, that is—would vacation together. The succession of rentals with their curious, imposed decors (one house, named Safari, featured jungle-print sheets and giraffe-shaped salad tongs) had served and now outlived their purpose. When we started, fifteen years earlier, I was just out of college; I had nothing to call my own except what was in my head. My brother and I still brought home laundry. We brought home everything: That was the meaning of those summers. But even adjoining rooms could not disguise for long that we were all just individuals. It was nice to imagine us as a clubby clan—the kind Andy fantasized we might be—but we were not clubby and not much of a clan. We were solitaries, each marked with a version of the species grain, but stained and buffed to his own chosen luster. We were not one family anymore, we were several.

Was it quixotic or just sentimental of me that I nevertheless wanted my grandmother to know what my new life was like? I visited her in the nursing home later that summer. We sat in the so-called common room; our conversation went as it always had:

"Gotta girl?"

"Grandmom, please."

"Are you making money?"

"Yes."

"How much?"

"Enough to get by."

"How much is that?"

"Grandmom, please."

(A short pause, filled with the sounds of the television and nearby snoring.)

"Okay. Gotta girl?"

She was ninety-seven. The skin on her hands was like pleated silk, her eyes like goldfish behind her glasses. I showed her pictures: "This is my friend Andy," I said. "He has a son named Erez, which means cedar in Hebrew." She studied the snapshots as if they were hieroglyphs. She looked at me in bewilderment. "You see, Grandmom," I tried to explain, "Andy adopted the boy, and I—"

"I know more than you think I do," she said. She gripped my

hand so tight, I suddenly could feel what she must have been like as a young mother stocking shelves in the store. Then she let go. "Gotta girl?" she said.

If we don't always get to have our love in exactly the forms we desire it, it is love nevertheless. My parents, it is true, had so far been unable to enjoy the new life Andy and Erez were bringing me, but I knew that time would turn them around, if only I could tell them clearly enough where it was I meant to end up. I was less sure of my friends—my gay friends especially. None had yet seen the three of us together, though they'd heard the stories ad nauseam. That they had not met Andy and Erez was itself emblematic of my new circumstances. Had Andy been an ordinary boyfriend, he would surely have been going to movies and dinners and publishing parties soon after we met. As a father, though, he had few freedoms. Even I, a father-in-training, watched helplessly as my social identity got nibbled and then swallowed by our co-identity as parents. We had so little in common with most gay people now, except when we were too tired to do anything about it. Those we managed to see had kids or at least didn't mind them; if they owned a sandbox or a pool, so much the better.

My fears about my friends proved groundless, however; though the "community" may have been vaguely hostile, individuals understood, from their own lifelong struggles, that happiness is never political. They freely offered the gift of their delight. Some were even encouraged in their own quest for children by Andy's evident success. Others immediately recategorized themselves as uncles; if there was any chagrin involved, they did me the favor of hiding it. The most enthusiastic response came from John, my ex, who seemed relieved: a little for himself but especially for me. "Now you can be the father you always wanted to be," he said. "Which I never could have given you." I waved that off; I *hadn't* always wanted to be a father. Or had I?

And *was* I? My straight friends didn't seem to think so. Meg, who with her husband, Richard, now had two boys, pointed out that as long as I did not live with Andy, Erez would never be my son. "If you're not trapped, you're not a parent," she said exhaustedly.

TWENTY-TWO

After Labor Day—the summer over, the fall not quite begun—
Andy returned to work for the first time since Erez came home,
eighteen months earlier. I returned to my apartment in the Village, which suddenly seemed empty despite its overcrowding.
Much of the summer we were a family whether we wanted to be
or not; now we would have to scramble and commute (and, in
Erez's case, wait) to be together for just a few hours. Erez would
spend the majority of his waking day, happily enough, with
Eliane, one of the Haitian women who'd helped care for Janet
and whom Andy now hired full-time. Meanwhile, Andy would
spend his waking day with other people's kids.

I had hoped we might continue to escape to Long Island on
weekends, but the place had to be rented to pay Eliane. We did
manage to eke out one last visit before the winter renter took over.
It was mid-September, golden and vast, still warm enough for
shorts at noon, cool enough at night for fires. I am not the sort of
person who remembers much unadulterated happiness, but I remember the glow of that weekend, and the glow of us within it.

Mercedes, who had a little house not far from Least Hampton,
invited us to join her and some friends for a walk that Sunday at
Cedar Point, a crooked finger of land jutting into Gardiners Bay.
Erez was perched in a carrier high above Andy's shoulders; the
contraption was backbreaking, like wearing a scaffold, but it allowed a baby to see (for once) even farther than the adult who
bore him. It also kept him out of trouble: off the slippery sand
paths, away from the sheer drops down to the bay. The views were
exhilarating, if scary; from our height the water seemed like a fish
on its side, with millions of whitecap scales.

Mercedes and her friends—a young straight couple, a gay widower—were, of course, interested in Erez's adoption, and Andy
told the story he loved: How the child now towering above him
had been handed over like a precious message of hope from a war
zone. Though the birth parents could not themselves escape,

they saw to it that their little boy did, and with him some sort of
coded instructions, woven into the web of his heart. He would
never learn the names of the people who had sent him out to freedom; they knew it was better that way.

"Never?" asked Mercedes.

Andy explained that this had been a closed adoption: He knew
little about the birth parents and they knew even less about him.
There was only one way they could legitimately find each other,
and it was complicated. Erez, after he turned twenty-one, would
have to register with an agency in the state where he had been
adopted. When the youngest of his biological siblings, if any sur-
vived, turned twenty-one, too—and if both his birth parents had
also registered—the state might make a match. Information provided by Erez would then be released to his birth parents, and
vice versa; the information might or might not include a means of
making contact. In any case, if any of the people involved decided not to register, the match could never be made. Whether
Erez would register would be his choice, of course, but Andy and
I did not intend to make him feel the need to.

"You don't want him ever to know his mother?" Mercedes
asked.

"You mean his birth mother," said Andy.

The path narrowed; we separated into pairs to get by. I asked
Mercedes why she was so interested in the issue: Was she considering adoption herself?

Yes, she said, she was considering it. She was considering
adopting a child, since it was unclear at this point whether she
would find an appropriate father in time. But she was considering
adoption in another sense, too: She was remembering it.

"What do you mean?"

When she was an aspiring actress just out of college, she now
told me, she had become pregnant by an all-too-dashing boyfriend. Abortion was legal, but Mercedes, who had been raised
Catholic and had attended a college run by Ursuline nuns, chose
to carry the pregnancy to term; she gave birth to a boy she named
Christopher. Though her plan had been to place him for adoption, she found she could not bear to do it: He was so beautiful,
and he was hers. Still, after a few tortured weeks of indecision, she

acquiesced to the sad facts of the situation. She had no money, no support, no stability. She let him go, never to see him again.

It had now been twenty-one years, exactly. She had done many wonderful things in that time: played great parts, suffered great loves, received great attention for her work. But she had never stopped wondering what had happened to Christopher—though that would no longer be his name.

"I'm thinking of trying to find him," she said. "Now that he's twenty-one."

The path pitched steeply down toward the beach; we descended it in silence. Perhaps it was from the tenuousness of my position as an *éminence mauve*, but I was pained by the idea of her seeking the boy. Of course he isn't a boy anymore, he's a young man, and I trusted Mercedes's motives. But for myself, I was glad of Erez's closed adoption, not because I feared that anyone would take Erez away, but because I did not want him to grow up thinking there was anyone who *might* ever take him. Rescue him, even; he had to learn to live with his disappointments as well as his successes. A child is better off without having to hold open the possibility that some secret mother may descend from the sky at any moment. He must be whole in his life; Andy and I must be always sufficient.

"You did the right thing back then," I eventually said. "For you and for him."

"Yes," said Mercedes.

The sun was low above the water as we reached the squishy sand. "Boeud, boeud," said Erez, pointing to the gulls. Andy let him out of the scaffold to run on the beach and chase the tide, while out of someone's canvas knapsack came a bottle of nice champagne. Erez startled to hear it pop, and everybody laughed.

"To children!" Mercedes toasted.

TWENTY-THREE

If you're not trapped, you're not a parent—but I *was* trapped. True, the trap was not physical: Now that the summer was fully over, I did not live with Andy. Under no other circumstance would anyone think it was sane that I should; we had only been dating (though that's hardly the word) since the beginning of June, and neither of us had the kind of apartment that could accommodate the other. Our apartments could hardly accommodate ourselves.

But even *potential* fatherhood trumps gayness, trumps single-ness, too; people who learned of my relationship with Erez started asking, regardless of my relationship with Andy, how soon I would move in with them. A few acquaintances even seemed slightly offended by the notion that I might begin to consider myself some sort of father without at once relinquishing all remnants of my former life. "You *must* move in: A child is involved here!" one married woman exclaimed, betraying her prejudice that Andy, single and (worse yet) male, was ipso facto insufficient. Others were concerned because they accurately surmised that I could not tolerate too much confusion in my role. Already the commute between my world and Andy's—from Manhattan to Brooklyn, from single freelancer to family man—was becoming disorienting, like the feeling you get after entering an afternoon movie in winter and emerging two hours later in total darkness.

There was a child involved, but there were also two adults. The pervasive idea of what was best for the former was at odds with my own idea of what was best for the latter. A child wants (or so we are told) to draw his world, like a blanket, tight around him: He wants you to go fast, regardless of safety. But the seriousness of the situation—the child, in fact—made it more necessary than ever for me to go slow. That was my trap. I could not do both and I could not do neither, yet people's assumptions (not to mention my own) assured there was no middle ground. Strangers already called Erez my son when they saw us together; should I do less? It seemed defiant somehow, a kind of hubris, to proclaim what clearly wasn't true, or even to acquiesce passively in someone's misunderstanding. But I could not move forward toward the goal of real fatherhood without presuming on it in the meantime.

Sticky as this was, it was not the trap Meg had in mind. She meant that a person was a parent only if she could never again *not* be one: not for one moment, not for the rest of her life. She was right in some fundamental sense, of course, but the formulation begged the question, like defining a rabbit not by its ears but by its propensity to remain a rabbit. What made it a rabbit in the first place? What made a real parent? It was relatively uncomplicated for Meg: She had wanted a child so clearly and fiercely that she had overcome the doubts of her skeptical husband to make it happen, and happen again. She became an unassailably real parent to the world on the day she gave birth, and to herself even earlier. As the writer Barbara Jones put it in an essay about adopting a daughter: "The irrevocable moment in becoming a parent is not the moment you conceive a child; it's the moment you conceive of her." I saw how this was so for others, but knew it didn't account for me. Andy had conceived of Erez by himself. I had not had the chance.

Though in the abstract we regard the bright red line of birth as marking the clearest claim on parenthood, in reality it is inadequate to all but the most traditional configurations. People who adopt, or marry into a preexisting brood, find the birth definition useless. Conversely, that definition goes too far in crediting as parents those who abandon their biological offspring. Why are deadbeat dads called dads? Perhaps to tempt them with the wistful possibility that they could still be real fathers, if only they'd pay the bills. Is it money, then, that makes you real? Most of the children born to the teenaged girls Andy counsels are supported by the U.S. government. Yet no one dares say the girls aren't mothers, even when they don't live in the same house with their babies. Often a grandmother has custody, legal or otherwise; is *she* now the mother? And what if she has to work, and so turns the child over to a series of day care workers and aunts—are *they* now the parents? If not, who is? And if so, who's to say I wasn't a father the whole long summer? I already spent more time with Erez than most of the fathers I knew spent with their children.

Not biology, not money, not cohabitation, not some running total of minutes per day, not the law, certainly; what then makes a real parent? Is it love? But anyone can love a child. Is it a *special* love? Pedophiles profess a special love. Is it the *child's* love, then? Perhaps in part. But a young enough child is promiscuous and will plant his kisses anywhere. Erez loved me and a dozen others, more or less. So how would I know when I was a real father by the only definition that mattered—his?

TWENTY-FOUR

I already knew quite a lot about Erez's definitions—his derivations, pronunciations, and substandard usage as well. I had reconstructed, from Andy's memory, a record of his early language, and was now compiling from direct observation a detailed lexicon as his vocabulary blossomed. His first clear word, of course, had been "dada." He also on occasion said "da," but this was for men other than Andy, as if they weren't worth the extra syllable. "Ma," as I've already related, had ages ago been tried and abandoned, there being no one who answered to that sound. By persistent conditioning, we managed by November to force "Abba" into retirement, in favor of something that sounded like "Elliot"; Eliane was called "Dom" (or so we think), perhaps from the French for "lady." With that, Erez's job of naming the major characters in his drama was almost complete, including "dibee" for Chauncey (or sometimes "urf") and, for himself, with joy in the mirror after a bath, "Baybee! Baybee!" Soon we realized that this could also mean the mirror itself (with or without his image in it) and, to our embarrassment, bald, chubby men. "Baybee!" he crowed when one passed in the street. But he did not have a word for me.

By the time he was twenty-one months old, his vocabulary consisted of seventy-five words. Very soon he'd be old enough that we'd start counting his age in years, not months; his vocabulary would be too large to count at all. But for the moment I had its entirety on paper, including "Ma'am" the stuffed cat; "bruller" for umbrella; "bahpour" for diaper; "zhip" for zipper, especially the one on his pale blue pajamas; "rah" for rice, his favorite food; "bolly" for broccoli, which he occasionally tolerated; "ow," inexplicably, for his cousin Michael; "me-me" for "excuse me," when trying to get by; and "hoo-hoo," the ever-popular mystery spirit that lived near the door—was it an owl? Or was it just a variant of "laloo," the apparently French wolf who lived in the hall as well?

But knowing the name of each of his spooks was not the same as knowing *him*. Nor was knowing his daily schedule: when he awoke, when he ate, when he usually needed a clean diaper, when he could not keep his eyes open for want of a nap, when he could not take a nap for want of diversion. As an uncle and a godfather, I had contented myself with mastering these mechanical details, but now such expertise seemed insufficient. It could not answer the central questions, which until recently I had not needed to ask: Who am I to him? Who does he want me to be?

For Andy those questions had been long since asked and answered. It did not take any expertise to see that father and son were each other's everything. To Erez, Andy was complete and sufficient and abundant and permanent, even when he went back to work; Erez's days were divided into *Daddy Is Here* and *Daddy Is Coming Back Soon*. The rest of us were icing—not even on the cake but on top of other icing. If Erez delighted in me, it was largely because I provided a different form of entertainment. I talked to him more than Andy did and engaged him in specific, structured games. Do you want to play Tickle? Do you want to play Train? Andy would sometimes forget to talk to Erez for very long stretches, would just go about his cooking or diapering or tenth load of laundry. But it didn't matter; they did not need to be engaged in conversation. They were engaged in each other, without out a word spoken.

I knew this because I saw it so often. By Thanksgiving we had settled into a pattern: Friday afternoons I came to Brooklyn and stayed through the weekend; one other night each week I tried to visit, at least for the evening. On those occasions, I gave Erez his bath and shared in all the domestic duties—except washing dishes, a scary task in a murky sink I could not fathom. But as much as Erez welcomed me in all these roles, I was, even with him, an *éminence mauve*. You may have my ear, he seemed to say, but my eyes are elsewhere; you may hover importantly, but you have no name. When I handed him to Andy after the bath, he stuck to his father like an overcooked noodle.

Not that it didn't make me happy to see such happiness—and I don't mean Erez's. Is there anything sexier, more powerful in a man than his joy in apogee? The handsomest smile I have ever witnessed is the one that blooms on Andy's face when Erez comes running into his arms. Alas, it is therefore handsomer than the smile elicited by anyone else, running or leaping or twirling batons. There are many things, important things, I can do for Andy that a child cannot, but there is one big thing Erez can do that I never can: make him a father. In that light it has often seemed cruel to want to break into the perfectly cozy room of their love, whence come invitations but no keys.

TWENTY-FIVE

Don't trust patterns. Once you get used to a situation, the situation changes. The moment you reframe its shocks and discomforts as joys and benefits, it shocks and discomfits you over again. This never fails; there is something in a pattern that begs for undoing, that scatters the seeds of its own supplanting.

"I want another child," said Andy.

This was around Thanksgiving; we were making plans for the coming holidays. Though I had been raised more traditionally than Andy, he was now more observant than I, which was saying very little. He liked anything to do with candles and dressing nicely and scarfing down blintzes: the tribal aspects of Judaism. This year, the first since his mother had died, he proposed to spend time with his family—Frank and his wife and their two kids, that is—at Klezcamp, a six-day retreat for Jewish culture held at a resort hotel in the Catskill Mountains that had once been grand and was now just grandiose. There would be traditional Eastern European music, he told me, plus lectures and crafts and nightly dancing. "I want Erez to have more time with my family, and I want more time with them as well. They're all I have left."

I wasn't offended; I knew what he meant.

"I'd love it if you came, too," he added.

"I think it would be too cold for me," I said, "what with hell freezing over."

"The thing is, we won't get back until right before my birthday."

"So what's the problem? We'll be together then."

The problem was that Andy was about to turn forty-six—or really, that he was about to stop being forty-five. According to its application forms, the adoption agency that had placed Erez with Andy only dealt with would-be parents who were forty-five or under. Back at the time of Erez's adoption, a social worker had made vague assurances that the rule was not adhered to strictly, especially in cases where they'd already made what they considered a successful placement. But there had been some turnover in the staff since then, and Andy's situation was unusual enough without requiring a special variance regarding his age. He could not take the chance.

"I have to send in the application now," he said. "There won't be time when I get back. So we have to decide if we're going to do this."

"We?" I said.

It's not as if I didn't know. Andy had told me on our very first date, at our very first meeting in fact, on the dock. He had even bought his car with two child seats built in. But I had forgotten, or deemed the desire gestural: something safely locked behind a door of the imagination. His wish to have another child had seemed no more real to me than the always imminent, never material plan to renovate his apartment. Indeed, as we spoke, the ancient washer was moaning so vociferously we had to wait until it spun itself out to continue the conversation. What I had forgotten is that however scattered and flexible Andy could be about schedules and bills and repairing appliances, he was determined enough about becoming a parent to have turned himself inside-out in the process. He might wait until the last minute, but he would not wait longer.

"Are you sure?" I asked.

He nodded yes. "I am a second son," he said.

"But so am I."

"I can't explain it. It's just what I see when I see a family. I see two kids."

"And two adults?"

"If you'll do it."

I had not even known I wanted one child until I loved the one that came to me unplanned. But two? I could hardly keep afloat as it was. Andy and I had so few moments alone; what would a newborn do to us? And what about Erez? Not even two, he was just beginning to exult in his capacities; wasn't this just the wrong moment to shock him with the arrival of a rival? Not that the classic boomer spacing—Andy was three and a half years younger than his brother, as was I—had done much for us in our respective youths. Neither of us felt as close as we wanted to the alien male who shared our bedrooms; someone was always out of synch. Perhaps a tighter spacing wouldn't be so bad; perhaps there was no "right" time but the right time you made. In any case it was the right time, the last time, the only time for Andy.

"I'm scared," I said. "I'm already a shadow; I don't want to disappear totally. On the other hand, I know that whatever child arrives I will love just as I learned to love Erez. I won't stand in your way. Maybe it's even my way."

"Right now I'm only making the application," said Andy. "It'll be months, maybe even a year or more before anything happens."

"That's what you thought with Erez," I said.

"But that was a fluke."

"Well, in any case, after this, I want your tubes tied."

"Okay, but not yours," Andy replied. "Maybe you'll want to adopt one later. A little girl. You've got years yet to think about it."

My grandmother's voice arose from my throat. "Oy gevalt."

Andy mailed the application the day before he took off for Klezcamp. He requested a boy—a second son—who might not look too unlike Erez.

"It'll be months," he repeated. "Even longer."

I saw them off to Klezcamp in the velvet dark of a chilly evening. Erez was playing with a dreidel in one of the child seats; the other was still tucked tightly shut. Without me (I was going to Philadelphia) and without the putative second son, the car, I noted, was precisely half filled. Or was it half empty?

"Bye-bye, hon," said Andy. "Have a great trip."

"Bye-bye, sweetheart," I said through the window.

"Bah-bah, Juzhee," said Erez suddenly, and smiled to see what he had done.

IV

Dreft
and
Kwell

ONE

The boy was born six days later, though we were still, as far as we knew, unpregnant. My biggest concern at the moment was only whether Erez, having learned my name so recently, would remember it when he returned from Klezcamp. (He did.) Otherwise we trusted our patterns. Andy had his forty-sixth birthday, and Hanukkah passed, and the year turned over. Nothing would ever change, it seemed, in this frozen corner of the calendar. The radiators banged and squealed; we snuggled beneath ourselves.

Messages at Andy's house have a way of wandering through purgatory before they reach him; the wait may be hours or years. Thus, by the time he found the inscrutable message from the adoption agency, on a Thursday evening in early January, it was too late to call back. "It's probably nothing," he told me later, after Erez was asleep that night. "Something they need for my application." At work the next day he dialed the number; how strange to call an adoption agency in just the way you called a Chinese restaurant. The same few digits in a different order, and instead of dim sum you got a baby. But no, no, it would not be a baby. It would be a problem with his deposit check, a missing form, a clerical error: a delay, he told himself, not an offer.

But it *was* an offer: a boy now thirteen days old. He had been born a bit premature, after thirty-eight instead of forty weeks of gestation, but at almost six pounds he was not exactly small. Bigger than Erez had been, Andy noted. This boy was jaundiced, however—the whites of his eyes were yellowish—and his blood sugar was low; did he have an infection? In any case, the hospital had put him under ultraviolet lights and pricked him constantly with needles; when his color and numbers normalized, they sent him out into the world with a seven-thousand-dollar bill of good health. Since then, two days now, he had been living with a foster mother in a nearby town, waiting for someone to want him.

His birth parents were Hispanic Catholic Mexicans. He himself was dark-haired and light-skinned and of course "very cute"; the social workers always said that. They thought he might grow up to be tall, because his birth father was tall; they always said that, too. In fact, what we know of the birth father's height, like everything else about him, is only what the birth mother chose to reveal; it was she who had crossed the border, made the deal, and filled out the forms. Whether the birth father knew of her actions (or even her pregnancy), and whether he approved of them if so, are matters of conjecture. There was even the risk (the social worker told Andy) that the man might, between now and the time the adoption was finalized, show up and assert a paternal claim. But no one expected this to happen. The pair weren't married, and the mother herself had returned to Mexico, seemingly ending the matter.

I reconstruct this information from Andy's hieroglyphs, which are scrawled on the backs of the computerized forms he uses at work to notate schedules for hundreds of students. Strangely, these so-called bubble sheets seem an apt memento of this new conception. On the front of one, a girl named Roxell has been assigned to USHSGOV1B and KYBDNG2CLG; on another a boy named Kerean takes HOE:CORE3. On the backs, nearly as indecipherable, an as-yet-unnamed boy is put together from snippets of blood tests and genetic guesses. Apgar 7; Apgar 9. Birth mother's half-sister: blond and fair. But an unseen child is untranslatable; Andy already knew that from Erez. What did a random collection of "facts" mean? Nineteen inches; Mexican; short, straight hair; father liked to play ball: This could be a Chihuahua.

"You mentioned that you were hoping for a boy who might look like your other son," the social worker told Andy. "This may be the one, with his coloring and height. Do you think you want him?"

"How long do I have to decide?"

"We can give you until tomorrow morning."

I have little memory of Andy calling me that morning with news of the offer. I know I would have been in my apartment, at my computer, when the phone rang. I would have nervously started typing whatever he started saying, my fingers acting independently of my brain. In any case, the file has disappeared into an electronic netherworld along with the afterglow of my fear and excitement. I do remember flipping pages on my on-screen calendar, trying to figure the sequence of events. "He was born on the twenty-ninth?" I asked.

"Yes. Two weeks premature," said Andy.

"The day before you turned forty-six, then."

"As if he knew . . ."

In theory, you can consult. In theory, you can choose. In reality, you only do what you must. Andy asked me what I thought, and I said, "What do *you* think?" and he said, "I don't know," and I said, "I don't either." But each of us knew what each of us thought. When I asked him where he would stay when he got there, he told me he already had the name of a hotel not far from the foster mother.

TWO

"You're going to have a little brother!" we told Erez the next day, hoping to prepare him, in less than a week, for an event most children have almost a year to consider. "A baby brother!" we said. "A little baby? Brother?" He smiled uncomprehendingly.

If he was not yet ready to grasp the import of these words, neither were we. What did it mean to prepare for a new life? Well, cleaning, of course; we cleaned all weekend. And rearranging. Fortunately we had already begun the game of musical beds in Andy's apartment. After months of urging, I had recently convinced him to move his heavy Mission bed into the living room; it took three hired men to do it. The result was less than charming when guests were over, but afforded us a little privacy once they left. Erez now had privacy, too, perhaps more than he wanted; what had previously been the communal bedroom now became solely a nursery, with Erez's crib in one corner and his new "big-boy" bed in another. When the three of us had all been sleeping there it was virtually claustrophobic; now it seemed too vast for one toddler. "Perhaps we should order Procrustean beds," Andy e-mailed me while we were considering various schemes, "and adapt kids instead of adopting them."

But Erez had taken the new situation in stride. Each bedtime for weeks, after his stories, we asked him to indicate where he wanted to sleep by tossing Ma'am the cat either into the crib or onto the bed; he always chose the crib, until one night he finally didn't. "Are you sure?" we asked, proud and nostalgic. He climbed right in. Since then, the spurned crib had become a storage pen, filled with overstocked toys and stuffed animals. Silly me, I thought it was a stroke of good luck that we'd managed to vacate it in time for the new baby; I had not read enough books to know better. Andy explained that, according to experts, putting the new boy in Erez's old crib would provoke jealousy. "Erez will have enough issues to work through as it is," Andy said. This seemed ridiculous until I remembered the pair of white buck shoes my parents had been required to buy my brother for his marching band uniform; I cried for weeks until they bought me an identical pair, which never left my closet.

So we would have to get another crib, wholly redundant; the new boy would not even use it for the first few months. During that period he would sleep in a Moses basket or bassinet, Andy told me, which would have to be kept in the living room with us so that the frequent nighttime feedings would not awaken Erez. Later we could move the new boy into the new crib, disassemble the old crib, give away the bassinet . . . my mind boggled. Not only at the excess of it all but at the years of perpetual reconfiguration that now began to seem my fate. Life with one child was confusing enough; what would life with two be like? I suddenly thought of those little puzzles consisting of tiles you had to slide from space to space until they formed the desired pattern—except that getting any one tile into alignment meant disrupting the order of the others, and the damn things kept popping out anyway.

"You're going to have a baby brother!" we told Erez again the next day. No response.

We read him books that featured new siblings. "See, Arthur has a baby sister! Which is kind of like a brother," I said. We drew him drawings. We told him how Daddy was returning to the same place Erez himself had come from once, only this time he would bring back a new little boy and Erez would get to stay home with Jesse. Wouldn't that be fun? He smiled compliantly.

"You're going to have a baby brother!" we tried again, with three days left.

We screwed new furniture together, aired old coverlets, snaked recalcitrant pieces of lace over bent metal frames and laughed at the frippery. We emptied some drawers and consolidated others; we put out the call for hand-me-downs. We did not think about what was happening, for what would we have thought? Besides, there wasn't any time. It was all Andy could do, after work, to buy his airline tickets, notify the aunties, engage the mohel, and put a check for twenty-three thousand dollars, borrowed against securities, in a FedEx envelope to send to the agency.

"You're going to have a baby brother!"

Two days later, it seemed as if our play-acting and picture books had begun to pay off, for Erez was dancing merrily around the apartment singing "Baby bruller, baby bruller!" But on the rainy day of Andy's departure, we discovered our mistake when Andy walked in with his umbrella dripping and Erez delightedly pointed to it. "Baby bruller, baby bruller!" he exclaimed. "Me baby bruller!" Apparently he thought he was getting a baby umbrella; he had successfully learned to expect the wrong thing. As who does not?

THREE

One week after he first heard the little boy described, Andy was on a plane to pick him up. He could still back out, if necessary, for any reason or no reason at all: *He's too sick. He's too little. He looks like a monkey.* People had changed their minds for less. It was really a matter of imagination. Some birth parents instantaneously loved the little blob handed over to them: They saw it come from the mother's own body, and could find their own features in its shrieking face. Adopting parents had to take a leap of faith. They had to believe that the child handed over all neat in his swaddling would some day grow to look like them, or feel like them at least.

Andy arrived, late that night, at the cheap motel the foster mother had suggested. He brought with him little more than a book and a comb and a diaper bag waiting to be filled. He called me to see how Erez was doing (he was asleep) and to say good night. Then there was a knock at his door. "Is everything all right?" the desk clerk asked. "Do you have enough blankets?" He lingered, smiling and sheepish.

"Thank you, yes," said Andy, closing him out politely.

It would not have been apparent to the desk clerk that Andy was here to pick up a son and that he had another one back home, not to mention a spouse. He would have seen a handsome man with a New York accent and almost no luggage. He would have seen availability, whereas what Andy saw in himself was satiety. Fear and exhaustion, of course, but mostly a sense of impending completion. The construction of his life was almost topped off (as builders of skyscrapers like to say): A flag could be planted on the uppermost beam, and the rest of the work would be details.

Nevertheless, ringing the bell at the foster mother's shiny house in a wooded suburban development the next morning, he was almost sick with nervousness; perhaps the breakfast of *huevos rancheros* at a Mexican diner hadn't helped matters. But Pat turned out to be a cool blonde in her late thirties with a calmingly matter-of-fact attitude, as if Andy had answered an ad for a grandfather clock she was hoping to sell, and had come to inspect it. Foster parenting was her business if not her passion; taking in a newborn from time to time, at fifty-five dollars a day plus expenses, allowed her to stay at home with her own brood of four, the youngest an adopted "special needs" child who was even now creeping around on the floor, watching the interesting transaction.

Pat went into her sales pitch, though it wasn't anything so crude; her interest in closing the deal was largely unselfish. It would have been to her financial advantage to hold on to her visiting babies longer, but emotionally she must have learned not to get too attached. She knew it was best for everyone involved if the baby was placed as soon as possible, so she did what she could to make that happen. "He sleeps well, eats heartily, and is sweet as can be," she told Andy while leading him to the bassinet. "One of my kids even said, 'Oh, this one's cute, we ought to keep him,'" which led Andy to expect another Erez.

We all learn to expect the wrong thing. The three-week-old baby was asleep in the bassinet; how many other babies had slept there? This one had a bright-red scrunched-up face and a stripe of black hair across his skull like a Mohawk. When he opened his eyes a few minutes later they were almond, feline, tiny slits in a pie. He weighed nothing, of course, and yet he was solid, and then he let out an enormous cry. He was healthy, all right. Andy fed him a demi-bottle of formula that Pat had prepared, then changed his diaper, the size of a thank-you note. He did all this somewhat mechanically, worried he was not bonding quickly enough (though less than twenty minutes had passed) and looking constantly into the baby's face for a sign that this was his son.

"He's all red and scrunchy," he whispered on the phone. "I know I'm not supposed to care, but Erez was so cute."

"Erez was a cesarean, right? They're always cute," I answered. "And this one was two weeks premature, so it's really like he's just a week old, and lots of babies look squashed at that age."

"I suppose . . ."

But why was I arguing on the side of the baby—if it *was* the side of the baby? I had not seen him, could barely picture him; even if I had and could, on what basis would I form an opinion? Yet I had an opinion. This is the child fate offered; let us acquiesce, as a shtetl bride acquiesces to a marriage arranged by her father. In an age of individuality and romance, of children virtually by design, this was, of course, a throwback, a submission. But for once in my life I felt submissive. Let us take him, I said, and wait for the love to come later.

FOUR

It would not take long. By the time they landed at Newark Airport that night, Andy and the boy were father and son. Not yet officially: Though he had signed temporary custody papers ("I agree to take this child into my home in the same manner as if the child had been born to me . . ."), Andy would not be his legal father until the adoption was "finalized," before a state judge, six months to a year down the road. But the emotional bond had begun to set the minute Andy left Pat's house—a bond not like a manacle but like glue. It had taken time for the two halves to marry, but not much time. Now they were one; even the stewardesses said so.

I arrived at the airport early, having hired a car service on the assumption that Andy would be too tired (and I too nervous) to drive. I was right about myself at least: I waited for fifteen minutes by the carousels, my heart jumping at every baby's squeal, but forgetting that Andy had checked no luggage. When I finally realized my mistake I raced in a panic around the terminal. Finally I spotted them in the glassy emptiness of the departures instead of the arrivals concourse: Andy in a leather jacket bulging with bottles, the baby in a tiny car seat that TWA had helpfully labeled "Special Handling."

I could hardly see the little boy, all but mummified in the puffy down sack in which Andy had dressed him. He was, remarkably, asleep. I pushed aside a piece of the hood in order to get a closer view; he looked a bit like an angry monkey, but it didn't matter. I kissed him on his hot plum cheek, and so I kissed his father.

"He's here," he said. We stood crying in the vast concourse.

After a few minutes, we transferred the baby and ourselves into the hired car. The driver tried to help, but there was little we would let him do. He did take extra care to avoid sharp turns and sudden stops as we headed toward the Verrazano, and smiled at us, or raised an eyebrow, in the rearview mirror. Did he want to speak? In any case, I did not want to hear him; on the ride to the airport we'd already had a disturbing conversation. He'd seemed eager to be friendly. Perhaps, having picked me up at my apartment in the Village, he made some quick assumptions, just as the motel desk clerk made some quick assumptions about Andy. "You are meeting a friend?" he asked; from his accent he seemed to be an Arab.

"Yes," I said, instantly flummoxed. "My friend is just returning with the new baby . . . that is being adopted." I had not tried to use this kind of passive, genderless construction in years, and was rusty at it. What did I think it would accomplish, anyway? He'd see Andy soon enough. But I'd rather him see than have me explain, so I said what I said with a tone of finality in hopes it would derail the discussion.

"Your girlfriend?" he asked, doubtfully.

"No. A guy." I felt myself blush.

We were stuck in line for the Holland Tunnel, moving only ten feet a minute; at this rate the conversation seemed likely to continue until I actually died.

"And you do that guy-guy thing?" asked the driver.

Though the wording was creepy, he did not seem hostile. His English was good but not good enough to make clear the nature of his curiosity. Was he personally interested in the guy-guy thing? Just making chitchat?

Before I could answer—and I have no idea what I would have said—he added, sadly, or so I thought, "In my country, you know what they do to you?"

I wasn't sure whether he meant me personally, or people like me, or even people like him. In any case, I warily shook my head no.

He made a gesture with his right hand, removing it from the steering wheel and slashing six inches of air. "See?"

"I think so."

Now he drove in silence as I grilled Andy about the trip just completed: What did you sign? What did people say? Between us, the boy in his car seat was all but inanimate: an expensive shopping bag. Ahead of us, the driver's eyebrow popping up in the mirror from time to time reminded me that the happiness Andy and I felt in each other, let alone in this sleeping monkey-baby, was a happiness much of the world would punish severely. It made me feel that the little boy wasn't the only delicate package being transferred to safety. We, too, were adoptees, remanded into our own adult care, charged with creating, over and over, better worlds to live in.

Erez and the baby-sitter were both asleep when we got back to Andy's, but Chauncey wasn't. He came over and sniffed the boy, whom we had laid on a receiving blanket for his consideration. He seemed to find the new person acceptable; at any rate, he went back to his favorite spot and curled up. After putting the boy in the bassinet and winding up the musical clown, so did we. For one hour.

FIVE

"May the one who comes be blessed": Thus began the circumcision service two days later. Sixty people crowded into Andy's apartment for the noon affair, including dozens of delegates from Andy's rangy family and three from mine: my mother, father, and nephew. All were kind enough, upon arriving, not to mention that we looked wooden and sallow, with raccoon rings around our eyes; we had barely slept since the boy arrived forty hours before, and our hearts (I could feel Andy's, too) were clanking, loud and irregular, like the radiators.

At least the baby was getting cuter; what sleep we had lost, he had found and kept. His capuchin face had begun to unfold, his redness to recede. Everyone admired his sequin eyes: Is he Chinese? they asked.

"No, Jewish," I inevitably said. "As you will see."

Not *all* would see. We hired a sitter to keep Erez and my nephew busy in the nursery during the circumcision itself; if we had made our peace with the implications of the surgery on the baby, we were not so sure of its effect on a toddler who might catch a glimpse. Probably we should have hired a sitter for the adult men, too. They visibly blanched as the mohelet set out her arcane equipment, which looked both surgical and culinary. The adult women, more familiar with blood and cooking, were matter-of-fact and stalwart.

This was the same mohelet—a handsome woman in a nubbly pink suit—who had circumcised Erez twenty-two months earlier. With the air of someone used to explaining herself, she politely brushed aside nervous queries about her authority: "Did you

know," she countered, "that females performed the rite in ancient
Israel?" As a woman and a convert to Judaism (not to mention a
plastic surgeon) she had clearer ideas about her role than did run-
of-the-mill mohels, most of whom had inherited their ancient
sideline unthinkingly, as others inherit a dental practice. Few
would even perform a bris on a child born of Catholic parents, let
alone a child adopted by a gay man to be raised with his boyfriend. But this one did so happily, recognizing perforce an idea
of Judaism that is more inclusive than the one formulated by me-
dieval rabbis. Indeed, in her mimeographed script for the service,
she had slightly doctored the traditional prayers so as to include
among the litany of patriarchs the names of suppressed matri-
archs as well. Perhaps this was only fitting, since the mother had
been suppressed in our story, too. Still, in the manner of all things
defensive and politically correct, it was as awkward as it was moving: Sarah, Rebekah, Leah, and Rachel had been pieced into the
Hebrew text by hand, unevenly, like a ransom note.

There was nothing politically correct about what followed.
Onto her forehead, the mohelet strapped a lamp, which glowed
and shimmered like a halogen diadem. Then she withdrew from
her satchel a large flat board fitted with Velcro restraints. Calmly
she instructed me how to hold the baby utterly still upon the
board, lest his legs close and ruin the job. In the event, this took all
my strength, for he struggled mightily—not, it seemed, from any
pain, but from the insult of being butterflied. After saying a prayer,
the mohelet dipped the edge of a napkin into a glass of sweet red
wine, twisted it into the shape of a nipple and offered it as a mild
anesthetic—to the baby, that is, though I could have used it.
While he sucked hungrily, she leaned forward and completed the
cutting, at which point the baby pooped and promptly fell asleep.

"Our God and God of our mothers and fathers," the mohelet
chanted, having added the mothers, "sustain this child and let
him be known in the house of Israel as . . ."

Here the script offered only a blank, as life did, too. Andy had
wanted to name the child Juan, a nod to Janet and to the boy's
Mexican origins. Zev and Wolf, rejected for Erez, poked up their
feral heads again, only to be heartlessly quashed. "You're over-
compensating," I told Andy. I suggested honoring his mother with

her maiden name—Emanuel—instead; if this were the boy's middle name it would leave us free to choose something pretty and preferably nonanimal for the first. Andy agreed, in part because he liked my suggestion—Lucas, for light—and in part because he thought it sounded ever so slightly like a name that might still mean "wolf."

". . . let him be known in the house of Israel as Lucas Emanuel," the mohelet continued. "May he bring much joy to his parents in the months and years to come."

With that and a few more prayers, Lucas was a proper Jew, if not to the Orthodox at least to us. But what did that mean: a proper Jew? I was too weak to consider—and oddly famished. I knelt beside my mother's chair and burst out crying. She patted my head, as she always had; my father offered to get me some food from the deli spread Andy had ordered.

"Where do you think it went?" asked my mother a moment later. "You know: *it*. I saw her put it in a napkin, then suddenly it was gone."

"Oh my God," I said, scanning the room for Chauncey.

SIX

Unable to afford another family leave, and ineligible for another sabbatical until the year 2000, Andy could manage only a few sick days during the following weeks to stay at home with Lucas. He worried that even that much absence would annoy some of his colleagues, who had not been very supportive when he took time off for Erez, and were even less so now. "I understand you have a part-time job," one supervisor commented, referring to Andy's frequent tardiness during Lucas's first six weeks. This man and others must have felt that Andy had breached his contract, in a way: He had been embraced on the understanding that as a gay man he would be more, not less, available; he would take on extra projects and stay late when crises involving kids arose after school. Now he was insisting on taking care of his own kids—what did he think he was, a woman?

Luckily, Lucas was relatively easy to care for. He sucked at his bottle easily, slept soundly for longer and longer cycles, and though he had a bloodcurdling cry it was easily assuaged. He didn't much care for his bath at first, but everything else in his world seemed tolerable. He became more alert. He learned to smile. Still, as any parent of a second child quickly learns—no matter how easygoing that second child is—the work is not twice but several times harder than the work involved in caring for one. It isn't like cooking: You do not simply double the recipe. You make entirely separate meals. And two babies in a bath might as well be twenty.

Is that why second children are so poorly documented? My parents faithfully kept a baby book for my older brother's first three years: locks of hair, logs of gifts, notations about diet and activities and words. There is no such book for me, nor even many pictures. Andy, too, barely exists in his family archive: The job was too taxing and the novelty had worn off. I had always resented this inequity, and swore not to perpetuate it; until I met Andy, I had pretty much succeeded. But it has been one of the many insults to my perfectionism that I managed to keep the second son's baby book no better than my parents did. Though I remember major milestones and random splinters of daily life, much of Lucas's first year is therefore a blank. My journal is no help, it having given out around this time; my calendar lists our travels but none of our travails.

Perhaps this is one way (there turn out to be several) in which an adopting parent is luckier than others: What he might otherwise forget in his exhaustion, the law forces him to remember. Aside from the two court-mandated "postplacement" evaluations, performed by a social worker in February and August, Andy himself was required to provide the agency with a narrative of Lucas's progress at one, three, and five months of age. Taken together, the reports provide at least as complete a picture as my brother's fill-in-the-blank baby books—complete except for me, of course, necessarily elided as I am from Andy's poignant descriptions.

One month: "Lucas weighs nine pounds. . . . When he first came home, he seemed not to cry; I was a little worried because I remember Erez crying a lot. Now, Luke's caught on, and cries whenever he wants something. I feel better—and recently he's begun to have tears. . . . He sometimes coos at people who speak to him. He also watches his brother intently, and reaches for it when Erez hands him a toy. Life is pretty busy with two kids, but I feel we're doing very well."

Three months: "Lucas weighs fourteen pounds, two ounces. . . . He's never had diaper rash and is getting along without a pacifier. . . . We spend time out and about, with Luke in a Snugli, facing outward. He watches the world with interest, takes bottles in that position, and sometimes chews on my finger while we walk down the street or shop for groceries. . . . To date, we've encountered no real problems, and things seem to be going very well."

Five months: "Lucas weighs nineteen pounds, one ounce. . . . He smiles all the time, vocalizes to himself, and laughs outright when you amuse him with gestures and sounds. Even his brother can now make him laugh. . . . He looks very, very healthy, especially since he was such a skinny little peanut when he came here. Now he looks like the littlest football player. . . . He has a tooth (bottom, front) and another one on the way. . . . Everything seems to be going very well."

Lucas (often called Luke or Lukie) was basically a placid baby; when he teethed we hardly knew it. He didn't get frightened, wasn't moody, liked people but was perfectly happy to entertain himself for long periods of time with just a few toys. The outlines of his personality were all there the day he arrived, but now life was coloring them in—just as it was completing the painting of his physical being, so sketchy once in its prematurity. His Mohawk turned into a shiny, jet-black Beatles shag; his face opened up to the world like a pale magnolia. His eyes became merry. Despite Andy's characteristic hedge (things *seem* to go well, but one never knows for sure), he felt he had won the lottery—again. I, too, felt I had won a lottery, and not one for which I had even bought a ticket.

SEVEN

Lottery winners are famously undone by their fortune, and in Least Hampton that summer it was sometimes all we could do to keep afloat on our happiness. Wanting to be together as much as possible, we spent five days a week there, which wasn't hard for Andy, since he was on vacation. For me, the commute between my familiar life of silent work and my still-new (always new) family circus was bumpier than ever, in part because it was so literal. Monday nights after dinner and baths we packed up the car with pajamified kids and drove from the country to the city, where for the next forty-eight hours I kept to a madly condensed schedule of meetings, interviews, and feeble attempts at writing. Wednesday nights we packed up again and headed back out. Not that the ride itself was unpleasant: We avoided the heavy weekend traffic and the kids fell asleep at once, calm and happy. It was a happy time for the adults as well: two hours to talk uninterrupted or listen to children snoring mildly or just hold hands as the pink light failed.

Come Thursday morning in Least Hampton, the work began; though I was still doing less of it than Andy, it was grueling enough to put my "real" work in perspective. That real work, however all-consuming and vague, at least had beginnings and ends and familiar signposts in between: I began a project, it was eventually due, a revision was requested, the result appeared. *Rinse and repeat.* Working with children was utterly different. All tasks were simultaneous and never-ending; it was like swimming far out in an ocean. Daily patterns—not to be trusted!—gave way to long-term mystery. You could read in books what should happen when a child turned two (as Erez now had) or when to expect an infant to walk (not until around his first birthday), but books were of little use in appreciating an actual, individual child. Nothing but your instinct, which was often faulty, told you how to finesse disappointment or how much dessert to allow or when to lay down the law and when to relent. I constantly made the most obvious and the most subtle mistakes, and in so doing I made myself miserable.

Perfectionism, which in my work had proved a useful trait (if annoying to colleagues), turned out to be a boondoggle with children. It served me well only when a combination of organizational skill and brute perseverance could make a difference: teaching the kids to clean up their toys, getting them into happy sleep patterns. We had easily trained Lucas to Erez's schedule be-

fore he was even three months old; he went down at seven-thirty
and stayed that way for eleven hours. But the territory of childhood is mostly irrational, not susceptible to legislation; problems
are too interwoven with pleasures to extricate cleanly. Confounding my dire predictions, for instance, Erez turned out to be a loving older brother to Lucas. Too loving, sometimes: We would
awaken many nights that summer to a loud thud and then a
scream; rushing into their room we'd find Luke crying in shock
and hot outrage, Erez lying atop him, asleep. Apparently Erez
had climbed out of bed, scaled Luke's crib, and plopped himself
over. What should we do about this frequent and exhausting dis-
play of affection? We just put Erez back in his bed and comforted
Luke for a minute or two, which didn't really address the problem
and left me wide awake.

But my exhaustion was more moral than physical. If I resigned
myself to the boys' voracious appetites—for love, for time, for entertainment—I would disappear into parenthood; if I recused myself too successfully, I would be no parent at all. The middle
ground was incoherent, a place I couldn't live for long. Where
should I go? Having answered the door when children knocked,
I could not close it now without damage: It had swelled upon
opening and never fit into its frame again. But an open door is no
guarantee of a comfortable room. Maybe there was a reason, all
those years, I had kept the door shut, with only a frosted pane to
look through.

Was it just twelve months ago that I had seen myself in the
same boat as those single career women who wondered how they
would ever find a suitable man, let alone a sustainable child?
Now I was more like those late-to-motherhood career-track
women so much in the news, who rushed back to work soon after
delivery, the milk fairly dripping from their breasts, torn by their
conflicting desires to be perfect parents, endlessly available, while
remaining meaningful adults on their own terms. I was like them
and yet I was, to my shock, as much like their lucky, working husbands: letting the spouse bear the brunt of the conflict, while
hoping a toy every now and then, and a kiss at bedtime, would
keep them viable. Well, I did far more than that, of course, but in

relation to Andy's supernatural energy for mothering his kids—
and in relation to my own impossible standards—I was virtually
Darrin Stevens.

EIGHT

In my previous life, if a deadline ran late, if I got home at midnight without having eaten, I could call it a diet and go to bed
hungry. As a parent, you learn you cannot skip *Sesame Street*, let
alone a meal, without repercussions. In the precincts of Dreft and
Kwell, there are no excuses and there's no forgiveness; no emergency matters, other than the child's.

When you try to forget this, you pay in the end, one way or another. One day late that summer, enjoying the unusual luxury of
having hired a baby-sitter for the whole afternoon, Andy and I
took a few hours off. We drove to a quiet beach, quieter that day
than usual because the air was unseasonally cool and the ocean
was loud and dramatic. We picnicked on delicious, rich sandwiches and tiramisù from a fancy takeout. We had been to this
beach many times before, kids in tow, and were always the subject
of obvious speculation. Today no one paid attention to us as we
napped on a blanket, holding hands, unafraid beneath the low
sun. Oh, we were happy! And so were the kids when we returned;
they had delighted in tiring the tireless baby-sitter and did not
seem to resent us for the brief abandonment.

But soon after we put them to bed, Andy started complaining,
a little, of sharp subcostal pains. He showed me where, and I
flinched with concern, because seven years earlier I had had similar symptoms that resulted in emergency gallbladder surgery. Of
course, my pains had been monumental, I could hardly speak,
while Andy said his were mildly unpleasant. On the other hand,
Andy was in general a stoic, for himself and especially for others:
He did not believe in your headache and did not indulge his own.
So when, hours later, he started to moan, I knew something must
be very wrong. We called the emergency room at the hospital,
seeking advice; what advice could they give but "Come right

away"? I remained calm externally but began to feel frantic. What should we do? We could not, of course, leave the boys home alone, and though neighbors would later tell us we should have asked them for help, we did not at the time feel we knew them well enough to call so long past midnight. In the end, Andy drove himself to the hospital, squirming and stretching and cradling his side, and I had no choice but to let him. Such disloyalty to a spouse, inconceivable in my previous life, turned out to be mandatory now.

It *was* his gallbladder—an attack brought on by the rich food he'd eaten. The pain resolved itself by morning, and he drove himself home. He would need surgery at some point, he told me, but right now all he needed was sleep. He climbed into bed a few minutes before the kids, full of energy and optimism, woke up.

"Boys, we have to be very quiet today," I told them. "Daddy had a tummyache and he needs to stay in bed for a while. But we'll have fun by ourselves, okay?" They looked at me doubtfully.

At first I dreaded taking over the full day's burden of child care while Andy slept off his adventure. My eyes were already hard-boiled before breakfast was over. But gradually I found myself relaxing. If you resigned yourself to it—as the emergency had forced me to do—the eddying currents of hard play and quiet exploring, of food and diaper, even of wailing and comforting, could be enjoyable. Without the noise of your other life (or the need to earn money to support this one), you could discern a rhythm in what otherwise seemed chaos. It was a faint, complex rhythm to be sure, but catchy. I did not think about my laptop computer, sleeping shut near Andy in the bedroom, even once that day.

Pleasant as it was, this outing into the land of unambivalent parenting was, I knew, temporary. When the emergency was over I would have to get back to work, for money and for myself. I was grateful this was the kind of emergency that *would* be over, in just a few hours. But what if it hadn't been? What if Andy had gone to the hospital and never come back? Or come back incapacitated? How would I manage to run the family, while running myself, without him?

And then too: Would I be allowed to? I had no legal relationship to Andy, let alone to Erez and Luke. Wills naming unmarried partners as guardians for children were often invalidated by the courts—and Andy did not even have a will. Parenting was supposed to insure you against the disasters of life by providing a death benefit in the form of descendants. But it also exposed you to the possibility of disasters you might not otherwise have faced. Perhaps I was especially aware of this because of the friends who came to visit that day. Myron and Jerry were two men I'd introduced years before; recently they had broken new legal ground by becoming the first gay couple in the country to adopt a baby *as a couple*: openly and together. Little Ethan was Lucas's age, blond and pink and marble-eyed. *He* had two parents.

By the time Andy arose that afternoon, sore and relieved, I was ready to sleep but unable to. Not just because of the questions provoked by our little emergency, but because of something much simpler: the heat. Andy did not have air-conditioning—did not "believe" in it; sometimes I touched the closed bedroom door and worried that the house was actually on fire. As I often did when I felt this way, I sought out the refuge of the damp, quiet basement and the anesthetic pleasure of doing the children's laundry.

NINE

In the time it takes me to fold a tiny waffle-weave onesie—and with approximately the same intricate movement of the hands—I could produce an entire colony of origami macaques. Instead, all I make is a neat bundle of piqué: a perfect baby without the baby. Even so, the seams do not align at the shoulders, and the whole fabric contraption comes apart as I lift it from the laundry table. Andy typically finesses this problem by throwing all such incorrigible apparel into a drawer, helter-skelter, direct from the dryer. Why should an eight-month-old care if his romper wrinkles? I, on the other hand, have daydreamed of applying the tools of microsurgery to the riddle of underwear that has the approximate dimensions and tensility of a pancake.

I did not expect to spend my peak years wading waist-deep in laundry, all of it filthy, all of it cute. *(Look, smeared on Elmo, a curd of vomit!)* Oh, I had shopped for the odd christening gift, of course: a knit jester's cap, a pair of doll shoes. But no one could have told me, or the rest of my generation, that we would one day, childless or childful, end up cruising the aisles of Baby Gap like Donna Reed on Prozac. We recognize each other stalking the wee sweaters, arms zombily outstretched toward the bright merchandise. We are proud and yet a little embarrassed to be seen: Proud because we have, for the first time, something we profoundly care about that isn't attached to our body. Embarrassed because the experience is as private as pornography. Indeed, the enterprise is fullest when there is no actual child in tow to distract you from drinking in the *essence* of childhood. "Oh!" you murmur, hand to heart, as the clamshell smile of demented Gaplove develops on your face. "How adorable—and how superbly folded!"

We were not supposed to care about such things, yet some people now require twelve-step programs to get this particular monkey, in its stretch-knit leggings, off their back. (Step Three: God grant me the serenity to accept what I cannot exchange.) When I first became aware of the Gap it was just a place for teenaged would-be hipsters to buy jeans. The name itself seemed to refer to the newly popular *generation* gap, which I at thirteen was on the desirable side of. But the rules of the generation gap gradually changed; when the first boomers got close to the divide, the divide started moving, and hasn't stopped since. The traditional demarcation—parenthood—lost its iconic, bright-line status, as science and society opened the doors of procreation ever wider. We were all swept into the cute new world, and merchandisers brilliantly repositioned themselves to address this continuum of youthfulness. Which is why it will not come as a surprise to read, in the not too distant future, an advertisement celebrating the grand opening of Gap for Crones or Fetus Gap.

The successfully dressed child is offered to the world as a small monument to our own achievement, and a talisman of goodwill. Doesn't everyone on the street smile as we pass, first at the kids, then at us? The adorability we have squandered by aging still gleams brightly from babies in their outfits. *Wear this lovely chalk-*

striped flannel overall so that people will think we're good parents, honey. By the time we have Erez and Lucas beautifully wrapped for a Sunday-morning birthday party, it is all Andy and I can do to change from the underwear in which we slept into the jeans we wore Saturday night. Gap jeans, at that. As far as fashion goes, what we rarely grant ourselves we can regularly grant our children.

There is precious little in this world that lets us feel we can take care of them lavishly: Schools cannot be depended upon, camp and college are ruinously expensive, neighborhoods seem dangerous even when they aren't. The easy pleasure of ample time together, so common for the children of stay-at-home mothers only a generation ago, is largely a thing of the past, like cloth diapers. But even if we can no longer sustain that mid-century suburban vision of easy, unending plenty, we can still cocoon a child in pajamas that evoke parallel visions of comfort and warmth — and not have to explain ourselves to the bank in the morning. While he sleeps, warm and aromatic as a fresh croissant, we can say to ourselves that we have given him at least one perfect thing, if only until the zipper sticks or his toe pokes a hole in the foot.

And we've been given something too, as I'm reminded in the laundry room. The stains of childhood are dark but not deep; they lift away quickly if treated in time. Here is a problem, for once, that is solvable, unlike the problem of why your child bites, or others bite him — and is that a tic starting? In the laundry room, every mess is unmakable, or if it isn't, we can just start over. *(Attention, shoppers: Flannel shirts size XXS now reduced to $4.99!)* We dress our children as lovingly as we do because we want to believe that we, too, are looked after. We want to believe that, harried and imperfect as we are, we can nevertheless be fresh and new, day after day: remade in optimism, safe in our fireproof pajamas, at least as long as the seams hold out.

TEN

Once upon a time, in the land of Dreft and Kwell, there lived a people who rode in silver spaceships and spoke a foreign language. No one was native to the land; all were immigrants. At first, each newcomer was overcome by the strangeness of the country. Oh, everything looked the same on the surface, but it was ruled by a race of giant babies whose tiniest internal doings shook the ground for miles.

The language of the people was not unlike English, and yet it was not English. For one thing, it had far more x's and z's. In the olden days when a greenhorn arrived, he was taught to speak it— though you couldn't really call it teaching—by a cruel and largely random process of total immersion. Now there was night school. In any case, after a short period of time, the greenhorn had to take a test to become a citizen; the test included language skills and critical thinking and was administered by a faculty of aged basset hounds based near Princeton, New Jersey. They kept the questions, which changed constantly, a secret, and the formula for the curve proprietary. In time, of course, samizdat study guides appeared on the black market, and these are excerpts from one of them. (When finished, add up all your correct answers and multiply by zero; this is your preparedness index.)

Pronounce and identify: amoxicillin, Bathinette, cephalosporin, doodyhead, erythromycin, Ferberization, Grover, Huggies, ipecac, jaundice, Kimberly (the Power Ranger, even though you don't let them watch), lanugo, mohelet, nystatin, otitis media, projectile vomit, quality time, rubella, sulfamethoxazole, Thomas the Tank Engine (and innumerable friends), Umbro, varicella, Wet Ones, xylophone (the x word of last resort in every primer), Yodels (a/k/a Ho-Hos), Zithromax.

Explain the following proverbs: A waterproof mattress pad makes a lumpy bed. Neither a sleeper nor a waker be. Home is where the toy is.

Analogous relationships: "Food" is to "floor" as "crayon" is to ____? (Wall.) "Toast" is to "guns" as "sticks" is to ____? (Guns.) "Nice crystal" is to "your life" as "Elvis" is to ____? (The building.)

Logic: If there are two toy trains and two little boys, how many trains will each boy get? (None.) The local public school isn't very good but private school is too expensive. What should you do? (Move.) If a child was conceived by Mexican Catholics but raised by New York Jews, whom will he sound like when he starts to talk? (Cookie Monster.)

Match each of the stories above with the appropriate title below: "Roach Spray Is Never a Lotion, Honey," "No! Don't Jump on Daddy There," "Your Penis Is Fun: But Not in Public," "Ghosts Are Only Make-Believe," "Because the Legos Were Too Small."

Correct the error in each term below: Percules (the Disney hero), sukermarpet, the Statue of Lickety, hangurber, bacooter (laptop or otherwise), Katie's (the Underworld; see Percules).

Math and Science: How many toys will fit in a toilet? Who can fold this; can you? How does a plunger work? With what force will a body falling from the height of a coffee table—get off that!— strike the floor? Can a tiny person scream louder than a big person? What is the composition of a baby's breath?

Multiple choice: What hurts? Did you have a bad dream? Do you want some water? Do you want me to stay with you for a minute? I told you you'd hurt yourself. That's okay. I love you, sweetheart. Talk in words, please. Ouch –don't pull my nose like that. Here comes a kitty! Here comes a mouse! Again with "The Itsy-Bitsy Spider"? Are you asleep?

Short essay questions: How would you comfort a child who was afraid of a woman walking down the street? Of a stuffed turtle? Of an empty chair? Of Edvard Munch? Give specific examples McDonald's: anteroom to Hell? Discuss. How would you administer eyedrops to a child who won't open his eyes? Oh, really? You try it. Are Brussels sprouts worth a scene? Is anything? What is that wet stuff? What is that green stuff?

ELEVEN

Erez's first crush was on Mercedes. He had encountered her on a few occasions since our walk on the beach a year before and had gabbled merrily in her presence—though neither more nor less than he would for any other interesting visitor to his realm. But on a fine summer evening when he was two, he fell in love, and he has never recovered.

Six friends had come for dinner; they sat on the porch with us, eating ice cream as the evening hovered. Luke had drifted off already, and Erez was winding down. "Time for books and bedtime, sweetie," I suggested, picking him up. He started to protest, mildly.

"May I do it?" Mercedes asked. She was still hoping to adopt a baby—and to find the baby she had once given up; the childlust in her was rising.

They disappeared into the house. I expected mayhem; Mercedes did not know Erez's patterns, how to divert the mad discharge of energy that sometimes sent him speeding in the wrong direction, away from instead of toward sleep. After a while, though, I realized that I heard no human whoops and hollers, just the noise of our party: sighs and gossip and ice cream spoons. What had she done to him?

They were not even in the bedroom, I discovered. They were on the sofa in the living room, he with his head in her lap, she leaning over his face. They were not speaking, or not very much. Erez just stared and stared, occasionally reaching up to touch her admittedly voluptuous hair. He smiled moonily, as did she. This went on for a good half-hour, until he was all but asleep.

For months afterward, he said he dreamed of her. Often in these dreams she would arrive at the house in Least Hampton by train, sometimes with—oh, joy!—an elephant. Occasionally, she just "standed" in his bedroom, smiling. A woman in the street with long dark hair, it was always hoped, would turn out to be she.

But the next time he saw Mercedes in reality, he could not look. He hid his eyes with the backs of his hands. He quivered and shook when she tried to touch him, or even just speak. "No!" he quavered. Then when she went silent, or started to back away, he splayed his fingers and peered between them. If she left the room he took down his hands. "Where Mercedes? Where she go?" Later it took only the mention of her name to make him blush. Lesser men have done as much.

Some psychologists believe that an early love imprint like the one Erez evidently felt marks a person's soul forever. Some believe that the soul is marked already, that the love object is significant only to the extent it matches a preexisting image. Whatever the case, Erez seemed to know that something wonderful and vivid had happened, something entirely his own. It was the beginning of his romantic persona. That this persona is evidently heterosexual is something we will have to make peace with. We tried our best: We played him Judy Garland records and showed him tapes of *West Side Story*. We were even affectionate in his presence. But the proselytization didn't take. The heart knows what it wants long before the body, and his wanted her.

Later it wanted Lourdes Lopez, a dancer he first saw on *Sesame Street*. She was the second in the chain of women he came to call "ballerinas." They didn't actually have to dance; what defined them was their height, their long dark hair (sometimes knotted on top of their heads), their large, still eyes, their self-possession. "Who that ballerina?" he'd ask, reverently, of a tall, thin woman on the street. Soon his whole female cosmology became clear. Women who weren't ballerinas were either "baby-sitters"—playful teenagers, that is—or else, alas, "grandmas": everyone else. When later he asked to take ballet (not just dance class, but the real thing) it was not, we soon realized, because he wanted to do pliés. He wanted to watch the girls in their tights, their backs so straight, their hair piled up. Still, he was so awed by the spectacle he could hardly do so without hiding behind a pole.

Well, I had a crush on my kindergarten teacher and it didn't make me straight. Nothing would have—as, I suspect, nothing will divert Erez from his sexual identity, whatever it is. Certainly not Andy and I; truth be told, we are relieved by and proud of his interest in girls. Not just because we thus disprove the right-wing dogma that says gay parents make gay children (as if this would be something shameful). And not just because it's easier to be straight; though with all the explaining he'll have to do about his family, perhaps he'll be grateful to be as mainstream as possible within the confines of his heart. No, we are proud of Erez's interest in girls because it proves that he is not embarrassed to be exactly who he is, even in a home that does not model the specific kind of passion he feels. Which is more than can be said for the millions of kids, both gay and straight, who grow up in homes that model no passion at all.

TWELVE

That summer, my parents finally moved from the arresting but
difficult house I grew up in. They were thinking about their old
age, among other things: how not to end up as a burden on their
children, a burden on each other. They therefore looked for a
place that one of them could manage alone, if need be: a place
on one floor, a place with wide halls, a place without a driveway
to shovel. They did not like to imagine what events might someday make all this necessary, and yet, because they acted before it
became an emergency (they were still in their sixties), they could
make the change optimistically: a vigorous step up, not a grim de
cline. The new place they found, ten minutes away, was suitably
glamorous, at once obliterating all nostalgia for their forty-two
years on Greentree Lane. It was a beautiful move, and just in
time: Soon after the last box was empty and the stickers were
peeled from the last new appliance, my mother was diagnosed
with colon cancer.

Her first surgery, that September—there would be four over
the next two years, plus six months of chemotherapy—took place
on the same day and at the same time as Andy's long-planned
gallbladder removal. It is perhaps the most salient indicator of my
new life status that I did not go to Philadelphia. As I had not been
able to attend to Andy when he rushed himself to the hospital
that summer, I could not attend to my mother now, and for the
same reason: Erez and Lucas. "Don't worry about me," my
mother rasped through a druggy haze as she lay recovering from
her ordeal. "I'm in good hands, and they need you there."

This was not a cartoon of Jewish self-abnegation but a gracious
acceptance of new realities. My mother was letting me choose,
without guilt, to be where my future evidently lay. As I hung up
the phone and dashed back to Andy, still asleep from his ordeal, I
could not help but feel the weight, the almost physical sadness of
adulthood, at least for a child with loving parents: You cannot
face two ways at once.

Let alone three ways. Luckily, Erez was by then going to preschool several mornings a week, two doors from Andy's house. Eliane took care of him when he returned, and took care of Lucas all day. As I had learned so often already, there was nothing too difficult about keeping kids going as long as you had plenty of help and totally halted the rest of your life. "We'll have special fun alone together," I told the boys, over and over, wondering how long I could let my work slide. When I had my gallbladder removed, I was out of commission for several weeks. I could barely care for myself, let alone children. But the advent of laparoscopic surgery had revolutionized the whole procedure; Andy was discharged in two days and was able to celebrate with a French bistro lunch. Erez examined the boo-boos minutely: four short lines, like inchworms.

I could never look at my mother's scars; by the time the doctors considered her cured, her belly (she told me) resembled a railroad yard. All of us with our marks upon us! And yet the more painful marks are the ones I imagine on Erez and Luke someday in the future, if one of them stumbles with a pencil in his pocket or plays near a lit barbecue. How does a parent survive a child's emergency? Of course, we are especially vigilant about sharp objects and open flames; even so, there are a thousand dangers we are not sensitized to and therefore barely notice. Against most of them even around-the-clock surveillance would prove useless anyway; who can protect against what grows, or does not grow well, within us? Erez, when he was ten months old, underwent surgery to repair a congenital hernia. I'm not sure how I could have borne that, but it was before I knew him, and the scar can no longer be seen. His body, like Luke's, remains perfect all over: unseamed, unstained, unabused by life.

Though I hope never to see that perfection dismantled, I know it will be, if only by adolescence. This is one reason becoming a parent is so fearful: You volunteer to be robbed. On the other hand, it is my perversity (is it only mine?) that the awareness of danger is what gives safety its glow, as salt enhances sweet. Love, forged by hand, is annealed in the fire of loss. I am never so ferociously supportive of Andy as when he seems to be under attack.

Which does not mean I am very effective. When a nurse questioned my presence in his room one morning—"Friends aren't supposed to be here yet"—I idiotically snarled: "I am *not* his friend!" She shrugged and backed off as I dug through my briefcase for his health-care proxy: then, as now, the only legal document connecting us. Even so, it is not always enough. During his subsequent colonoscopy, I was not permitted to sit with Andy in the procedure room as he awoke from sedation, even though every other waiting spouse did, nor was I briefed (as they were) by the doctor, despite our having made clear beforehand that I was Andy's partner. Or perhaps because of it.

If my relationship to Andy could be so easily passed over, how much more easily could my relationship to Erez and Luke? Stories of children removed from even biological parents—parents who had been outed by their exes—were constantly in the news. What would the law make of me? Not much. At least Andy had written a will, in anticipation of his cholecystectomy, but it named his brother as the boys' guardian if he should die while under the knife. This was a mutual decision of ours, an intermediate step. In any case, we could hardly legalize my role before we had legalized Andy's.

THIRTEEN

Though he has been through this before, Andy cannot get himself calm. He yanks his tie in and out of alignment, mops his forehead with a ragged handkerchief; it's now January, but it's hot down here and we've just had Mexican food for lunch. He hands Lucas to me so he can shuffle fruitlessly once again through his date book, which offers the fact of the appointment—FINALIZATION 1:30 P.M.—but no instructions as to where. Lucas, having started walking on his first birthday, a month ago, wants to climb the steps to the courthouse, so I let him down; he is already up the two stone flights and pawing at the massive doors by the time Andy gives up his search. "Never mind," Andy says. He remembers that the courtroom (the same one in which he finalized

Erez, a year and a half earlier) was on the sixth floor, and except for the fact that the building, when we enter it, has only four, he could be right.

A panicky call to the adoption agency leads us to their lawyer, a crisp woman with extremely dark and lacquered hair in the manner of early Lady Bird Johnson. She is waiting for us at the second-floor elevators—or waiting for Andy, really; by now he holds Luke, and I hover behind, once again an *éminence mauve*. As far as the law is concerned I don't exist, but lawyers are not the law. When Andy, making introductions, says to Lady Bird, "Maybe you remember finalizing my other son's adoption, he's almost three now," she gives me a quick once-over and dryly responds: "Oh, now, he looks older than *that*."

Lady Bird clacks down the hall in her stout black patent-leather pumps, informing us, rather too casually, that the agency has misplaced the relevant papers and that she needs to tend to another matter just now. "But don't y'all worry," she continues without looking back, "the whole thing is basically pro forma. Anyway, you'll be in good hands with Maggie." And now she hands us over to a different lawyer—this one, herself an adoptive mother, as casual and warm as Lady Bird is crowlike. Maggie introduces us to another client finalizing that day, who in turn shows us pictures of her *four* adopted children, some with "special needs" and some with needs that are presumably more ordinary. "This one's from Colombia, this one Ecuador . . ." After the tour she introduces us to the woman of unexplained provenance at her side; we raise eyebrows at each other, inconclusively.

Andy waits in the hallway, playing with Luke, while I sit in Courtroom 218 listening for our case to be called. Presiding at the front of the room is District Judge Edna Monroe; Her Honor has a blond flip, a pointy face, and sharp blue eyes behind frameless glasses. Pinned to the lapels of her robe are several dozen miniature gold charms: hearts, flowers, musical instruments, bees. But she is no pushover. However many years she has been handling family court cases, she is not sentimental beyond her wardrobe. As I enter, she is addressing a twelve-year-old girl without condescension: "Are you here willingly? Were you under any type of duress?" The girl looks down, confused, for she is wearing slacks. "Not dress, *duress*," says the judge, stretching the syllables. "Did anyone *make* you?" The girl nods uncertainly, yes then no.

The courtroom must have been handsome once but is now somehow both overpolished and undermaintained, like the pocky, silver-haired lawyers waiting their turns in the pews. The pews themselves, half filled with various clumps of hopeful or hateful families, are scratched with the markings of decades of children's bored feet. Despite the penitential furniture—and the dark paneling and the pageant of flags—this is not a place of awe; it's less like a church than like a church kitchen, with brown linoleum floors, buzzing overhead fluorescent fixtures, and frequent but totally ineffectual shushings. The families come and go at will. Some are toting cameras, some videos, some a dime-store picture of their child in lieu of the child himself; others, here not for happy events like adoptions but for inevitable events like divorces, have only grim, sarcastic smiles to show for themselves. The divorce cases, when called, are palindromic in their recrimination: *Zabloski v. Zabloski, Iming v. Iming, Ortega v. Ortega, McCloud v. McCloud*. After the gavel comes down on one of them, a lawyer leads a man and a woman back down the aisle away from the judge. "Well, that's done," mutters the new ex-wife, as if it were the first task she ever got her husband to complete on time.

The adoption cases are called according to a kinder if quainter legal formula: *In the Interest of Baby Boy, a Child*. When the bailiff utters this curious phrase, it takes some sorting out among lawyers and judge to determine which baby boy here is currently of interest. Eventually, it is Luke; Maggie directs me to fetch him and Andy from the hall and then to stay put in a pew at the back of the room until the judge indicates it's time to take pictures. I nod eagerly, trying not to think too much about how I've come these thousand miles to record a happiness not my own. But that isn't right, that's the law speaking; my happiness or lack thereof is not the court's to adjudicate and will take place elsewhere anyway. I'm a *special needs* parent. I may have thought that as a gay man I would never have children, I may even have convinced myself that I therefore did not want them, but here they were, want them or not. They came with Andy. Whatever the law said, they were now mine, too—and yet: As Luke enters the courtroom in Andy's arms, smiling his usual jolly smile and looking around at these interesting new surroundings, he sees and then reaches to me in my pew, and I feel I must wave him past.

FOURTEEN

Andy takes the oath, though I can't hear him; what I can see is that in order to raise his right hand he must shift Luke into his left. There then ensues a kind of litany, which I can only make out as mime, in which Maggie reads a list of questions to be answered by Andy and approved by the judge. Later Andy will tell me that the questions are like these: "Are you Andrew M—— of Brooklyn, New York?" "Have you been caring for this baby boy known as Lucas since January 18, 1996?" "Do you understand that the adoption that is about to be completed is irrevocable?" "Do you attest that you want it to be permanent, for the rest of your natural life?" "Do you understand that though you may disinherit your birth children, you may never disinherit your adoptive children?"

This last must be the question that elicits from Andy a look of surprise and a few blinked-back tears, for he does not remember from Erez's finalization how the state puts a higher responsibility on adopting parents than it does—or can—on biological parents. The reason is hard for me to fathom: It is not because adopted children are felt to be more precious, but because they are often felt to be less so. In short, the state does not want them tossed back in the lake. The procedure is therefore constructed to formalize a compact not of ownership but of attachment, and in this the law seems beautiful. And symmetrical, too: What are the divorces that precede and follow us but Zabloski detaching herself from Zabloski, Ortega from Ortega? If the room lacks intrinsic sacral gravity, the counterpoint of divorce and adoption provides it. Up at the altar they seem to feel it: Maggie tilting her head with each question, Andy nodding yes, the judge turning from one to another and starting the cycle again. Even without hearing the words, I find it a very moving dance.

Of course I have always been more comfortable watching others dance than getting onto the floor and doing the hustle myself. To all my twitching college friends, I was the forgiving uncle on the sidelines—forgiving, if dour. Even at twenty, as if I were sixty, I watched their marvelous gyrations (and now I don't just mean at a mixer) with a wholly unwarranted sense of regret. These were the dancers, the procreators; they would have lovers—already did—and, one day, lapfuls of gyrating children. Whereas I, I had lost so much already (though I couldn't say what) and had borne it so bravely; if I were to be a parent, it would only be to my own rue. Call me Mother Discourage, and yet I would never have believed, had you told me then, how much more there was to lose and, even stranger, how much to gain.

For the blinked-back tears I can just make out in Andy's eyes as the court records his affirmations are my tears by proxy. This is the joy of watching the person I love become more fully who he is—a father—but it is something else, too. Erez was already fourteen months old when I joined his life; I treasure him but was not a part of his conception. Lucas I chose. Perhaps not while in my right mind: Did I really think it would not be hard? Still, a year later, I had to admit it all turned out well. By the luck of the draw, Lucas was such a good, happy baby, beautiful and self-sufficient, a pleasure to hold and behold. He was something more, too. I had been so concerned about what his arrival would do to Erez that I had neglected to consider what it might do *for* him: open him up to a kind of love that is not dependent, not looking upward, but next to him and forever. He does not remember, does not want to remember, a time when he was alone in his room, and only rarely do I think he still wishes his brother were an umbrella.

Many tears have rained down on Luke since that wet night Andy first showed him to me near the TWA ticket counter at Newark Airport. I gave him his name, in honor of light, and held him down as the mohelet taught him a lesson he will never forget, or remember. She taught me a lesson, too: There are pains more real than adolescent rue, and the realer they are, the more lightly they hover. *To be real!*—the phrase from an old gay disco tune haunts my parenthood. A child makes you real, if you meet him halfway: if you come to him when he comes to you. Which isn't to say there aren't other methods of inhabiting one's outlines. But as Andy keeps answering yes, yes, yes, I finally realize that this is my method. Finalizing Luke means finalizing me. Becoming a parent—the pun can't be helped—means becoming apparent. Not to the law; the law can never make you real, though it can make the process easier or harder. Apparent to myself, I mean.

FIFTEEN

Three minutes after it began, the hearing is over; the judge claps her hands together and says, loudly enough to be heard where I sit, "Okay now, lemme have him." Luke is duly transferred into her arms; she has clearly done this hundreds of times and knows how to commandeer an infant. Luke obliges with a giggle and a leer. Only now does Maggie motion for me to approach, which I do, content in the role of cameraman. "Smile," I say, my only line, as the judge instructs me from long experience which angles work best in the harsh overhead light. Even so, only one photo eventually develops, and neither I nor Andy is in it: just a jolly baby and a woman with gold charms.

"I want to see this one again," she drawls.

"We'd like him to come back," Andy says, leaving that "we" to hang in the air. "Maybe we'll send him back for college."

"But not for law school. We don't need any more lawyers here." The lawyers in the gallery laugh obligingly if bitterly, and another case is called.

We hasten from the courtroom and stand vibrating in the hall-way. Luke needs his diaper changed, but we have forgotten how to move. The only thing I can think to do is to keep playing my supporting role: I ask Maggie to take a picture of the three of us before the moment passes. "I guess there's no danger now," I venture to add as I hand her the camera.

"There was no danger before, either," she replies.

And indeed Edna Monroe, tough old bird, knew the score. *Everybody* knew the score. The agency, the social workers, the lawyers, the clerk, the studiously nonjudgmental reservationist at the motel. They need only have looked at us—and not cared. No lie was spoken. Everything proceeded pro forma, as Lady Bird predicted it would; but how could a gay man find it less than profound to become a parent *according to form?* If the system required of us a little discretion in return, of whom does it not? In our hearts we are enough indiscreet to cherish the child discretion gave us. That certain politicians and preachers may not be so kindly disposed to our happiness is moot for the moment. It can't be ignored—which is why I've changed the name of almost everyone in this book, except ourselves. But it can't be allowed to be decisive, either. As far as adoption goes, process finally is nothing; we're all de facto in our homes. If the law is a ass, as Dickens wrote, it is sometimes a nice one.

Maggie knows this. She retrieves some papers from her bag and pushes them toward us. "These are the forms from which the new birth certificate will be produced, so I think it's important that you look them over carefully and make sure everything's spelled properly, because the clerks are not necessarily the most careful spellers. A lot of lawyers don't do this," she adds pointedly, "but I think it's important that you look these papers over carefully and make certain you've seen that everything's right." She hands the buff-colored forms to me first. "Look carefully," she repeats.

I immediately see why she's placed so much emphasis on our studying these papers. It's not the spelling, which is fairly straightforward. It's that they list quite plainly the names of the birth parents—names we are not supposed to know, names we could never learn later. I immediately feel my temples dampen as I look at the neatly typed information, which includes, I now notice, not just their names but their city of origin. I hand the bundle to Andy and say, "Look at this. Carefully." And as casually as I can, I take out my notebook.

Unfortunately, my hands are shaky; the next day I am unable to make out what I wrote. Elaborate graphological experiments later suggest several viable candidates for the birth mother's name—

Delores Bel Reese, Belinda Rodríguez, Olivia Beria, Doris del
Rio—and that she's from somewhere in Mexico that begins with
a "Q." No matter how I combine and recombine the letters, she
sounds like an aquatic movie star, or a kerchiefed worker in a
maquiladora, when in fact we had learned at the time of the
placement that she is a young woman with a college degree in—
can it be?—tourism. I content myself not to know what I am not
supposed to know anyway, but one day months later, I suddenly
do crack the code of my scrawl and decipher the names, and the
hometown, too. A quick look at my atlas shows that the tourism
student must have traveled some five hundred miles to cross the
border—not, like her clients, for a swanky vacation, but so her
child could be born in the United States and find a loving home
there.

SIXTEEN

Perhaps ours is not the kind of loving home she had in mind. She
did not, after all, indicate on her forms a preference for gay urban
Jews. On the other hand, she didn't exclude the possibility. This
is not a facetious distinction. Some women, in open adoptions,
actually choose a gay couple over other applicants. Perhaps they
think the gay couple will make better parents because they're
more fun or more cultured; or perhaps the woman had a gay
friend she loved, or is a lesbian herself, or is just a rebel. Still, I
imagine, she's the exception. If she weren't, adoption agencies
would be banging the drums for people like Andy instead of
drumming them out.

If Luke's birth mother had the power, would she take him from
us? I doubt it. Women especially, I have found, defer to their
child's attachments. One night as their foster child Alex lay dying
of AIDS in the hospital, Frank and Dante—the first gay couple
with children I knew—encountered a strung-out, emaciated
specter from the boy's first life: his birth mother. The three of
them sat silently in the intensive care unit while Alex's tiny body
began to shut down. Eventually, the woman spoke: "You guys

want some stuff?" She showed them a plastic bag of vials. "I gotta make a living, you know." The men were horrified, but even so asked if she'd like to hold Alex, and helped situate the boy in her arms. After a little while, though, he started reaching for Dante, and she knew what this meant. "You take him," she said. "You're his parent."

You do not have to be a miserable addict to understand that a child is better off with the people he loves. Lucas's love is unmistakable; to the extent he is partly the creation of his birth mother, is his love not hers as well? Mightn't she love us, too, then? At any rate, she loved him in the moment she let him go, as the document we've just been shown proves heartbreakingly.

Looking at it, Andy and I do not dare to look at each other. We feel, we both feel, that we have been handed something dangerous, fissionable; why else would it normally be locked in steel safes forever? And yet we are grateful to have seen the names. Somehow, instead of making us feel that we have been trumped by biology, it makes us feel that we have been handed the deck. This is not an entirely comfortable sensation, especially for me; shadowy as I am in the transaction, I am more sympathetic than Andy to the fate of the woman now to be erased from the record. I can almost feel her disappearing, becoming invisible just as he becomes visible, in a way *permitting* him to become visible. For the state enforces its legal fiction to the last degree; the three copies of the birth certificate that arrive by certified mail two months later are inexpertly doctored to render "father" where "mother" once had been, and Andy's name is typed there. As for the birth father, the court decree includes a heart-stopping paragraph entitled NO EXISTING PARENTAL RIGHTS—parse it how you will: "The Court finds that the child has no living parent, and no living alleged or probable father whose paternity has not been adjudicated, whose parental rights have not been terminated by final judicial decree."

We gasp at its brutality, but not every gain achieved in the world is accompanied by an equivalent loss. Adoption has given Lucas's birth parents, no less than Andy, something they apparently wanted dearly: in their case, the right not to have a child at this time. Perhaps it was a hard decision, motivated by unfortunate factors of religion or economics, but would the pregnant woman who hied herself five hundred miles to cross the border really have balked at the paragraph entitled ADOPTION GRANTED?

> IT IS ORDERED AND DECREED that the above-described child the subject of this suit by Petitioner is GRANTED and that the parent-child relationship shall henceforth exist between the child and the Petitioner. IT IS FURTHER ORDERED AND DECREED that the child the subject of this suit shall henceforth have the legal name of LUCAS. . . .

We'll never know. Almost as an afterthought, the decree states that "all other papers and records, including the minutes of the Court, in this case are ordered sealed"—and with that swipe of legalese, Lucas's first birth disappears into the state's machinery. Back home in Brooklyn, Andy is elated; he clasps the manila envelope with a blush of pride, as if it contained a cum laude diploma. But I am ambivalent. Could not an instrument so arrogant, so unreal, abrogate me as easily as it did Delores?

However arrogant, however unreal, the gesture doesn't seem to have fazed the judge, who has been through this a million times and accepts without cavil the dirty business of joy. She has signed the document, just her first name and last initial, with loopy flair, it would seem almost girlishly.

SEVENTEEN

"Lose something every day," the poet Elizabeth Bishop recommended. "Then practice losing farther, losing faster." That same cold winter, two weeks before we finalized Luke, poor old Chauncey got finalized too. He had been breaking down for a while, barely wanting to go outside, peeing indiscriminately. Erez, who at almost three was beginning to use the toilet, found this part hysterical. But soon Chauncey just stopped eating, and Andy began to grieve. The dog had carried him from his old life into his new one and would not be around for the next transformation, whatever it might be. One night in Least Hampton—I was in Philadelphia, where my mother had just been released from the hospital after one of her operations—Andy held him for hours as he shivered, and the next day took him to die.

Chauncey was fifteen, though we only told Erez, who could count that high, that the dog was extremely old. ("Ten?" "No, older." "Twenty?" "Even more than that, in dog years.") How much should a child be asked to handle? Some would have us say the whole truth: "Everything that lives, passes; death is the end of everything; it can happen at any moment." Others would have us tell a small child only that Doggie went to a happy heaven—in which case, why was Andy crying? We decided to be frank if incomplete. Over the next days we mentioned repeatedly but without undue emphasis that Chauncey had died, which meant he was gone and would never come back; though this was very sad, we told the boys, we could always remember how much he loved us and how much we loved him. This seemed to satisfy Erez, at least in the moment; he looked interested but not worried, and quickly changed the subject. Still, at bedtime, he would sometimes try again: "Chauncey come home tomorrow?"

"No, sweetie," we repeated, "Chauncey has died. He will never come back." We put a picture on the refrigerator. Luckily, Erez did not ask where the body had gone, and we did not offer the information that it had been turned into ashes, which were now in a jar on a shelf in the garage. Luke did not ask about anything, of course; his entire vocabulary at that time consisted of "datun" (daddy), "banah" (banana), "bah" (bottle), "buh" (book), "hah" (hi), "guh" (got it!—a ball, that is), and "hod" (hot: my morning teacup). By the time he acquired a word for "dog," it applied only to dogs in books; would this mean he'd never remember Chauncey?

Would Erez? When he quite soon stopped asking about Chauncey's return, we were humbled by the speed at which he let go of a sadness, but pleased that we had managed to impart the difficult news with minimal upset and confusion. This was hubris, of course. Had we so quickly forgotten the lesson of the baby umbrella? It was impossible to know what went on in a child's head—he was barely sane by any adult standard, let alone coherent. Erez had not let go, of course, had not forgotten the difficult news; he was performing some mad experiment on it. A few weeks later, out of the blue, he shared with us the results of his thinking: "Chauncey dived," he said.

"Died, honey. Died."

"*Dived*," he insisted.

We laughed, and then we thought about it: Erez loved to swim but would not dive into a pool; adults dived; adults were old; Chauncey was old; Chauncey had dived. It made perfect sense. But did that mean Daddy and Jesse might disappear as Chauncey had? Is that why Erez had recently started asking us how old we were?

"Diving is when you go into a pool with your head first," we told him. "It's a fun part of swimming. Dying is totally different. But you don't have to worry about it now. Nobody's diving *or* dying."

Except that, a few weeks later, just shy of her ninety-ninth birthday, my grandmother dived, too. Never was a woman readier to take the plunge: She had been in the posture for years. And yet my family—especially my mother, who threw the first handful of dirt on the coffin—was not ready to have her go. She was our seawall against the flood of the future, our bulwark against mortality. We watched her sink into the earth, following her husband so many years gone, while torrents of rain engulfed us all, despite the canopy.

Not all, of course. We had left Erez and Lucas with Eliane for the day. They had been to cemeteries; in fact, they had several times visited the one where Andy's parents are buried. But it was one thing to show them the quiet place we sometimes visited to think about people we loved, like Grandma Janet. It was another thing to let them see a sealed box lowered into the ground. That shocking news would be absorbed soon enough; one of the things about becoming a parent closer to forty than twenty (and about being a gay parent, for that matter) is that death is likely to hover near your family more closely than it otherwise might. Erez and Luke, as I had seen, would learn to manage what they could manage and garble the rest; but what about me? Having children was supposed to provide you with a new bulwark against mortality, to replace the ones crashing down behind you; a child took you into the future. But a child also forced you to live your losses with extra intensity. I could not tread water as I had before on the fundamental questions. I had to dive.

EIGHTEEN

The landscape of a child's mind, however poetic, is terrifying—perhaps not to himself, but to an adult. You explore it at your own risk, all but blind; at best, you learn to interpret rocks and fossils (if you don't crack your head on them) that hint at the ancient formation of his world. Even then, you are as likely to recreate your own ancient world as his. That summer in Least Hampton a friend told us how she dreaded the inevitable day her daughter, whom she had adopted in China, would start longing for her birth mother and begin seething with resentment.

"But why inevitable?" I asked.

"How could a child *not* grieve her lost mother?" replied Emily. "Don't you think Erez and Luke will have some kind of hole in their hearts, wondering who their mother is?" She did not say "father." "Don't you think they'll resent you for it?"

"When the time comes for them to resent us," Andy said, "that will be as good a thing to resent us for as anything else."

"Opportunistic resentment," I allowed. "But I don't agree that it's inevitable or that there will be a hole in their hearts. Not if we don't encourage them to make the hole themselves, by teaching them that it must be there."

"But don't you think, whether we teach it or not, they know the loss, deep inside them?" Emily asked.

"No," I said. "I really don't. But I think *you* might."

Emily considered this; she was frank and undefensive. "You're right," she said. "My mother and father divorced when I was young. I lived with my father. I missed my mother all my life."

Her daughter, Lulu, was chasing Erez around the yard while

Lucas tried to keep up. The two older children—they were both three—had met at day camp and, in the way of determined kids everywhere, made quick friends of their parents. At first the "alternativity" of our families was a bond; later it was just a curiosity. Mostly what made us click was Emily herself, who had more energy alone than Andy and I put together on our very best day. She knew fun things to do with kids, things they actually enjoyed, whereas we generally tried to convince them that what needed doing (trekking to the dump, say) was entertainment. *(Look, boys, this is where corrosive stuff goes!)* Under Emily's tutelage, we broadened our horizons. One day we visited a petting zoo, where the kids spent an hour hugging stoned-looking animals; the girl in charge then uttered the sentence you least want to hear in such circumstances: "I hope nobody touched the cow."

"Why?" I asked warily.

"Oh, probably nothing. We think it has a fungus."

I wondered how this girl would decode our entourage if she set her mind to it: two haggard male adults with one sexy, whip-thin female; two pretty, tannish boys with an elegant Asian girl. A UNICEF delegation? She could never have guessed right, and yet she had probably seen many such inexplicable ménages tromp through her mangy corrals. Without even trying, we had uncarthed dozens of nontraditional families that summer, and not just nontraditional in the traditional way. Some were gay, some transracial, some single-parent, some adoptive, and some, like ours, almost all of the above.

And then there was Mercedes's. That July we all attended, at a church in Least Hampton, the christening of her new baby boy. Jake Javier, the priest pronounced him, or J.J. for short—the "Javier" at the request of the Portuguese-born birth mother. Mercedes was elated, and not just because the open adoption had been so successful. She was also happy with little J.J.'s godfather: a tall, handsome, quiet young man who looked a bit like Mercedes herself—with good reason. The previous winter she had located the boy placed for adoption twenty-one years earlier; after gaining his parents' approval, she met him over Christmas. He had known he was adopted, of course, but not that his birth mother had gone on to become a well-known actress; was it humbling to Mercedes that he was not familiar with her work? In any case, he and his friends quickly rented some of her movies to see what this biological mother was like—a terrifying notion. ("Give me the fucking ticket, dickhead!") But if her name had not rung a bell with him, *his* did with her. It was still Christopher: the name she had given him so long ago, though no one ever knew.

Now he was here, godfather to the son his birth mother had adopted. How's that for nontraditional? Though I always felt normal in my daily life, scenes like this—Erez handing Mercedes a gift, his eyes fast shut—reminded me that we were in fact living at ground zero for alternativity. Or were we? I was surprised to read, soon thereafter, of a momentous demographic shift. Fewer than half of American families, a report stated, now consist of a married man and woman, both of the same race, living in one home with their biological offspring. If this is true, and I hope it is, more of us are alternative than not, which really means we all are.

NINETEEN

Even the most alternative parent still has to do the laundry. That summer, while Erez attended camp each morning, Andy took Lucas errandizing so that I could, in theory, have three hours for work. Instead, I mostly ended up washing dishes, folding onesies, straightening toys, and making beds. By the time the house (and thus my head) was clear, I'd hear the boys come scampering home. In a way it was a comfort that child care was turning my brain to mush: It proved that I was responding to parenthood in pretty much the normal way. My lists of things to do grew so profuse that they had to be indexed with master lists. And still the tub remained uncaulked. You could be a perfectionist, you could have children, you could have a career; you could even choose two from the list. But not three.

If this was classically a woman's predicament—and most of the mothers I knew were in the same boat—it was also more and more a father's. Unavoidably, Andy and I were poster boys for the dissolution of rigid gender roles. Since we could not divide the household duties along traditional lines, we divided them according to preference and ability. Andy prepared the food, I did the laundry (stereotypically female jobs); he tended the yard, I made the repairs (stereotypically male). Of course, we often traded hats, and took on most roles interchangeably: bather, succorer, disciplinarian, chauffeur. Nevertheless, people wanted to categorize us according to existing templates; they asked which one of us was the mother and which the father, just as people used to ask me, about gay sex, which was the boy, which the girl.

As far as that went, we were both both. Is that what disturbed some people about us? That we couldn't be put into prelabeled boxes? For as much as neighbors and friends accepted us—delighted in us, even—we were all too often forced to listen to the disparagement of strangers. Even leaving aside the psychotic vitriol of dim editorialists and skinhead counterdemonstrators, there was the much more dangerous, because calm, opinionizing of buttoned-down flacks for conservative front groups. Especially in the months after a Hawaiian court opened the door to the possibility of gay marriage (a possibility that now seems remote), the radical right went into overdrive. A spokesman for the disingenuously named Family Research Council got plenty of airtime talking about a nonexistent "mountain of evidence" proving that "homosexuality is destructive to individuals, families and society and that homosexuality is a changeable condition." Gay adoption, the same spokesman said, represents "a deep threat to children's well-being." Would other families, he wondered, "want their children to stay over with Johnny and Bobby for the weekend? To be openly exposed to that kind of lifestyle, that kind of behavior? I think it could create great tension among a lot of American families."

Gay people who have children create an almost insoluble problem for the radical right, since the premise of its disapproval is thereby undermined. Before they became media savvy, antigay ministries condemned homosexuality simply on the basis of its innate immorality: The Bible says so. But this approach eventually turned out to be ineffective in a secular country—a country of people, moreover, who did not want their behavior judged by ancient laws that seemed to prohibit not only gay sex but most of what straight people did in bed. So the radicals changed their tactics. Understanding that the fear and hatred of homosexuals derives not so much from what they traditionally do (have sex with each other) as from what they don't (procreate), they trotted out a new campaign: *Dangerous to children! Proselytizers! Causes tension among Johnny and Bobby's classmates!*

At least this inane approach laid bare the right's hypocrisy. Andy and I were "married" (as much as we could be), faithful, raising children, teaching them to love: Wasn't that what the clergy wanted? But no, what they wanted was that we stop being gay, the one thing not even God, if you believed in him, had ever managed to do. If the deepest cause of homophobia is envy—the gay man is punished for his supposed (or at any rate potential) freedoms—there was more, not less, to envy now. We were free, but with our freedom we had chosen obligation. And so it was back to turpitude. "A deep threat to children's well-being": Would that be because we fed the boys three times a day or because we read them *Goodnight Moon?*

I do not by habit climb on soapboxes or nauseate myself sniffing the foul winds of democracy. When I was a single gay man I contented myself to take the poison in tiny doses, and became resistant to it. I gave money to groups that fought these battles and wrote my pieces and tried to live my personal life, as we all must, personally. But now that I am a father I do not feel so complacent. The hatred aimed at me hits my children, or will any day. That the hatred is for the most part cynical—a fund-raising ploy—does not make it less dangerous: The charlatan is as bad as the lunatic. Both gladly fabricate what evidence the real world fails to provide; they are not genuinely interested in the real world at all. Conservative "family research" may not be a delusion, but it is still a fraud; how could it not be? They do not know us.

TWENTY

Of course, we do not know them either. They exist only on television and behind our turned backs. In person, to our faces, people are almost always cordial—even more so now that we have two kids. Do they think we're more serious because we're "in deep"? Or do they just like the symmetry of two and two? "Let me guess which one is whose," a stranger once said. And every day someone asks, just as they used to ask if Andy and I were brothers, if Erez and Luke are twins. In fact, they look nothing alike and are obviously not the same age. But there is something powerfully radiant about their brotherhood. Yes, they are dressed by the same hands and eyes, and learn their expressions from the same faces. But it's more than that. By the luck of the draw they also fit, like puzzle pieces or ideal mates, and they keep on shaping each other into complementary forms. When Erez stopped climbing into Lucas's bed, Lucas started climbing into Erez's. When one is crotchety, the other is smooth. The accident that made them brothers was a head-on collision, and left them forever entwined.

Still, that fall, at three and a half, Erez would be ready to go off alone to preschool five mornings a week. We had visited several local programs earlier in the year and made application. I was still disturbed by the idea that a child barely out of diapers had to be "interviewed" by an admissions director: *What strengths do you think you could contribute to the Li'l Kids community?* But these programs could afford to be selective. They had dozens of applicants for each of the few openings not already filled by current students or their siblings. They had endowments. They had stationery and mission statements and handsomely printed brochures.

The professionalization of early childhood education has not come without disadvantages. Erez was examined by people whose training seemed to have taught them to equate personality with pathology. At one interview, when asked if he wanted to enter a room in which older kids were playing, he sensibly enough shook his head no. Instead he chose to explore a different room, a room with no kids but filled with toys. "What's this one?" he asked, and then examined it for a minute or two. "What's that one?" The interviewer later interpreted this behavior for us: Erez was easily distracted; his refusal to play with strangers indicated that he felt overwhelmed when presented with too much input;

his method of moving from one toy to another revealed a tendency toward perseveration. "Perhaps you should have him evaluated for attention deficit disorder," the woman suggested.

We tried not to be defensive, though we were aware of a tendency of our own: to feel as if, for the sake of gay parenting worldwide, we had better be perfect, and Erez, too. But this was absurd. Erez did not have attention deficit disorder; he was a three-year-old boy with a three-year-old's energy. Choosing the unpopulated room was merely practical: more toys for himself. And if he was shy, that was practical, too: a useful (and temporary) way of managing his large emotions.

Andy was perhaps *too* adept at managing large emotions: He was furious but said nothing. He felt that Erez had come under invidious scrutiny as an adoptee and as the son of an openly gay man. What I saw operating here (and at other preschools that examined him, too) was just the opposite: a prejudice against boyish boys. When I was a child, it was girlishness that was deemed suspicious; now the tables had turned. Schools wanted pupils who would be easy to control and would not challenge their established practice. I understood this: I, too, would have found it easier if Erez were (as I had been) ductile and grave. He simply wasn't. He was exuberant, moody, rambunctious, silly, clever, affectionate, joyful, bold. Whether this was merely being a boy, or being a nascent heterosexual, or the particular mischief of his own genes, he was himself and that's all there was to it. We could not take credit for his personality any more than we could take blame—and there was no blame to take. We adored who he was. So did everyone who met him without a clipboard in the way.

Still, we were demoralized. The fancy preschools may have been acting in bad faith, but the others we knew of were not in the neighborhood. I was dead set against shipping even an older child, let alone a toddler, to a school miles off; the sight each morning of kids collapsed over math books on the subway had always filled me with sadness. But what was our choice?

"Well, there is that other one," said Andy. "Just three blocks away."

"Oh, dear," I muttered. "I don't think so."

TWENTY-ONE

That preschool was housed in an Orthodox synagogue affiliated with the Hasidic Lubavitcher sect. The congregants called themselves *Modern* Orthodox, but they'd have to be very modern indeed to welcome the likes of us. In Israel, the Orthodox establishment was radically self-righteous; among other bigotries, they refused to recognize conversions performed by anyone but themselves. Even in America, most Orthodox did not think any better of homosexuality than did the Family Research Council. How would they ever accommodate Erez? On the other hand, the school did not require interviews or psychological evaluations and betrayed no prejudice against boys. If anything, boys were indulged; this was, after all, a patriarchal tradition. Married teachers, no matter how chic and casual otherwise, wore a modest wig—a *sheitel*—in public and (as we found out after several embarrassing attempts when we visited) were loath to shake our hands. Not because we were gay: just because we were men.

We sat on little chairs and watched a class of three-year-olds cut circles out of paper. Erez clung to us at first, though eyeing the rest of the room intently. The school's director—she was also the rabbi's wife, a young and pretty mother of four—did not mind that he was shy: "It's only natural," she said. She did not even mind that I was aggressive, engaging the salient issue at once. "Do you think you can make Erez feel comfortable here?" I asked. "Given your beliefs?"

"After you called," she said calmly, "I did some research. I talked to some rabbis. It's true that what you . . . do . . . is against our beliefs. But many of the parents of the kids in our school also do things that are against our beliefs. Some are unobservant: They don't keep Sabbath, they don't keep kosher. Some of the parents aren't even Jewish. It's not our job to judge people or change them. Our job is to teach. So, yes, I think we could make Erez feel comfortable."

Though this argument equated my love for Andy with someone else's taste for pork, it seemed fair enough. But it didn't really address the question of supporting Erez's reality. "What about if you were making, I don't know, Mother's Day cards?" I asked. "Have you given any thought to how you would handle that?"

"No. How would you *like* us to handle that?"

Andy and I looked at each other. "Well, we haven't given it any thought either," I admitted sheepishly. "We don't expect you to have answers that we don't have ourselves. But would you be willing to consult with us when issues like that came up, so we could figure out how best to handle them?"

"Of course," she said. "It will be a learning experience."

By now Erez had edged away from us and toward some toys near the ring of children. The room was bright and comfortable. Posters on the walls depicted themes both religious and patriotic, much as they had at my nursery school. Perhaps the portrait of the late Menachem Schneerson, whom Lubavitchers revere as the promised Messiah, was an unexpected touch in a world otherwise devoted to Barney. But at least Schneerson was smiling. Everyone was smiling. As we sat, two boys from an older class—one wearing a yarmulke and one evidently biracial—ran into the room with a challah they'd baked. They might have been bearing Schneerson himself, so great was the ensuing excitement.

Like the tiny chair I tried to perch on, a good school serves a child's needs first; adults have to shift for themselves. It wasn't necessary that I fit in, only that Erez might. Still, I had lived so long as the only designer of my fate that this was a strange and awkward position. I didn't even believe in God, let alone in a messiah. And yet, the other places we had toured all reeked of dour professionalism: welcome in a dentist's office, less so in a school. Erez, quite properly, had not liked them, no matter how fine their phonics curriculum. The highest aim of preschool—my mother had told me—would be fulfilled if Erez had a good time going, and of course she was right. Content, religious or otherwise, was irrelevant: His only job at three years old was to be as happy as possible.

Though we sent him there with trepidation, the school has been as good as its word. Handmade Hanukkah cards are addressed to Andy and me together; I am welcomed at conferences like any other parent. Yes, Erez comes home on Friday afternoons with Lubavitcher tracts in his lunchbox; Friday nights he waves his hands mystically over nonexistent Sabbath candles. And once, in the bath, he suddenly asked: "Can I have tzitzis like Mendy has?"—referring to the fringed prayer shawl that Orthodox men (and even some boys) wear beneath their shirts.

"No, sweetie. We don't do that here."

"Why not? Mendy does!"

"Yes, and that's great. But every family's different."

In truth, we have been delighted with all the *Yiddishkeit*. People often ask us how we will nurture Erez's (and, especially, Luke's) "Hispanic heritage"—heritage being a touchy subject in adoption circles these days. Especially for children like our friend Lulu: No matter how Emily raises her, the rest of the world (the white world, at least) will always see her as Chinese, and so she must be taught what that means. But Erez and Lucas do not have to shoulder quite the same burden. They can simply be what we are: Jews. We are their heritage. If later they want to learn Spanish, fine; first, they will learn a bit of Hebrew. But just a bit. We take a homeopathic approach to religion: A little prevents a lot. Children must learn to believe something about the most difficult human questions, even if only to unbelieve it later.

TWENTY-TWO

Letting a child into your life is like letting a monkey into your kitchen. He will gibber and grab, defecate anywhere, break every dish that isn't well hidden—and even some that are. The fine soufflé you constructed from scratch with so much care: Burst! Separated! The monkey is cute, though; when he someday leaves, you will look at your ruined life and not know how to build it again.

This, I thought in our first years together, would be my biggest problem: how to survive the kids' monkey antics. Not just the inevitable physical disorder but the primitive chaos of God and gob-

230 · Jesse Green

lins, icky cartoons, diapers, debt, unceasing laundry, and even the boisterous boyishness I had fled from in my youth. Now I was wedded to it. Even the best-behaved children (and Erez and Luke are quite well behaved) grow, like muscles, by breaking down. Within bounds you must let them fall on the sidewalk, fight over cookies, protest your power, mangle their toys. Of course it breaks you down, too, which is how I began to understand why Margaret Drabble had called her novel about motherhood *The Millstone*. ("It seemed so absurd, to have this small living extension of myself, so dangerous, so vulnerable, for whose injuries and crimes I alone had to suffer.") What would ten or twenty years of this constant grinding—however productive for them—do to me?

But then, in time, as Erez and Luke began testing limits in earnest, I worried instead about the opposite problem: What would ten or twenty years of me do to them? I have many good traits as a parent, it turns out: I'm clever at smoothing over transitions, at distraction and cajolery; I'm good at schedules and teaching and fun; I know how to make the boys understand that they have my attention and my love. But, to my shock, I've also discovered a painful fault in my parenting. At first I'd ignore it when I blew up at Erez for tearing a book, or when I was reduced to furious tears by Luke's refusal to share. I'd tell myself I was simply tired; but Andy was even more tired than I and rarely boiled over. Was I an angry person? I had thought of myself as someone who'd stilled all of his world's harsh weather and thus achieved a placid demeanor—but that was the problem exactly: It was a demeanor, and it was achieved. Now the demeanor seemed to be cracking, but what was I angry about? What did it have to do with the children? A subject, no doubt, for psychoanalysis, and yet I could not help but feel it had something to do with my own gay childhood: the circuitous back roads one had to take to avoid being beaten up by bullies, the innumerable main roads one never dared try.

Chekhov wrote (I paraphrase): If you want to understand true loneliness, get married. To which I would add: If you want to understand true childishness, become a parent. Approaching forty, I had nearly made my way back from the back roads onto the main, and found that my years of wandering had altered me in a way not visible until the wandering was all but over. This was the irony of Moses, permitted to see the Promised Land but not to inhabit it, after forty years in the wilderness. Of course this overstates my wrath; I yell no more than the average parent and rue it considerably more. But my perfectionism, designed as a kind of vaccine against anger, turns out to be worse than the disease itself. It leaves me standing at the threshold of my new life with an invitation I am too scared to accept. Am I truly fit to enter? And yet there is nowhere for me to go back to.

Nowhere to go back to. Is it surprising that my love and hope proved stronger than my fear? It surprised me, at least. Having spent every day of the summer *en famille*, I could not bear to spend the winter separate, and so, after eighteen years in that little apartment in the middle of everything, I moved to Brooklyn. Not into Andy's house, which was far too small for the three large souls already in it, let alone a finicky, work-at-home snob. Instead I found an apartment that possessed the one glorious thing I could never have in Manhattan: a view of Manhattan. (Erez stood on the deck and exclaimed: "The Statue of Lickety! What's she doing here?") Well, another glorious thing, of course: constant access to my family. They were just around the corner, a two-minute walk along an alley amazingly named Love Lane.

I know that people find this a peculiar solution to the problem of parenting: I am not trapped, not physically. But is the traditional family so successful that it cannot stand experimentation? If the question for many people of my generation has been how to become a parent while remaining in some ways recognizable as the adult they chose to be in the first place, this is my provisional answer. When the time is right, we will all live together; until then, I need only walk down Love Lane (as I do two or three times a day) to be with the kids for dinner and baths, for books and bedtime—and to be with Andy for after. I need only walk back up Love Lane to have a view and do my work. This is merely a literalization of what we all must find in families: a way to commute between necessary worlds. Love, not just in Brooklyn Heights, is always a thoroughfare.

TWENTY-THREE

I had read those studies in which moving was ranked as a cause of stress second only to one's own death; last winter, with its brokers and lawyers and decks of paint chips, I fully understood why. Like a potbound plant, I had set down roots too intricate to transfer without trauma. Still, the minute I shut the door for the very last time on my young adulthood in Greenwich Village, I knew there was nothing left to miss. Except Mercedes, but she'd moved, too, just a few days earlier.

Perhaps my parents would miss the Village; for them, its gaudy pageant was a novelty and not a nightly inconvenience. In any case, they made it possible for me to move by donating the down payment. This is what they had always done (though never before so literally): made me sufficient to my own odd choices. They were doing so with my parenthood, too. My father, despite his original doubts, had started referring, tentatively, to Erez and Luke as his grandchildren. His relationship to them was not the same as to my niece and nephew, who after all lived just eight minutes away; still, when we visited Philadelphia, he'd take the boys down to the tracks to watch the Main Line train go by. "The conductor waved!" they'd all come back shouting. "And tooted his horn!" And my father would be holding their hands.

My mother, too, was coming around. One day, in Brooklyn, out for a walk with Erez and Lucas, she watched me chase them to the Promenade and then said to me, "I like you with them."

"Really? Why?" I asked, somewhat startled.

She looked at me as if the answer was all too obvious. "Well, because they make you happy, of course."

It was true; I was smiling. There wasn't very much in the world more satisfying than showing a child a good time. Of course, you connect to a child differently from the way you connect to an adult; you engage directly and unblinkingly and in a kind of privacy too scary otherwise. You stare, make faces, chase, manhandle, sing nonsense songs quite publicly: things you'd be considered mad for doing if you did them to anyone else. They would be *in-trusions*, presumptions upon separateness. But a child's best gift (and his threat) is the piercing of that separateness. I didn't favor, any more than did my mother, piercing of any kind; had I not written a novel whose leitmotif was the anti-Forsterian "Only dis-connect"? Which is also a useful philosophy. But whatever lines we necessarily paint, we live together young and old and affect each other profoundly; our discrete apartments of quiet order may keep us from hearing the pitiful sounds of birth and death but cannot keep us off the road that leads from one to the other.

There are many ways to be an adult, and many more ways not to. Having children guarantees nothing. I don't recommend it ex-cept, like art, to those who feel they simply must. That's for the sake of the art, and the children, as much as for their perpetrators. In particular, unlike Andy, I do not stump for gay parenting; if being gay does not suggest any unfitness for raising a child, it does not suggest any genius for it, either. But to the extent gay men have abandoned younger people, whether because of the pain of their own youths or the intimidation of bigots, I hope they have the nerve to return. Not the way they returned to the gym—with a vengeance—but the way they returned from their long years of internal exile to the crowded field of the civic realm. What did all those demonstrations demonstrate if not connectedness?

"Take ye the sum of all the congregation of the children of Is-rael, by their families, by their fathers' houses, according to the number of names. . . ." The Torah portion I learned to read for my bar mitzvah was called "Bemidbar," which means "In the Wilderness." The stultifying text was little more than a census: "Those that were numbered of them, of the tribe of Judah, were threescore and fourteen thousand and six hundred." At least I would learn to count in Hebrew, the rabbi observed. But reciting the ancient names—which included, presumably, some ancestor of mine—I was forced to confront the vastness of humanity on both its axes: all of us living, horizontally, at one moment; each of us, vertically, with our parents and progeny. Smart-ass thirteen-year-old, I laughed off the implications; I would not be charting my life upon that particular graph. But having children returns you even to what you have rejected, and you love it a little more, now that you're free, as you would a friendly ex.

I was born the same year my parents' synagogue was founded; now it and I were nearing forty. In celebration, the synagogue was printing a "family" album; congregants were asked to sponsor pages and publish appropriate greetings thereon. My mother called me to ask permission for the wording she and my father devised, a wording that included me and Andy and our kids parallel to Tony and Mary and theirs.

"Are you sure you want to be so out there?" I asked.

"Oh yes. Let them deal with it."

But she called me a few days later and said she was having second thoughts.

"I understand," I said, a bit relieved. "You don't have to fight every battle."

"No, no, it isn't that. I'm just concerned that people might think Andy's a girl—short for 'Andrea.' Can we say 'Andrew'?"

And so I rejoined the generations.

TWENTY-FOUR

They run ahead and, truth be told, we let them. Not more than half a block, really, and never around a corner. But still, the blocks are long and they can get pretty far. A haggard street biddy occasionally scolds us for our insufficient stewardship; she'd have them on a leash. "They could fly out into the street, and then where would you be?" she says. If anything could make them fly, it would be her fearful asymmetry. But they never do fly out. Luke trips frequently on the uneven bluestone, and just lies there, not even whimpering, perhaps enjoying the cool hard resistance in his warm soft life. Then he scrambles back up and runs ahead again.

One early spring morning we toddle this way, all four of us, to school. Luke, who used to cry each day when his brother's classroom door shut him out, at two and a half is now happily enrolled with a younger group in the same building. Andy is antsy about the time; he has to be at work early and we are running late. For

my part, I am somewhat stupefied: It is not yet eight o'clock. But
today we have scheduled a parent-teacher conference, and I am
playing the parent since Andy cannot. We schlep our assorted accoutrements past the bakers and opticians opening their shops.
Do you have Luke's diaper bag? Erez's pinecones (plucked from
the woods that weekend, enough for each of his classmates)? Your
satchel? My notebook? The kids are unencumbered, far ahead of
us, rounding the bend.

"Don't turn that corner!"

They stop obediently, if not accurately, and wait. Erez hides behind nothing, then says, "Boo." Luke giggles.

The danger is not traffic.

Now we, too, round the corner. Ahead I see the school—and
on its stoop the rabbi in full phylactery. It's Thursday, a traditional
Bible-reading day, so I know he's out there trolling for minyan; a
minyan is a quorum of ten adult males who must be present to
make the reading proper. "Oh, thank God," the rabbi mutters,
tugging Andy up the steps like a Chicago ward heeler. "We're one
short."

"Actually," Andy says, "I can't stay. I'm late for work."

"Well, *you're* Jewish, aren't you," the rabbi declares—it's not
really a question—looking at me.

"Of course," I say inanely.

"I only need you for one Kaddish."

As Andy tosses me the diaper bag and the boys dash jabbering
into the building, the rabbi dragoons me into the sanctuary and
whacks a yarmulke on my head. The *mehiza* is up—the screen
that partitions the room, on sacred occasions, into separate areas
for men and women. But there are no women, of course, in an
Orthodox minyan. So why is it up? And why am I on the wrong
side of it?

To be fair, I'm not the only one. The nine other men are scattered about the sanctuary, seemingly oblivious of the giant screen;
it makes a distinction that is today irrelevant and so in effect does
not exist. That's Judaism for you. The relevant condition is solitude, or solitude with God, and as such even maleness, let alone
gayness, is, for the moment, invisible. Though I note that one of
the men has, beneath his tefillin, a very shapely arm.

We are saying a Kaddish; the word itself means "holy." It's an all-purpose prayer, repeated with slight variations throughout all Jewish services. This version is the Mourner's Kaddish, whose unforgettable (if unintelligible) words and implacable rhythms ring like chisels in even such stone hearts as mine. I have always known it.

Yitbarach, v'yishtabah, v'yitpaar, v'yitromam, v'yitnasei; v'yithadar, v'yitaleh, v'yithalal . . .

"Okay, thank you very much," says the rabbi, removing the prayer book from my hands and patting my back toward the door. But he leaves the white polyester yarmulke on my head.

Less than a minute has passed. Erez and Luke are still climbing the stairs, and I catch up to them. "What did he want?" Erez asks.

"They needed an extra man to pray," I explain, though Erez is not convinced. He makes a face; Luke giggles. They run up ahead.

It's five minutes past eight in the morning. I have just spoken ancient Hebrew in a room of believers—though my disbelief was as unimportant to them at that moment as was my gayness. I was a useful body, nothing more or less. Well, thank God, useful to someone. I am climbing the stairs to talk to a teacher about how well or poorly Erez performs each of the tasks symbolized by icons on his yellow report card: "I share and play cooperatively" (kids jumping rope); "I take care of my personal needs" (a lunch box, a zipper); "I indicate positive feelings for my traditions" (a boy beaming with some sort of pride). There is no pictogram for honoring thy father and thy father's partner, but there, too, I am the useful body. A child is no more particular than a rabbi on Thursday at one minute to eight. My gender, my gayness, my disbelief, my work: all irrelevant. At last.

TWENTY-FIVE

Children are pirates. They kidnap you to their wild den in the land of Dreft and Kwell. They don't do it because they're evil;

they do it because it must be done. Not that evil would bother them. They're as likely to root for Scar as for Simba when they watch *The Lion King*. One night, after the lights were out and Erez had fallen asleep, I leaned down into Lucas's neck and said, "Good night, my wonderful little boy. I love you so much." As I started to lift away, he grabbed my ears and pulled me down to his mouth. I could feel his sweet breath grazing my cheek. "I . . . killed . . . Mufasa," he whispered.

He and Erez had watched *The Lion King* possibly a hundred times by then. After baths and before reading, they sometimes request a video featuring Arthur or Gromit or the Cat in the Hat, or they might be in the mood for one of the train movies they gorge on like pornography: "Do you want to see my diesel? Look at my caboose!" But it was *The Lion King* they demanded most often; sometimes after a half-hour of it (that's all we allowed, generally) they wanted to read the book as well. There was clearly something in the story that Erez and Luke glommed on to—something beyond the flatulent warthog and burbly music. Was it the Oedipal theme? In the van one day, out of the blue as usual, Erez announced to all assembled, "Simba has two daddies." But Simba does not in fact have two daddies; he has one, who is killed by his uncle, named Scar.

That word again. Not "scar," but "uncle." The mother of one of Erez's classmates insists on describing me by that title: "Hon, you remember Erez's uncle," she tells her son. I have relaxed enough to let this go; if she wants to manufacture her family's reality, I can't stop her. Perhaps she really thinks I'm like the other men— Uncle Elliot, Uncle Wayne—she sometimes sees escorting the boys to school and playground, museum and movie. Perhaps she envies the wealth of male involvement in the boys' lives. Perhaps she's even suspicious of the lack of equivalent female involvement, though the women we know have kids of their own and aren't free for a day at the zoo. They're not, after all, gay men.

Well, it doesn't matter what the neighbors think. And Luke I don't worry about; he is content to throw open his arms when he sees me and shout, "My Jesse!"—as if that were not my name but my role. Whereas Erez, at four, is old enough to be confused; what does *he* think?

Walking him home from school one day ("walking" is a euphemism, as we usually end up chasing and hiding alternately), I suggest that we stop for a moment and talk. "Do you know who I am to you, sweetheart?" I ask.

"Jesse," he says.

"Yes. But like Andy is your daddy and Luke is your brother and Eliane is your housekeeper and Chauncey was your dog—what am I?"

He looks baffled. "A writer?" he offers.

"That's true. But what do you say when you say who I am? 'Here comes Jesse, he's my . . .'—what?"

A sneaky look comes over his eyes. "My chasing man?" And he starts to run, screaming with pleasure.

When I catch up with him, I persevere one more minute. "How about if I tell you what you can call me if you want to? Would you like that?" He nods. "Well, you can call me your daddy's partner, because that's true."

"I know that," he says smugly.

"But if you want, you can also call me your other daddy. Or just your daddy. What do you think?"

He smiles unknowably. "Can we chase now?" he asks.

I run ahead.

And then, a few days later, he emerges from school wearing a paper tiara. It's called, he tells me, his Family Hat. He has pasted figurines representing himself and Lucas, holding hands, on the left side of an oaktag strip; on the right (according to the legend) are Daddy and "Jessie"—misspelled, but still. He insists on wearing it all the way home, as what king with such a crown would not?

Can one reliably interpret these dispatches from the imagination? Another day he brings home from school a drawing that seems to feature a sun, a bird, and a clarinet. But the dictated caption, in the teacher's jaunty print, tells a different story: "I live in an apartment house. I live with Daddy and Jessie and Lucas. I sleep in a room with Lucas. My apartment is very big." Only one of these four sentences is accurate (he *does* sleep in a room with Lucas), but I am happy if this is the reality he is writing for himself.

It is often said that writers write to find out what they think.

Compiling a memoir is a way of deciding which of the lives one has had are true and which life to have in the future. It is also a way of pruning lives. Andy would see much of this differently: He was not quite so chaotic before he met me, not quite so neat after; he wasn't so nervous at the courthouse, so callow back in college. But these alternative realities get overwritten; choosing the version to tell eliminates the others. Which is part of why one does it. This is the story I want to have lived. Nevertheless, I come to what should be the final moment, still asking: How should this story end?

TWENTY-SIX

There comes a day, some years, when summer and the awareness of summer arrive together. Other years, you may catch up to the season a few weeks late, when you suddenly realize that your windows need washing, or that the asparagus has disappeared from the supermarket, or that you haven't retrieved your shorts from storage—and look, it's eighty-five degrees. Or you may become aware of summer too soon: pining for tomatoes when the vines are barely up; ready, a few weeks before the networks permit it, for the blessed surcease of sitcoms.

But some years, due to vagaries of weather and love, the day arrives and you arrive with it. Thursday it was spring, still crisp at midday, and the birds were new in their nests. And then Friday, all at once, it is summer. The blooms on the roses, still in their plastic nursery pots, already start to crinkle and scorch. The day is so long that the children are confused by the light through the blinds as they go to bed: "Turn out the sun," says Erez, half asleep.

Alas, I cannot, but I stand in its way, protecting his eyes, at least for a time.

I do not know how easy or hard he and Luke will have it. If hard, it will not be because Andy and I are gay, but only because of what people think about that. Nor will it be because they lack a mother. Whatever else may trouble him, Erez does not ask for

Mommy anymore. He knows what the word means; he refers to his friends' mothers as such, and does not confuse them with the woman who grew him in her stomach so long ago. That he does not have a mother is a matter of only the most casual interest, much like having no dog (though he had one once) and having no sister, ever. (Ah, but somewhere . . .) What he knows, and knows joyfully, is what *is* so: his brother, his father, and me.

I call my lawyer.

Second-parent adoptions (or "stepparent adoptions," as New York State unhelpfully calls them) can take about a year, she says. The requests will be entered into the family court docket as separate petitions—one for Erez, one for Luke—but numbered sequentially, for convenience. I will have to hand over fingerprints, reference letters, hundreds of pieces of paperwork and thousands and thousands of dollars. Implanting a uterus might cost less. But it would not make me more real.

There comes a day, some years, when summer and the awareness of summer arrive together. This was such a year. Summer came to Brooklyn and I was there with it, and so was my newfangled family: my millstone, my crown, my tattoo.

Acknowledgments

I am grateful to the many people who have allowed me to put them in this book, whether under their real names or, for the sake of privacy, made-up or incomplete ones. In particular I must thank my parents, my brother and his family, and Andy (who shall remain surnameless) for consenting to long interviews and then letting me write whatever I felt like anyway.

Without the prompting of Cynthia Cannell, Susan Lyne, and Brian DeFiore, I would not have dared to write a memoir. Without the indulgence and expertise of Ann Godoff, Bruce Tracy, Benjamin Dreyer, Jolanta Benal, and the staff at Random House and Villard, doing so would not have been as happy an experience. If I have committed fewer gaffes than usual, that is largely thanks to my friends Sara Sklaroff, Tim Blackburn, and John Cantrell, who have lent me their ears, and eyes.

A portion of Part IV of this book first appeared as "Finalizing Luke" in the anthology *Wanting a Child* (Farrar, Straus and Giroux). My thanks to Jill Bialosky and Helen Schulman, who edited that collection. Elsewhere, passages ranging in size from a phrase to several pages are drawn from articles I have written over the last ten years for *GQ, 7 Days, The New York Times Magazine, Glamour, Mirabella, Out, New York,* and *W*—or from the research done to support those articles. All of the material thus reused has been radically recast; still, I want to acknowledge the contribution of the people who assigned, edited, fact-checked, re-punctuated, paid for, and otherwise midwifed the original stories, including: Chris Bagley, Diane Cardwell, Mark Carson, Pamela Erens, Michael Goff, Penelope Green, Elise Harris, Howard

Karren, Lisa Kogan, Adam Moss, Maer Roshan, and Patricia Towers. I especially wish to express my gratitude to Eliot Kaplan, then of GQ, who in 1988 assigned me to write "The Velveteen Uncle," an article about the birth of my niece, and to Bruce Buschel, who gave that essay (and thus this book) its inevitable title.

ABOUT THE AUTHOR

JESSE GREEN is a much-anthologized, award-winning journalist and a regular contributor to *The New York Times Magazine*; he has also written for such publications as *The New Yorker*, *New York*, *The Washington Post*, *Premiere*, *GQ*, *Mirabella*, and *Out*. His novel, *O Beautiful*, was called one of the best first novels of the year by *Entertainment Weekly*, and his short fiction has appeared in *Mademoiselle*, *Mississippi Review*, and *The American Voice*. He was born in Philadelphia, graduated from Yale University, and worked for several years as a music coordinator on Broadway shows; he now lives in New York City.